Nehemiah Williams

Twenty-Four Sermons on Various Useful Subjects

Nehemiah Williams

Twenty-Four Sermons on Various Useful Subjects

ISBN/EAN: 9783337087401

Printed in Europe, USA, Canada, Australia, Japan

Cover: Foto ©Lupo / pixelio.de

More available books at **www.hansebooks.com**

TWENTY FOUR
SERMONS,

ON

VARIOUS USEFUL SUBJECTS.

BY THE REVEREND
NEHEMIAH WILLIAMS, A. M. A. A. S.
LATE PASTOR OF THE CHURCH IN *BRIMFIELD*.

PRINTED AT *WORCESTER*,
BY LEONARD WORCESTER,

1797.

CONTENTS.

SERMON I.
Thankfulness for Existence.

PSALM cxxxiii. 14. *I will praise thee; for I am fearfully and wonderfully made.*   7

SERMON II.
The same Subject continued.   19

SERMON III.
The Moral State of the World.

1 JOHN, v. 19. *And the whole world lieth in wickedness.*   33

SERMON IV.
The same Subject continued.   45

SERMON V.
Conformity to God the Essence of true Religion.

MATT. v. 48. *Be ye therefore perfect, even as your Father which is in heaven is perfect.*   57

SERMON VI.
The same Subject continued.   70

CONTENTS.

SERMON VII.
The Benefit and Delight of drawing near to God.

Psalm lxxiii. 28. *But it is good for me to draw near to God.*   84

SERMON VIII.
The same Subject continued.   99

SERMON IX.
The restless Soul resting in God.

Psalm cxvi. 7. *Return unto thy rest, O my soul.*   112

SERMON X.
The same Subject continued.   124

SERMON XI.
The Friend of God.

James, ii. 23. *And he was called the friend of God.*   137

SERMON XII.
The same Subject continued.   149

SERMON XIII.
Self Knowledge, or Acquaintance with our own Hearts.

Psalm iv. 4. *Commune with your own heart.*   164

CONTENTS.

SERMON XIV.

Joy for the Happiness of Others.

LUKE, VX. 9. *And when she hath found it, she calleth her friends and neighbors together, saying, Rejoice with me; for I have found the piece which I had lost.* 177.

SERMON XV.

The Hypocrite.

JOB, xxxvi. 13. *But the hypocrites in heart heap up wrath.* 191.

SERMON XVI.

The same Subject continued. 205

SERMON XVII.

The unchanging Goodness and Mercy of God an everlasting Source of Gratitude and Praise.

PSALM CXXXVI. 1. *O give thanks unto the Lord, for he is good; for his mercy endureth forever.* 217

SERMON XVIII.

The Gospel Method of instituting and ordering Churches.

TITUS, i. 5. *For this cause left I thee in Crete, that thou shouldest set in order the things that are wanting, and ordain elders in every city, as I had appointed thee.* 232.

CONTENTS.

SERMON XIX.

Times of Refreshment.

Acts, iii. 19. *Repent ye, therefore, and be converted, that your sins may be blotted out, when the times of refreshing shall come, from the presence of the Lord.* 251

SERMON XX.

The same Subject continued. 264

SERMON XXI.

Fidelity in Preaching Desirable.

1 Sam. iii. 17. *And he said, What is the thing that the Lord hath said unto thee? I pray thee, hide it not from me: God do so to thee, and more also, if thou hide any thing from me, of all the things that he said unto thee.* 278

SERMON XXII.

The same Subject continued. 292

SERMON XXIII.

Truth Painful to a Wicked Heart.

Acts, ii. 37. *Now when they heard this, they were pricked in the heart, and said unto Peter, and to the rest of the apostles, Men and brethren, what shall we do.* 307

SERMON XXIV.

The same Subject continued. 322

SERMON

SERMON I.

Thankfulness for Existence.

PSALM cxxxix. 14.

I will praise thee; for I am fearfully and wonderfully made.

THE first idea, which occurs to mind on reading these words, is, that the psalmist feels disposed to bless God for his existence; not only that he has *an existence,* but that he has *such an existence.* "I will praise thee; for I am fearfully and wonderfully made." He was meditating upon the mysterious and wonderful formation of his body in the womb, how curiously every part was formed, according to the all perfect pattern in the divine book. And to the attentive and philosophic mind, the formation of the human body appears to be a work of surprising power and wisdom, far surpassing the reach of our comprehension. But the same

may

may be said, respecting the formation of the body of a beast, or insect; and therefore the power and wisdom of the Deity is no less manifest in the formation of the body of an animal, than in that of a man. But there is something in man, which is wanting in every other species of creatures on earth, that is, a rational and immortal soul. By this, we are made capable of contemplating ourselves, of knowing our own existence, and of knowing what kind of existence we have, and to whom we are indebted for it. This we can by no means suppose was out of the psalmist's mind, when he said unto God, in the words of the text, "I will praise thee; for I am fearfully and wonderfully made." To suppose, that he had no respect to the internal powers and faculties of soul, with which he was endowed, would be doing violence to reason; for without these, he would never have known to whom he was indebted for his existence, nor been capable of praising God for it. On the whole, it is clearly evident, that when the psalmist says to God, "I will praise thee; for I am fearfully and wonderfully made," he means to express his gratitude to him, not barely that he had given him such a curious and wonderful body; but that he had given him such a still more noble and admirable soul; or that he had given him *such an existence*, made him *such a creature*, as he found himself to be. And who, you may say, is there, who does not feel thankful, not only that he has an existence, but that he has a rational existence, that he is made man?

SERMON I.

I doubt not but mankind in general are glad, that they have an existence; that they esteem it a happiness, that they are men, and not beasts; that they are wiser than the beasts of the field, and have more understanding than the fowls of the air. But, still I believe, that a great part of mankind do but little consider what a being man is, and still less do they feel their obligation to praise God, that he has made them men. It is, undoubtedly, pleasing to the pride of the human heart, to think that we stand high in the scale of being; that man was made but a little lower than the angels, and crowned with glory and honor; that he is at the head of this lower world, and has dominion over all the creatures. Every thing that tends to swell the heart with pride, and make men feel important in their own view, is very pleasing to them. In this view, there are but very few of mankind but what are pleased with the idea, that they are men.

But there have been those among mankind, who, on account of some outward trouble and affliction, which has befallen them, or some inward anguish and horror, which has overwhelmed their spirits, have envied the beasts their happiness, and have wished, that they had been formed dogs, rather than men. Others, again, have been so overborne with the burdens of life, and felt existence so intolerable, that they have, with their own hands, cut the thread of life; vainly imagining, that there was no other state, beyond the present, and that

B death

death would reduce them to their original nothing. Such characters, however, have made but a very small part of mankind; most men esteem life a favor, are glad of existence, and wish to have it continued; and the greatest unhappiness they feel, arises from the thought, that they must die—that they must quit the present state, and enter an unknown world. This, I presume, is the case with the greater part of my present hearers. Life is not a burden to you; you do not wish to end your existence; but, on the contrary, you are glad, if not thankful, that you have been brought into being, that you have been made men, and that you are still continued in life. Permit me, then, to lead you to a view of man, and to a particular inquiry, whether you have felt your obligation to be thankful to God, that he has made you men. If we are thankful to God, that he has given us being, that he has made us men, we shall then be thankful,

1. That we are made rational creatures.

By the faculty of reason, man is distinguished from all the creatures that inhabit this world. Though there appears to be that sagacity in many kinds of animals, which approaches near to rationality; yet we cannot suppose, that they are truly and properly rational creatures. By the rational powers and faculties, which man possesses, he is not only raised above the beasts, but he is allied to angels, and may claim kindred with the hosts of heaven; yea, more, by being a rational creature, he is capable

of

of bearing the moral image of God, and being conformed to that all perfect Being. By *reason*, we are capacitated, not only to enjoy the good things of this life, with a greater relish, and higher degree of satisfaction; but we are capacitated for the purer and more sublime pleasures of true religion; we are capacitated to enjoy those rational and divine pleasures, with which God himself is delighted. Who then can help being pleased with the thought, that he is a rational creature, that he is possessed, not only of a body fearfully and wonderfully made, but of a soul still more wonderful and excellent? Who would be willing to exchange states with an idiot, or with a brute? And who can help feeling his obligation to bless God, that he has made him a man? Or to praise the sovereign Creator, who, having a right from the same clay to form one vessel to honor and another to dishonor, has formed him a vessel of honor, in this respect, that he has stamped his own image upon it, and made it fit for the highest and noblest use, even for rational and divine employment? That you are pleased with your existence, in this view of it, that you are glad that you are men, so far as we have already attended to the nature and character of man, I cannot doubt; but this may be, and yet you may not be truly thankful to God, that he has made you such creatures, nor ever once said in your hearts, "I will praise thee; for I am fearfully and wonderfully made." Strange as it may well seem, it is still true, that very few of

mankind

mankind are really thankful for their existence, though they are so greatly pleased with the thought, that they are men; and very few act worthily of the character of rational beings.

2. Those who are thankful, that they are made men, are thankful that they are made moral agents, and accountable creatures.

It is a truth, which admits of no dispute, that man is a moral agent, and therefore an accountable creature; and must give account to his Maker for the use and improvement of his moral powers and capacities, with which he is endowed, and for every talent, with which he is entrusted. We conceive it to be true, that God never did, and never can, consistently, make a rational creature, who is not a moral agent, and accountable for his conduct. Angels and men are the only rational creatures, the only moral agents, that we have any account of. These are necessarily under moral law, or moral obligation to love God, and obey all his commands. Little is said in the Bible, because little is necessary for us to know, concerning the moral obligation of angels, or the particular law, which they were under, and the particular sin, by which vast numbers of them fell from their original rectitude and happiness; yet enough is said respecting them, to prove, that they are rational beings, moral agents, and accountable to God for their conduct. Men, as we just observed, are all the rational creatures, except angels, that we have any account

account of, and probably all that God ever made. As to ourselves, we know, that by being made rational creatures, we are moral agents; that is, we are capable of acting of choice, and of being governed by motives presented to our view. Man has understanding, which capacitates him to judge of the nature of those motives, which are set before him; and natural conscience, which points out the difference between moral good and evil; so that he never needs to do wrong, and indeed never can do wrong, unless he does it freely and voluntarily. If man be a rational creature, if he be a moral agent, if he be capable of seeing and feeling the difference between right and wrong, (which no one will deny,) then he must necessarily be the subject of moral government; that is, he must necessarily be under obligation to that which is right and good, and to avoid that which is evil and sinful. This obligation every moral agent must necessarily be under, antecedently to any particular and positive command of his Maker. Nor can God himself, consistently with eternal truth and justice, or consistently with his own infinite perfection, release mankind from this natural obligation. Hence, if we be men, if we be rational beings and moral agents, we must be the subjects of moral government, and under moral obligation to love God with all our hearts, as a Being infinitely glorious and good. To do this is nothing more, than in heart to approve of that, which is infinitely right and fit. And the rule of duty therefore is, in every respect, and in all things, to act from this great principle, An hearty approbation of that which is right and good; which necessarily implies an hearty disapprobation of that which is evil or sinful. More than this God never did require, and less than this he never can require, because this would be contrary to immutable rectitude. Hence, it may with propriety be said, that that law of God, which requires us to love God with all our hearts, does not properly make it duty thus to love God; but it requires this love, because it is our duty, or because it was antecedently fit and proper. And if man be a moral agent, if he be under moral obligation to God, this must necessarily imply, that he is, in some way, accountable to God for his conduct. It does not, perhaps, necessarily imply, that there must be a particular formal trial and examination had; but it plainly implies, that man, who is under law to God, must be liable to the divine displeasure, if he violates his moral obligation to his Maker. These observations clearly prove, that men are moral agents, and therefore that they are accountable to God for their conduct.

And the least attention to the Bible will enable us to see, in a light as clear as the noon day sun, that *as men* we are moral agents, and accountable to God for all our conduct, at all times; that we must give an account to God, not only for our external

external actions, but for all the thoughts and affections of our hearts; for God will judge the secrets of men. This is true, not only of those who enjoy the light of the gospel, but of those who live in heathen lands; it is true of all mankind, of every rational and moral agent. He who is a man, he who belongs to the human race, is an accountable being. And he who is thankful for his existence, thankful that he is made a man, must, for the same reason, be thankful, that he is made a moral agent, and accountable to God for his conduct. If it be a favor, which demands our gratitude, that we are made men, that we are made rational creatures, then it equally demands our gratitude, that we are made accountable creatures; for these can never be separated. The very idea of man supposes a rational and accountable creature. And if men, though rational beings, do act irrationally, or contrary to reason, are they, on this account, free from all obligation to gratitude, for the reason which God has given them? And if moral and accountable agents do transgress the first law of creation, and expose themselves to the displeasure of their Creator, are they, therefore, under no obligation to bless God, that he has made them men? In this view of human nature, in this view of yourselves, may I not ask, Are you thankful, that you are made men? Can you say with the Psalmist, " I will praise thee; for I am fearfully and wonderfully made?"

It is probable that this question, before we proceed any further in the subject, may be sufficient to try many hearts. How many of mankind are there, who would gladly separate what God has joined together! They would gladly have the favor of reason, and be able to act as they please, and yet be under no moral obligation, nor liable to any accountableness to God. They wish to live like men, that is, as men do live, enjoying all the advantages of men in this life, and yet to die like brutes, or rather to be as unaccountable for their conduct as they are. But this can never be. To be a brute, is to be destitute of reason, incapable of moral obligation, and free from accountableness; but to be a man, is to be a rational creature, under moral obligation, and therefore accountable for his conduct. And, now, which state do you choose? Would you be a man? or would you be a beast? Are you truly glad, that you are made a man, and thankful to Him, who made you such? Let your life and conduct answer the question. I may here add,

3. That he, who is thankful for his existence, will be thankful, that he is a dependent creature.

It is true, indeed, man is not, in this respect, distinguished from any or every other creature, which God has made. This is common to angels, to men, and to beasts. God is the only independent Being in the universe. To be creatures, is necessarily to be
wholly

wholly dependent on God for our existence—for our continuance in existence—for the continuance of the free exercise of reason, and all the powers and capacities, which depend upon reason. In *every* respect, therefore, we are dependent on God: In him we live and move and have our being; and all our sufficiency, for any thing, is of God.

Man is no less dependent now for his existence, and for such an existence as he has, than he was antecedently to his beginning to exist. And during time and eternity, we shall be entirely dependent, on God, for our existence and happiness. By being made rational creatures, we are made capable of knowing our dependence, (which the brutes are not,) and ought to be willingly and thankfully dependent, rejoicing that we are capable of knowing that God, in whose hand our breath is, and whose are all our ways. I know that there is, in fallen man, that pride and haughtiness of heart, which leads him to aspire after independence. Gladly would he renounce all dependence on his Maker, and be as independent as God himself. But this is an unreasonable and sinful desire, and the source of every sin. Were it possible for him to be as independent as he could wish, he would only be the more unhappy and miserable; for there is nothing necessary to make him miserable, but for God to give him up to his own heart's lusts, and let him eat the fruit of his own ways, and be filled with his own devices.

devices. We ought, therefore, to be thankful to God, that he has made us dependent creatures, and cheerfully give up our soul and body, for time and eternity, to the divine disposal. Convinced that he only is truly happy, who has chosen God for his portion, and whose hope the Lord is, and possessed of a meek, humble, dependent spirit, we shall be really thankful for our existence; we shall rejoice, that we are made rational, accountable, immortal creatures, who are capable of being forever happy in the love and service of our Maker; and we shall be entirely willing to live in this world, or to be removed from it, just as the sovereign Disposer of all events shall see fit to order.

SERMON II.

Thankfulness for Existence.

PSALM cxxxix. 14.

I will praise thee; for I am fearfully and wonderfully made.

THE more attentively we survey the works of creation in general, and observe the infinite variety, beauty, and regularity, which is manifested therein, the more we shall be disposed to join the devout Psalmist, and say, "Great and marvellous are thy works, Lord God Almighty! in wisdom hast thou made them all." All God's works, in some way or other, praise him; for they all shew forth his glory. But rational creatures, who are capable of seeing God in all things, who are capable of knowing from whom all things proceeded, and for whom they were all made, are under the greatest obligation to praise God, for what he is in himself, and for all the manifestations, which he has made of his adorable character, to the view of his intelligent creatures; and to bless him, that he

has

has made them capable of beholding his glory, and of shewing forth his praise. And where is the creature of God to be found, who is under greater obligation to praise him than his creature man? If he was made, at first, a little lower than the angels; yet, by his redemption, he may be raised higher than they. For, to which of the angels said he at any time, "Sit thou at my right hand?" But unto man he saith, "He that overcometh, to him will I grant, that he shall sit with me on my throne, even as I also have overcome, and am sit down with my Father on his throne." " And know ye not also that we shall judge angels?" Man, therefore, is under the highest obligation to praise God, that he has given him existence, and that he has given him such an existence, made him such a creature. But in order to feel our obligation to bless God, that he has given us such an existence, we ought to know and consider what creatures we are. Many, without thinking or knowing what creatures they are, are ready to imagine, that they are glad, and even thankful, that they are men. But what is man? He is a rational creature, possessed of a soul endowed with high and noble powers and capacities, by which he is allied to spirits of another world, and even connected with God himself. He is, moreover, a moral agent; he has a will to choose, or refuse; he is capable of judging of the motives set before him, and of acting accordingly; and therefore he is an accountable creature.

Thus

SERMON II.

Thus far we proceeded in our difcourfe in the former part of the day, and endeavored to fhow man's obligation to be thankful, that he was made fuch a being. But it would be injuftice to our fubject, to ftop here; and therefore we proceed to add,

4. He, who is thankful to God, that he has made him a man, is thankful that he was made for an endlefs duration—that he fhall never ceafe to be.

In this, man is diftinguifhed from all the creatures that inhabit this world. They were formed for the ufe of man, during his abode on earth, and they have bodies endowed only with animal and fenfitive life. They have no immortal fpirits within; when they die, they ceafe forever to exift, having nothing within them to furvive the body, or to exift in a future ftate. But man is poffeffed, not only of a body fearfully and wonderfully made, which muft foon turn to duft, and moulder in the grave; but this body is actuated by a fpirit, which can never die, never ceafe to be, nor ever be in a ftate of infenfibility. Philofophers have argued the immortality of the foul, from its immateriality, from its being a pure or fimple fpirit, and partaking of nothing in its nature, which is or can be corruptible or diffoluble. But though this be a probable, yet it is not a conclufive argument. For every being, whether material or immaterial, whether body or fpirit, depends entirely on the power and pleafure of the Deity, for its continuance in exiftence. It is, however, clearly evident from Scripture,

ture, that the soul of man is immortal; that when it has once begun to exist, it shall never cease to exist. And it appears probable at least, if not certain, that God never yet created a rational being, for a temporary or finite existence; for every rational being must be a moral agent, and every moral agent must be accountable, and therefore must exist beyond his state of trial and probation, in order to receive the recompense of his works. But, as I just observed, the word of God leaves no room to question, whether the soul of man shall exist forever. Life and immortality are brought to light in the gospel; yea, the gospel assures us, that these bodies, which we see turning to corruption, and buried in the dust, shall hereafter be raised from the grave, be formed spiritual and incorruptible, and the souls which had been separated from them, shall be reunited to them, and both exist together in a state unchangeable and eternal. So that all mankind, who have once begun to exist, shall continue to exist forever.

If it be a favor to have existence, it is a favor to have that existence continued; and mankind in general are as glad that their life is continued, as that they were brought into life, at first. Men naturally dread the thought of dying, and still more of ceasing forever to exist. Annihilation is a dreadful thought! It is granted, however, that some men are more afraid of existence than of ceasing forever to be; nor is it to be doubted, but that the existence

SERMON II.

ence of some, will be much more terrible than annihilation. "And how, may one and another say, do I know, that this will not be my case? How do I know, but that my misery, in another world, will be such, as that I shall wish I had never been born?" This is, indeed, a solemn and important thought! It demands attention! For this will undoubtedly be the case with many of mankind, and probably with some of you. But, notwithstanding this, are you not under obligation now to bless God, that he has given you existence, and such an existence as you have? Is it not a favor to enjoy such existence as you now enjoy? Would you be willing to exchange your present condition with a beast? Would you be willing, this moment, to be struck out of existence, and cease forever to be? No, you would not. You are, then, this moment, under obligation to bless God for your present existence, as a rational and accountable creature; and you ought to be thankful, that you have entered upon an existence, which shall never cease, though *the present state* of it may and will come to an end. For it is certain, that God has placed you in such a situation, that your future existence will be infinitely more happy than the present, if it be not your own fault. And if you should abuse your present life, so as to render your future state awfully miserable, will this lessen your obligation to bless God, that he has put you into a situation, in which you may secure eternal life and happiness,

if

if you will only comply with the terms of the gospel? Was Adam under less obligation to bless God that he had made him, after he fell, than he was before? No, certainly. Suppose I confer a favor upon you, which, if rightly improved, will render you completely happy, but you abuse it and become the more miserable; is your obligation to me, on this account, the less? No, certainly. Such is the case between God and your own soul. God has made you a man, a rational and accountable creature, has made you for an endless existence, and has placed you in such a situation, as that you may enjoy endless felicity, if it be not your own fault. What gratitude, what praise is due from you to God on this account! Who can help seeing his obligation to bless God, that he has made him, not for a momentary existence in this life only, and then to sink into his original nothing; but that he has made him for an endless and unchangeable state, and given him now an opportunity of securing eternal peace and happiness? This leads me to add,

5. He who is truly thankful to God, that he has made him a man, made him such a creature as he is, will be thankful that he is now placed in a state of trial and probation for eternity.

We have before observed, that every rational creature, every moral agent, must necessarily be under moral obligation to do that which is right and good, and to avoid that which is evil and sinful, and therefore must be accountable to God for

his

his conduct. This supposes, that every rational creature must, for a *time*, be in a state of trial and probation. This term of trial and probation may be longer or shorter, as infinite wisdom shall see fit to order. But it does not appear consistent, that God should ever make a rational creature, a moral agent, and immediately confirm him in an unchanging state of holiness and happiness, without his passing through a state of previous trial. And we are pretty certain, that he never did do it; for it is evident, that both angels and men (who are all the moral agents that we have any account of) were placed in a state of trial and probation. Nor does it appear proper, that they should be always continued in such a state. Though no rational creature can ever be discharged from moral obligation to do that which is right and good, and to avoid that which is evil and sinful, and therefore can never be without law to God; yet God may and does confirm creatures in a state of holiness and happiness, after passing through a state of trial, by which it becomes certain, that they never shall sin, because they are secured by the power and oath of God. Previously to this confirmation in holiness, we say, every moral agent must pass through a state of trial and probation. This state of trial and probation mankind are in, while in this world. This is abundantly evident from the whole tenor of sacred Scripture, as well as from many particular passages, which need not (it is presumed) be here recited. It is true, that the very first act of sin, the first violation of the moral law of God, might end the state of trial with every moral agent, and sink him down into endless misery, as the just punishment of his criminal conduct. This certainly was the case with the fallen angels; and fallen man would have been doomed to endless misery, on the first offence, if it had not been for the intervention of a Redeemer, and that method of grace, which God has instituted through him. And now, though every transgression of the moral law deserves the wrath and curse of God forever, as much as if there had been no Savior provided for us, yet God has been pleased to place us under a different trial from that in which man was placed in a state of innocence. So that whoever of the guilty race of man shall truly repent of his sin, and believe in the Lord Jesus Christ, shall obtain the pardon of his many and aggravated offences, and receive eternal life. Mankind are, therefore, each and every one of them, as really and truly in a state of trial and probation, as Adam was while in the garden of Eden. And God has been pleased to assure us in his word, how long this state of trial and probation shall last; that is, so long as this life shall last, or during our continuance on earth, and no longer. We are, therefore, each of us, under the greatest obligation to bless God, that we are now in such a state of trial and probation, and to be concerned that we improve it wisely and well. There is a

disposition,

disposition, too natural to mankind, to complain of God himself, that in consequence of the first sin of Adam, we are prone to sin, and have not a fair opportunity to regain the divine favor. But this complaint and objection is infinitely unreasonable, not only as our proneness to sin does not lessen the evil of sin, or the criminality in it; but especially as we are under that gracious dispensation, which provides a pardon for our many offences, if we repent and believe the gospel, and accept God's offered grace. Therefore, though many will abuse the day and means of grace, and though we may do it, and continue in sin through the whole time of our trial and probation on earth, and sink down into endless and remediless misery, so that it would have been good for us, if we had never been born; yet, as we are now probationers for eternity, as we now have an opportunity, in which we may secure endless glory and felicity; we are under infinite obligation to bless God, that he has made us men; that he has made us rational creatures, moral agents; that he has made us for an endless state of existence; that he has sent us into this world on a state of trial and probation; and that the happiness or misery of eternity depends on the improvement of the present short and uncertain life.

And now let me ask you, in this view of the subject, are you thankful to God, that he has made you men? that he has made you such creatures as we have represented mankind to be? Are you really

glad

glad that you are men? Or do you wish that you had never been born? Or that you had been beasts, or been any thing else, rather than men?

The question is certainly of real importance, and calculated to prove and try your hearts. If you are really thankful, that you are men, that you are such beings as God has made you, or even if you are only glad, that you are made such, you will wish and desire to live like men, to act agreeably to the character you sustain, and the rank which God has given you among his creatures. But do you act, or wish and desire to act thus? Alas! man being in honor abideth not; he is like the beasts that perish. How low is human nature capable of falling, and how low must he be fallen, who, possessing a rational and immortal soul, lives like a brute, desiring and indulging sensual enjoyments and gratifications only! And some there have been so lost to all the dignity of man, as to wish to exchange conditions even with a dog. And probably there are many more, who have wished, or who will wish, that they had never been born. But, however this may be, and whether this is, or will be the case with you, or me, it is certainly important for us to remember what beings we are, and to live and act like men.

Whether we are thankful to God or not, that we were made men, whether we are pleased or displeased with our existence, certain it is, the sovereign Creator of the universe, who made all beings

and

and things according to his pleasure, has made us men; he has given us a rational and immortal soul, which must exist forever; he has made us moral agents and accountable creatures; he has placed us in a state of trial and probation, and suspended the happiness or misery of a never ending eternity, upon our conduct in this world. Hence it is, that he addresses us in these words, "Shew yourselves men;" that is, live and act like men. Only act in character, act like men, like such rational, immortal, and accountable creatures as you are, and you will then feel that you have reason, through the ceaseless ages of eternity, to bless God, that he has given you existence, and that he has made you men. Often examine your conduct, ask your own hearts, whether such and such conduct is worthy a rational, an immortal, an accountable creature? Ask your own hearts, how such and such actions will appear to you, when viewed in the eternal world? Whether it will then be a pleasing thought, that you have acted thus and thus? And remember, that the present life is short and momentary, in comparison with eternity, for which you were made, and in which you must exist. Remember, that all the joys and sorrows, all the pleasures and pains, of the present state, are not worthy to be compared with those of eternity.

It may with propriety be said, that God requires nothing more of any of his creatures than this, that they act agreeably to the character, which he has

has given them, agreeably to the rank in which he has placed them; and less than this he cannot require. Complain not, that you were not made angels; for then angelic service would have been required of you; and angels too, as well as men, have fallen. Complain not, that you were not made brutes; for you are raised far above them, by a rational and immortal soul. Rather bless God, that he has made you men, and live and act worthy of such a character, and eternity shall crown you with immortal glory, honor and felicity!

The subject, which I have written and delivered to you this day, was particularly chosen by me, because I wished, for my own sake, to attend to it, and preach it over to my own heart, the last week, in the view of the day of my nativity. Last Friday was the anniversary day of my birth, on which day I completed the 45th year of my age. On such days, it becomes us particularly to recognize the goodness of God, in giving us life, as well as continuing us in it. But, how can we give thanks to God for life, unless we know and consider what a life, what an existence we have? Can he be thankful to God for continuance in life, who is not thankful that life, or existence, was given to him? And can he be thankful for existence, who is not thankful for just such an existence as he has? Certainly, it is more than time for us all to consider who and what we are, and for what we were

brought

brought into being, and whether we are acting our part well or not.

Permit me to remind you also, that this day completes nineteen years of my ministry among you. On this 9th day of February, nineteen years ago, I was solemnly set apart to the work of the gospel ministry among you. It becomes me today, to bless God, not only that he has made me a man, but that he has made me a minister of the gospel, to testify the grace of God to you, and that he has continued me so long in life, and so long in this work. I know, that it becomes me to be deeply humble, that I have spent so many years, in so unworthy and unprofitable a manner, and solemnly to give up myself to the mercy, the power, and the grace of God. And let me ask of every praying christian in this assembly, that, when he is nearest the throne of grace, and most fervently imploring grace for himself, that he would then remember his minister.

To conclude; let us all realize, that we are accountable creatures, and that the great day of account is just at hand (how near God only knows) when you and I, must each stand in his lot, and be judged, by that Being, who has " formed us of clay, and made us men," and " who will render to every man according to his works. To them who, by patient continuance in well doing, seek for glory, and honor, and immortality, eternal life : But unto them who are contentious and do not obey the truth, but obey unrighteousness, indignation and wrath; tribulation and anguish upon every soul of man that doeth evil, of the Jew first and also of the Gentile; but glory, honor, and peace to every man that worketh good; to the Jew first and also to the Gentile; for there is no respect of persons with God."

SERMON III.

The Moral State of the World.

I. JOHN, v. 19.

And the whole world lieth in wickedness.

AND thus it would forever have lain, in wickedness and misery, had not the God of all grace, devised a way for the recovery of some of the fallen children of men, through the death and mediation of his own Son. Yea, St. John says, that this is even now the state of the world, notwithstanding Christ has actually come, and made atonement for sin, and wrought out an everlasting righteousness, for all who believe in him. "The whole world lieth in wickedness." This represents the natural state and character of mankind. And considering the expression in this sense, it justly applies to the whole world, even to every individual of the human race, without a single exception; for "they are together become unprofitable, there is none that doeth good, no not *one*, they are all gone out of the way." And in this state the whole world lieth;

lieth ; *i e.* remaineth, or continueth, without any effort to recover itself, until God is pleased, by his power and grace, to raise here and there one to spiritual and divine life. Some there are, who are the happy subjects of such a saving change. Of such the apostle speaks in the former clause of this verse. " And we know that we are of God, and the whole world lieth in wickedness." So that when he says, " *we know that we are of God,*" he must mean to exclude himself, and his fellow christians, from the general character of the world of mankind, or when he says " *the whole world,*" he must mean the world at large, or mankind in general. A part, by far the greatest part, being put for the whole. These ideas are immediately suggested, by the words of our text :

I. That this world is a wicked world.

II. That not only some parts or places of the world, but all parts and places of it, are wicked. And,

III. That it lieth or remaineth in wickedness, notwithstanding all the means or methods made use of to reform and amend it.

I. The first idea, which occurs to mind from the words of our text, is, that this world, in which we live, is a wicked world ; that there is not only some wickedness in it, but a great deal of wickedness in it ; that wickedness prevails and abounds in it, much more than virtue, holiness or goodness. That there is wickedness in the world, we all know,

and

SERMON III.

and confess daily; we do not need to go to the Bible to find the truth of this. Every person, who has grown to years of knowledge and observation, finds it true, with respect to himself, that he is a sinner, and has done many actions, for which his conscience condemns him. It is presumed, that there is scarcely a child of six years old, but what is conscious to himself, that he has often done wickedly. Children, as well as men, know, that there is much wickedness in the world. By wickedness here, we mean that outward conduct, which is injurious to mankind, and which all agree to call criminal. There are many, who seem to be totally ignorant of sin in the heart; and therefore have little or no sense how sinful mankind really are. All their ideas of sin seem to be confined to outward acts of wickedness, which are expressly forbidden, either by the laws of God, or man. But even in this sense, they will allow that there is much wickedness in the world; yea, that the world is full of wickedness. Indeed, we must deny our own senses, to deny this. For, how often do we hear of horrid murders, robberies, thefts, rapes, adulteries, fornications, blasphemies, drunkennesses, quarrels, contentions, and vices of so many kinds, that we can hardly find names for them! When we confine our attention to such species of barbarity and injustice, between man and man, we often find occasion to say, the world is full of wickedness; meaning that there is a great deal of wickedness in the world.

world. It is in this view, that the heathen nations have obferved the corruption and degeneracy of mankind, and have been utterly at a lofs to account for it. But when we fpeak of the wickednefs of the world, or the finfulnefs of mankind, we ought not to confine our thoughts to that kind of wickednefs, which is an iniquity to be punifhed by the judges among men; but to confider all the corruptions of the human heart, all fecret as well as open fins, all fins againft God, as well as acts of injuftice, unkindnefs, and uncharitablenefs towards our fellow creatures. When we confider the wickednefs of the world in this view, which is a juft view, we fhall then undoubtedly fay, the world is full of fin and iniquity. For, in this fenfe, no man is free from fin; even the beft of men have much fin remaining in them. " There is not a juft man upon earth, who doeth good, and finneth not." This leads to the fecond idea fuggefted by the text, viz.

II. That not only fome, but all parts of the world, are full of wickednefs. It is not only true, that there is wickednefs in the world, yea, much, very much wickednefs among men, and this in fome particular parts or places; but it is true of all places, of all parts of the world, and of all nations of mankind. The *whole world* is full of wickednefs. Men are fometimes ready to think, perhaps, that they live in the moft wicked part of the world, and in the moft degenerate day; that there never was a

time

time when the world was so wicked as it is now; and that there is no place so bad as that in which they live: But this is not true; it has always been so, and is so every where; for the whole world is full of wickedness. There is no reason to doubt, however, that vice and wickedness do much more abound and prevail at some times, and in some particular places, than others. The men of Sodom were evidently more corrupt than mankind in general, or else they would not have been so signally destroyed. Vice and wickedness, especially open immorality, more generally prevailed, in the days of Noah, than before that time; otherwise God would not, at once, have swept the world of its inhabitants by a flood. And the children of Israel were, at some times, more lost to all sense of the true God, and his worship, and more given up to idolatry, than at other times; which was the reason of their being punished, by particular judgments. And the history of the church contained in the Bible, as well as that given by common writers, abundantly proves, that religion flourishes more at some times than at others, and in some places more than in others. And the experience and observation of the aged among us, will undoubtedly teach them, that there have been times, when religion flourished more than at the present day; when vices appeared few and small to what they do now, in this land. And even in the present day, we can hear of some particular towns and

and places, where there appears to be a very great revival of religion, and many concerned to secure the one thing needful; while, in most places, religion appears to be very little, if at all, attended to, and vice and immorality greatly prevail. But, notwithstanding these things must be granted, yet there is not, perhaps, that difference, which many seem to imagine. Different vices prevail in different places, and at different periods. In one age, or in one place, the prevailing and fashionable vice is gaming; in another place we hear nothing of this, but there drinking prevails; in another place, or at another time, quarrels and contentions prevail. Custom and fashion mark the differently prevailing vices and follies of mankind, in different countries, ages, and places; but, go where you will, you find the whole world lying in wickedness. Some men are much more abandoned to vice and wickedness than others; but perhaps there are not many more of this character in one age, or country, in proportion to its numbers, than in another. If we attend to the customs and manners, the vices and immoralities of the heathen nations, we are surprised at their idolatry, impiety, profaneness, and open acts of uncleanness, practised at their religious and solemn festivals. If we look among the Mahometans, the followers of the great impostor, we are surprised at their infatuation, their gross, absurd, and inconsistent ideas of religion and future happiness. If we

turn

turn our thoughts to the votaries of the Popish religion, we are no less shocked at their idolatry, superstition, vain ceremonies, and false refuges. But if we come to christian, and what are commonly called reformed, nations, have we less reason to be surprised? How many sects, and denominations, and persuasions, do we find among them? And is the moral character of christain nations any better than that of Papists, Mahometans, or Heathens? Are there not many infidels in a christian land? And are there not even more vices to be found among the civilized, and what we call christianized inhabitants of America, than among the savage nations? And are not those vices to be found among us, more infamous, and more pernicious to society, than those to be found among them? Why do we see the mote in another's eye, and not cast the beam out of our own eye? What reason have we to complain of the wickedness of others, when we are so wicked ourselves? Surely the whole world is buried in sin, wickedness, and guilt! But, when it is said, "the world *lieth* in wickedness," the expression may further suggest this idea,

III. That it continueth, or remaineth in wickedness, notwithstanding all the means or methods made use of, to reform, or amend it. This idea seems to be strongly expressed in the text; because lying down denotes a state of quietude and rest, or a fixed and steady continuance in the same state. And, in this

this sense, the apostle might, with great propriety, say, that the whole world *lieth* in wickedness; for it has lain or remained in such a state, for almost six thousand years, notwithstanding every thing, which has been done, to reclaim or reform it. Sin began in our world with the first human pair; nor has a single generation continued free from it, though God made man upright. And it seems probable, that our first parents did not continue many days in a state of holiness, before they fell. From that day to this, all flesh have corrupted their ways, and the whole world of mankind have lain in wickedness. Not one of the human race has been free from sin. No place, no age, has been free from wickedness. Even in the family of Adam, the most abominable acts of wickedness were found. Cain, his first born son, inhumanly imbrued his hands in his brother's blood. And very soon again, even before Adam's death, we find Lamech confessing, " I have slain a man to my wounding, and a young man to my hurt ;" and saying, " if Cain shall be avenged seven fold, surely Lamech seventy and seven fold." It appears from the short history contained in the former part of the book of Genesis, that when men mutiplied and became numerous, the earth was filled with violence, and the wickedness of man was so great upon the earth, that God determined to sweep the world of its inhabitants, and to save none but Noah and his family, even eight persons, who were the only right-

cous

SERMON III.

eous persons to be found on earth. Among all the many millions of inhabitants, which the earth then contained, it is evident, that these eight were all that had any fear of God before their eyes—any religion at all. Nor does it appear, that even the family of Noah were real saints. They might be saved only for Noah's sake; for God says to him, "*Thee only* have I seen righteous before me, in this generation." And the history of the Bible, together with other histories, is a clear demonstration, that the world has lain in wickedness ever since; that there has been no age, nor part of the world, free from sin, from that day to this; and this notwithstanding all that has been done, by God and man, to teach the world the evil and awful danger of sin; and the infinite beauty, excellency, and happiness of virtue and holiness.

What has not God done, by way of motive and excitement, to induce mankind to forsake sin? Or (if I may use the expression) what pains has he not taken, to reform and amend the world? When he first made man, though he made him holy and upright; yet, as though he would effectually guard him against every danger and temptation, he plainly told him what would be, and what should be, the consequences of sinning. And then, as soon as he had sinned, though he gave him encouragement to hope for pardon, yet he caused him to feel the bitter effects of sin, by dooming him to hard labor, pain, and death, and by cursing the ground

D for

for his sake, and driving him from the delightful garden of Eden. Adam now saw and felt the dreadful consequences of sin; he knew the awful difference between a state of sin and a state of holiness. And was it not that we know that the nature of sin is to lead further into sin, we should suppose, that Adam never would have committed another sin after the first. God's treatment of Adam was calculated to deter his immediate descendants, his family, from sin; and yet Cain, though he had often heard of his father's fate, what his original state was, how he fell, and what was the consequence of it, presumed to murder his own brother. God then brought such heavy judgments upon Cain as led him to say, " My punishment is greater than I can bear;" yet this did not cure him of his sinful disposition, nor put a stop to his wickedness. And though God has, in every age of the world, and in every part of the world, been visiting sinners with his judgments, and inflicting his wrath upon the wicked, yet they have generally remained incorrigible. Though he has, at one time, swept the whole world of its sinful inhabitants by a flood, and, at another, destroyed whole cities by fire; though he has caused the earth to open her mouth and swallow up the wicked; and though he has tried every calamity and judgment, in order to teach mankind the evil and danger of sin; yet the whole world lieth in wickedness. Every generation has an opportunity of learning the destructive nature of sin, from such awful

awful difplays of the divine difpleafure againft it. And all thefe things are written for our admonition, to the intent, that we fhould not luft after evil things, as others have lufted, and perifhed.

But this is not all; in addition to all the admonitions and warnings, which God has given to mankind, by his providential dealings, he has been calling upon a wicked world, in every age, by his fervants the prophets, rifing up early and fending them, faying, " O do not that abominable thing which I hate." Every argument and motive has been made ufe of, which is calculated to excite the hopes, to alarm the fears, or touch any of the feelings of the human heart; and yet, notwithftanding all thefe things, the whole world lieth and remaineth in the fame ftate of wickednefs.

God has, alfo, at the fame time, been endeavoring to teach mankind the fafety, the comfort, and happinefs of fuch as forfake fin, return unto him, and fecure his favor. For this purpofe, he has, in every age, by the power of his grace and the influence of his Holy Spirit, taken poffeffion of the hearts of fome, and made them the objects of his love. In them, and by his conduct towards them, he has taught a wicked world, in every age, what good they may enjoy, if they forfake their fins, and return to him in the way he has appointed. How ftrikingly did he teach this, in his prefervation of Noah and Lot, and in his conduct towards the patriarchs, prophets, and apoftles? How many and how rich are his promises to all penitent, returning sinners! Yet, notwithstanding all God has done for his friends in particular, and though he has given his Son to die for mankind in general, still the whole world lieth in wickedness. It appears not but that the world in general is now as wicked as before Christ came into it, to enlighten and reform it.

Great have been human efforts to reform the world; and reformations have taken place, in many things, and in many respects. Many important and useful improvements have been made, and are rapidly making, in agriculture, in manufactures, in the science of politics, and indeed in all the arts and sciences. But these do not mend the heart, nor root out wickedness from the world. Vice and wickedness, it is true, have often changed their names and altered their complexion; but still they remain the same, in their nature and tendency. The truth is, men only grow more refined in wickedness, and more subtle in the arts of iniquity. An open disregard to real religion, and a contempt of real vital piety, take place, under the pretence of casting off superstition, and of imbibing a more liberal spirit. So that, as to any real alteration for the better, I see not the least appearance of it; but still the whole world lieth in wickedness.

SERMON.

SERMON IV.

The Moral State of the World.

I. JOHN, v. 19.

And the whole world lieth in wickedness.

WHAT a melancholy reflection is this! If we consider this world as made by God, and peopled with a race of intelligent creatures, who are formed for the service and enjoyment of their Maker, what a melancholy reflection is it, that they have all apostatized from him, deserted his service, turned to be his enemies, and lie dead in trespasses and sins! How many generations of such rational and immortal creatures have already been on the earth! And how many millions and millions are still in the world, lying in wickedness! This is not only the case with us in Brimfield, but it is so in the towns around us; it is so over all this state; it is so in all the states in the nation; it is so in every nation on earth—for the whole world lieth in wickedness. Melancholy thought! Enough to fill our hearts with grief, and our eyes with tears! " And is it thus, O thou kind and beneficent Parent of the univerſe, that thy creatures requite thee for thy numerous favors to them! Is it thus, that they treat thine adorable Majeſty! Haſt thou no wrath for them to fear, nor grace for them to ſeek!" But what will the conſequence of all this be? Shall God forever loſe that glory, which is due to him from his creature man? Shall he loſe the world, which he hath made, and the many millions of rational beings, whom he hath formed to ſhew forth his praiſe? No, he will not do it. Could we turn aſide the veil which hides eternity from our view, we ſhould there ſee the glory of God ſhining forth in the eternal deſtruction of his enemies. Here, then, we are led again to ſay, how melancholy the thought, that the whole world lieth in wickedneſs, when we conſider how many millions of mankind there are, who are ſtanding on the verge of eternity, and juſt ready to fall into endleſs miſery!

> On what a ſlippery ſteep,
> The thoughtleſs creatures go!
> And, O! that dreadful fiery deep,
> That waits their fall below!

We have already obſerved, agreeably to the ſpirit of our text, that this world is a wicked world—that it is ſo in all parts and places of it—and that it ſtill continues in wickedneſs, notwithſtanding all the means and methods, which have been made uſe of to reform and amend it. Theſe thoughts naturally ſuggeſt ſome important inferences and reflections, which claim our ſerious attention.

IMPROVEMENT.

IMPROVEMENT.

1. It is obvious to remark, that all mankind are, by nature, univerfally and totally corrupt and depraved.

If this were not the cafe, furely the whole world would not be fo full of wickednefs, notwithftanding all that God and man have done to reftrain and reform it. It is a truth, I think, written as with a fun beam on every part of our world, that mankind are univerfally and totally corrupt. Their conduct confirms the divine declarations, that there is none that doeth good, no not one—that they are all gone out of the way; they are together become unprofitable. No part of the world has ever yet been difcovered, where its inhabitants have not been found to be vicious, wicked and depraved. If mankind were not univerfally corrupt, furely there would have been fome place found free from fin, and fome time found, when men did not do wickedly. But fuch a time and place has not yet been difcovered. Though this world has been groaning under the burden of fin, for almoft fix thoufand years, and all mankind have been feeling the evil effects of it, ftill the caufe remains; fin continues and reigns in full dominion. Though the world has been called, in every age, to witnefs the marks of God's awful difpleafure againft fin; yet it ftill remains the fame wicked world. The temper and difpofition of mankind has ever been like

like that of the wicked Israelites, who, when they had just been smarting under the rod of divine chastisement for their sinful murmurs, yet instantly murmured again. When Korah and his company murmured against Moses and Aaron, as assuming too much power and authority, God caused the earth to open its mouth, and swallow them up. But though the people were affrighted and fled away from the place; yet, we are informed, " on the morrow, all the congregation of the children of Israel murmured against Moses and Aaron, saying, Ye have killed the people of the Lord." So it is with all mankind; though they know the judgments of God against the wicked, yet they do the same things, which have brought misery and ruin upon others. This was the conduct of Belshazzar. Daniel tells him, after reminding him of the pride and fall of his father, " And thou, his son, O Belshazzar, hast not humbled thine heart, *though thou knewest all this,* but hast lifted up thyself against the Lord of heaven." Though men know the judgments, which God has brought upon the wicked, in ages past, and the awful threatenings, which lie against sinners, in the world to come; and though they know the good, which God has heretofore conferred upon his friends, and the great and precious promises, which he makes to the righteous, yet still the world lieth in wickedness. Now, is it possible to account for all this, unless we suppose, that all mankind are corrupt and depraved, prone to evil, and

to

to that only and continually? Is it possible, that a man, who has his eyes open, and sees the world around him, can deny the universal and total corruption and apostasy of the human race? Are not mankind evidently resolved on sin, and determined in wickedness, notwithstanding all that can be done or said to reform them? O how fallen, how corrupt, how sinful is human nature!

2. It is natural to reflect, that human nature is the same, in every age, and in every part of the world; for it has operated in the same manner, and produced the same effects, every where, and at all times.

There have been some persons who have appeared seriously to question, whether certain nations, who differ from the generality of mankind in their complexion, or the color of their skin, belong to the human race, or are the descendants of Adam. But are they not evidently possessed of the same nature, and do they not discover the same moral complexion, that is generally visible in our world? It may well be presumed, that God never yet made two different races of beings so nearly resembling each other, as the different forms and complexions of men do. But if the inhabitants of the world in no other way discover themselves to be of the same race, yet they sufficiently discover it, in their hearts and lives.

It is true, sin is essentially the same in all beings. It is the same in fallen angels and in fallen men.

The fallen angels, it is probable, from their being incorporeal, are incapable of some external acts of wickedness, which men commit while in the body, and which they will be incapable of committing, when they are absent from it, in a future world. But still the nature of sin will remain the same there as here. In this world, sin has ever been the same. In every age, and in every part of the world, it has manifested itself much in the same way. Different vices may have more especially prevailed in different times and places among mankind; but the same vices, the same acts of wickedness, are found now among us, which were found in the early ages of the world, and have been found in every age since. From hence too we see, that human nature is the same now, that it was near six thousand years ago. Customs and manners may vary in various ages. Men may make improvements in knowledge; nations may be civilized, who were once barbarous and ignorant; still human nature remains the same. Though the fatal poison of sin has been transmitted from age to age, and has passed through so many millions of millions of mankind; yet its fatal malignity does not appear to be in the least abated, nor the quantity of it diminished. And notwithstanding all that has been done to destroy the works of the devil, he still reigns in every heart, until Christ comes by his Spirit, and takes possession of it for himself. Mankind are now, by nature, just the same wicked creatures, which they would have been,

had

SERMON IV.

had there been no Savior provided for them. Hence we may add as a further inference,

3. That mankind do not grow weary of sin, by continuing in it; nor become more disposed to forsake it, by seeing and feeling the evil effects of it.

Such is the nature of human depravity, and such the influence of it upon the human mind, that though men see and know the evil of sin, and complain of its bitter effects and consequences; yet they are not, on this account, at all disposed to forsake it. Though we know, that sin has produced a long train of calamities in this world; though we know, that it has swept off whole generations and nations of men from the face of the earth; and though we have all possible evidence, that it has plunged millions of mankind into endless misery; yet we are no more afraid of sin now, than mankind were five thousand years ago. Men love sin now as much as they did then. And even the same person, who has for many years lived a life of sin and wickedness, is not, on this account, any more disposed to forsake it, but, on the contrary, much more hardened in it. Such is the scripture representation of the matter. " Can the Ethiopian change his skin, or the Leopard his spots? Then may ye also do good, that are accustomed to do evil." And such is the truth of fact. We see individuals grow more and more hardened in sin, the longer they continue in it. And though they feel the sad effects of their folly, yet they are no more
disposed

disposed to forsake it. The drunkard will not reform, though he feels the fatal effects of his vice. The thief will not cease to steal, though he be detected and punished for his crime. Indeed, we sometimes see, though very rarely, a man forsaking some particular vice, because he finds it will ruin him, if he does not; but generally, when men forsake any particular way of sinning, it is because it agrees not with a change in their circumstances, or condition of life. In this case, they commonly exchange one vice for another, which is more convenient. But even when age, or bodily infirmity, incapacitates a man for the indulgence of any particular sin, he commonly discovers the same love to wickedness, though not the same ability to act it out. Suffering the evil consequences of sin, may lead men to hate them and guard against them; while yet the heart remains as sinful as ever. Nor did suffering for sin, ever yet, of itself, lead a man to hate sin itself, on account of the moral evil of it. Indeed, it is easy to see, that if a man forsakes any vicious practice, merely because he feels the ill effects of it, this has nothing of the nature of true repentance for sin, or hatred of it. This he may do from the very same principle, which leads another to continue in sin, that is, personal and present pleasure, comfort, or happiness. Hence it appears, that there is no foundation for the opinion of some, that the future punishment of hell will bring men to repentance, and lead them

SERMON IV.

to hate sin and forsake it. On the contrary, there is reason to believe, that their punishment will tend only to exasperate them the more against God. Besides, whatever the nature and tendency of divine judgments in this world may be, it appears, that the punishment of sinners in another world, is not designed as a discipline to reform those, but as a manifestation of the divine displeasure against them forever. Again,

4. It appears, that mankind are strongly and totally resolved on sin, and determined to continue in it.

If mankind were not very strongly set in wickedness and resolved to continue in it, surely the world would have been, at least in some measure, reformed and amended before now, by the various methods which have been used for that purpose. How many means does God now use to reform the world, and what various methods does he now take to reclaim sinners, without producing any salutary effect! Can you, my friends, imagine, that it would be possible for sinners to oppose and resist all the means of grace, and continue secure in sin, if they were not resolved and determined to continue in it? Why do not you, with all your heart, reject sin, and resolve never more to have any thing to do with this dreadful evil? Why do you not hate it, and watch, and pray, and strive, with all your might, against it? The truth is, your hearts are under the full power and dominion of it; you

hold

hold it faſt, and refuſe to let it go. But, probably you will ſay, We are certainly not determined to continue in it; nay, we are determined we will, by and by, forſake it. Fatal deception! Are you not determined to continue, at leaſt a little longer? The very ſaying that you are reſolved, hereafter, to forſake it, is ſaying that you are reſolved, at preſent, to continue in it. If you form any reſolution at all about it now, it muſt be either to forſake it now, or to continue in it now. And the diſpoſition to put off your reformation to a more convenient ſeaſon, is a preſent reſolution not to forſake ſin. You muſt own, therefore, that you are, at preſent, fixed and reſolved to continue in your enmity and oppoſition to God. Hence we are led to reflect,

5. That there muſt be a divine power to ſubdue and deſtroy ſin in the human heart.

Nothing but the almighty power of God can reform and reclaim the world, and bring men back from the paths of ſin. External means are in themſelves ineffectual. The means which God himſelf has inſtituted, and which he has made uſe of, are in themſelves ineffectual. They will do nothing, unleſs accompanied with his divine power. What means has God been uſing, ever ſince the fall of man? And what effect have thoſe means had? The world in general remains as wicked as ever. It is true, indeed, means have been effectual in many inſtances. Millions and millions have, at one time and another, been reclaimed, and brought home

SERMON IV.

home to God. But, in all those instances, the means used have been accompanied with a special divine influence. Men are made willing only in the day of God's power. This is agreeable to the whole tenor of sacred Scripture, which always ascribes the conversion of a sinner to the power of the Deity, even to that power, which was exerted in raising Christ from the dead.

6. We learn how great the patience, forbearance, and long suffering of God, towards sinners of mankind, has been and still is.

Is it not justly surprising, that God has so long borne with this wicked world, which has all the time lain in wickedness? How many enemies has he had here! How obstinately have they opposed all the means, which he has used to reclaim them! How greatly have they abused and provoked him! And yet he has endured them with much long suffering. Surely he has with propriety said, that he is slow to anger, gracious and merciful, abundant in goodness. He is indeed a long suffering God, and waits to be gracious to the most unworthy and ill deserving creatures. But if, notwithstanding all his patience and long suffering, they will lie in wickedness, then,

7. The time must and will come, when he will destroy the world.

It is inconsistent to suppose, that God will always uphold this sinful world, and continue to bring into existence a race of rebellious creatures. This would

would be to act out of character, and even to contradict his word. The awful judgments, which he has already inflicted upon the world, are a prelude of its future and final destruction. Besides, he has plainly and expressly told us, that this world shall be burnt up, that it is reserved unto fire, against the day of judgment, and perdition of ungodly men. O! let us remember, therefore, who, and what, and where we are. We are now inhabitants of a world, which lieth in wickedness. We belong to a race of fallen, perishing creatures. And, unless we come out from this sinful world, we must sink down into endless misery. We justly deserve this misery; but God yet invites us to turn and live. Let us immediately forsake all our evil ways and thoughts, and turn unto the Lord, who will have mercy upon us, and to our God, who will abundantly pardon.

SERMON.

SERMON V.

Conformity to God the Essence of True Religion.

MATTHEW, v. 48.

Be ye therefore perfect, even as your Father which is in heaven is perfect.

To every one, who believes the being of God, and the reality and importance of religion, it must be an interesting inquiry, What is true religion? Or wherein does it consist? The importance of rightly determining this question appears, not only from considering, that it is the almost unanimous opinion of all mankind, in every age and every nation, that some religion is necessary; but also from the very different ideas of mankind concerning religion. Almost all nations differ from one another in the modes and forms of religion, if not in their ideas of the nature of religion. And among the reformed christian nations, what a diversity of modes and forms are to be found among the same people? There is not, perhaps, a nation or people on earth, among whom there is a greater variety of religions, or outward modes and forms of religion, than among the inhabitants of this American land. And it is but too much the case, that each sect is disposed to confine pure and undefiled religion to those of its own denomination; or, at least, to imagine that they come nearest to perfection in it. In this view, therefore, the inquiry appears still more important, What is true religion? Or wherein does it consist? To determine this important question, we must have recourse to the word of God: *There*, undoubtedly, true religion is delineated. To this, however, all professing christians resort, and *there* imagine they find the particularities of their respective denominations. But our present inquiry is not concerning the outward modes and forms of religion; but concerning the real nature and essence of it. For though there be a right and a wrong, respecting modes and forms; yet there may be, and doubtless are, some who hold to different modes and forms, who will, notwithstanding, agree in the real nature of religion. For however many the modes and forms may be, which consist with true religion; yet religion itself is but one and the same thing, wherever it is found.

Religion is essentially the same thing in angels, in saints above, and in men on earth; yea, if there be myriads of worlds peopled with intelligent beings of different capacities, and yet moral agents, capable

capable of religion, religion is effentially the fame in them all. Nay more, religion is the fame in God, and in all rational creatures; for religion in the creature confifts in its conformity to God. We do not indeed fpeak of the religion of God, becaufe, when we fpeak of religion, we fpeak of that in the creature, which is its conformity to God; or the exercifes of heart, which the creature feels towards God. But, fo far as thefe exercifes of heart, in the creature, towards God, are truly religious, they are conformable to God, and conftitute the creature's refemblance of God. This, we truft, will be made to appear, in the important fubject before us, which is defigned to exhibit the nature of true religion, from the paffage juft read: " Be ye therefore perfect, even as your Father which is in heaven is perfect." Thefe words evidently inculcate on us a conformity to God, and the higheft poffible refemblance of him; and therefore naturally lead us to this obfervation, viz.

That religion confifts in a conformity to God, in the inward exercifes of our hearts, and in all the outward actions of our lives.

To fet this truth in the cleareft poffible point of light, it will be neceffary to make the following obfervations.

1. God is an infinitely perfect being. This is certainly fuppofed, if not expreffed, in the text. " Be ye therefore perfect, even as your Father which is in heaven is perfect." The perfection of God is here fet up as the ftandard of all perfection,

which

which the creature is directed to copy after and endeavor to imitate. And reason as well as revelation teaches us, that God is an infinitely perfect being; that the highest possible perfection dwells in him; that he is perfect, to such a degree as no other being is or can possibly be. All the perfection of created beings is derived from him, and dependent on him, and therefore cannot, in degree, equal the perfection of God. And the perfection of God consists in his goodness, in the infinite benevolence of his nature. Indeed all the natural and moral attributes of the Deity are necessary, to constitute the perfection of the divine character; but yet the perfection of the whole is completed by divine benevolence. Love is the sum of all moral beauty and excellence. The infinite purity, holiness, justice, and wisdom of the Deity, are only love in perfection. God is, therefore, infinitely perfect, because he is infinitely glorious in goodness. Hence,

2. The more any rational creature resembles God, the more perfect that creature is. This is a necessary consequence of the former observation. For, if God be infinitely perfect, if he be the sum and standard of moral excellence and perfection; then the more any creature resembles God, and the greater his conformity to God is, the more excellent and perfect a creature he is. And if the glory of the divine perfection consists in divine love and benevolence, then the glory, the honor, the dignity, and perfection, of every rational creature,
must

must also consist in the benevolence of that creature: Or in the measure and degree in which he feels and acts out the spirit of true benevolence. Furthermore,

3. As God is a being of such infinite perfection, of such infinite benevolence and love, he must be pleased with that in the creature, which most resembles himself; not only because it appears rational for every being to love itself, and that which resembles itself; but because it is necessary to the very essence of benevolence, to delight in benevolence, and in its greatest and most extensive spread and prevalence. For this reason, God, as an infinitely perfect and benevolent being, must be most pleased with the benevolence of his creatures; for in this they most of all resemble himself. Indeed, if we could make the supposition, that there were some kind of imperfection in God, in some other respects, and yet suppose him perfect in love; he would then be most pleased with that creature, which resembled him most in this benevolent spirit; for this is the fairest and brightest feature in his character. Hence there is nothing, which can be more pleasing to God, than the prevalence of the highest degree of benevolence and love; and nothing can be more pleasing to him in the creature, than its resemblance of himself in the perfection of love. For the same reason,

4. He must, if he require any thing, require this of those, who are capable of resembling him. If

God be such an infinitely perfect being, if he be so full of pure benevolence, and if he rejoice most of all in this resemblance of himself in his creatures; then he must use that authority, which he has over his creatures, in enjoining upon them a conformity to himself herein. If God have any authority over his creatures, any right to command them, (which none will deny;) then we might reasonably suppose, that he would require what was most agreeable to himself, and that in which they would most of all resemble him. Not to do this would argue imperfection in his character. But this he has done, as we shall find hereafter. These things being premised, we may now proceed more directly to the point, and show, that a conformity to God, in the inward exercises of our hearts, and in all the outward actions of our lives, is what constitutes true religion. And therefore I add,

5. That when God made man at first, he made him in his own image, conformed to himself in moral purity, holiness and love. We are particularly informed, that, when God made man, he created him after his own image. When God was about to create man, he said, " Let us make man in our image, after our likeness." And when he was created, it is said, " So God created man in his own image, in the image of God created he him, male and female created he them." Again it is said, " In the likeness of God made he him." But in what did this image or likeness to God consist? Not in the
form

form of his body, or features of his face; for God is a spirit: Not particularly in the natural powers and capacities of his soul; but in the moral rectitude, purity, and holiness of his heart. Hence Solomon tells us, that " God made man upright," *i. e.* in moral rectitude. The glory of God's character consists in his benevolence; hence, when God, at the request of Moses, would shew him his glory, he caused all his *goodness* to pass before him. That the image of God, in which man was first created, consisted in his moral purity and holiness, in the conformity of his heart to God, in the exercises of real love and benevolence, is evident from man's being recovered to this image of God in regeneration. In this change, he is born again; created anew in Christ Jesus unto good works; and renewed after the image of him who created him. It is abundantly evident, from the whole tenor of sacred Scripture, that the honor and dignity, the glory and felicity, of man's primitive state, consisted in his perfect and entire conformity to God, in the inward exercises of his heart. Man was then, in his measure and degree, perfect as his Father in heaven was perfect; *i. e.* there was no kind or degree of contrariety or opposition in his heart to God. He loved God with all his heart; he loved the same things which God loved; he hated the same things which God hated; though his nature and capacities were such, that he could not love in the same degree. But his heart was in perfect union and harmony with God; and in this confifted the image of God, in which man was firft created. This was his religion, and this is the religion of every rational being, whether angel, or man, as will more fully appear in this difcourfe. Again,

6. That religion confifts in a conformity of heart to God, a conformity to his moral image, or in the acts and exercifes of our hearts, is further evident from this confideration, that the great defign of man's redemption by Chrift, is to recover man to this image of God. The great defign of God, in the redemption of fallen man, was not merely nor principally to fave mankind from wrath, not efpecially to fave him from mifery; but to recover him to the moral image of God. Hence it is faid, that Chrift was manifefted to take away, or put away, fin, by the facrifice of himfelf; to deftroy the works of the devil; to redeem us from all iniquity, and to purify unto himfelf a peculiar people, zealous of good works. It is abundantly evident, from the whole complexion of the Bible, that the great end and defign of this, which may in a fenfe be faid to be the greateft of all God's works, the work of redemption, was to bring man back to God, from whom he had revolted; to recover him from the love of fin, to a love of holinefs; to recover him from a ftate of enmity and oppofition to God, to a ftate of reconciliation and peace with him. Hence Chrift is faid to have made peace, through the blood of his crofs; and the redeemed from among men

men in heaven, are represented as praising Christ, that he has redeemed them to God by his blood. Nothing can be more evident to any one really acquainted with the Bible than this; that the great design of man's redemption was, not to purchase for him a liberty to continue in a state of enmity and opposition to God; but, to recover him to a state of cordial reconciliation to God, to a state of union, harmony and peace with him. As the redemption of mankind by Christ is a manifestation of the infinite love and benevolence of the Deity; so it is designed to promote and increase the greatest love and benevolence among the creatures of God, and to excite the most ardent love in themselves towards God. And this effect it does and will have upon all those, who comply with and feel the genuine influence of it. We may observe,

7. That religion consists in a conformity of heart to God, is evident from this; that it is the work and office of the Holy Ghost in the economy of man's redemption and salvation, to renew the soul after the image of God, and to recover mankind to a Godlike spirit and temper. Man having, by sin, lost the moral image of God, being alienated from God, and become opposed to him in the temper and disposition of his mind, or in the inward exercises of his heart, it was necessary that he should become reconciled to God, in order to his enjoying eternal life and happiness. Hence there must not only be atonement made for sin, by the sufferings

ings and death of Christ, in order to support the honor and dignity of the divine law and government; but also the fallen sinner must be recovered to the moral image of God. The power and dominion of sin must be destroyed in his heart; all the contrariety and opposition of his heart must be removed; and he must become the cordial friend of God. Without this, God can never become reconciled to him, nor become his friend. Notwithstanding all the atonement made for sin, and reparation done to his injured law and government, it is impossible for God to become reconciled to the sinner, whose heart is opposed to him. God cannot become reconciled to sin, unless he deny himself, and act contrary to his own nature; nor to the sinner as such. There can be no friendship in God towards a creature opposed to him; but he is angry with the wicked every day. Hence, when God laid the plan of man's redemption, it was not only concerted, that Christ should die to make atonement for sin, but also that the Holy Ghost should renew, sanctify, and recover the redeemed from the power and dominion of sin, and restore them to the moral image of God. This change, wrought in the heart of the redeemed by the Spirit of God, is so great, and makes such an alteration in him, that he is said to be a new creature, old things are done away, behold all things are become new. And it is also called a new birth, or being born again. Hence Christ has said, and said it with

with the utmost solemnity, "Verily, verily, except a man be born again, born from above, born of God, born of the Spirit, he cannot see the kingdom of God." And all those who are indeed interested in the redemption wrought out by Christ, are thus renewed by the Spirit of God; and beholding as in a glass the glory of the Lord, are changed into the same image, from glory to glory, even as by the Spirit of the Lord. They are renewed after the image of him who created them, and have the spirit of God dwelling in them. The law of the Spirit of life in Christ Jesus hath made them free from the law of sin and death. They are washed, they are sanctified, they are justified in the name of the Lord Jesus, and by the Spirit of our God. Ye are not in the flesh, says St. Paul to the Romans, but in the spirit, if so be that the Spirit of God dwell in you. Now if any man have not the spirit of Christ he is none of his; *i. e.* if any man have not the same temper and disposition, which Christ possessed; if he have not the same or like heart; if he be not conformed to Christ in the exercises of his heart, he is not a christian. Hence it is, that real christians are said to be united to Christ, and to become one with him; because they are like to Christ in the temper and disposition of their hearts. They have the same mind in them, which was also in Christ Jesus; and he was one with the Father, not only in his divinity, but in all the exercises of his heart. Christians are also called ed the children of God; because, as the child bears the natural image or resemblance of his earthly parents, so the real christian, or child of God, bears the moral or spiritual image of his heavenly Father. The apostle to the Galatians says, "And because ye are sons, God hath sent forth the spirit of his Son into your hearts." There is such an union of affection and similarity of spirit, between Christ and believers, that the apostle, in another place, calls them the members of his body, of his flesh, and of his bones. In a word, it is evident, that God hath from the beginning chosen believers to salvation, through sanctification of the spirit, and belief of the truth; therefore he saves them, by the washing of regeneration and the renewing of the Holy Ghost, which he sheds on them abundantly, through Christ Jesus our Lord. And hereby all christians may know that God dwelleth in them, and they in him, because he hath given them of his spirit. At present, I observe only once more,

8. That true religion consists in a conformity of heart to God, is evident from this consideration; that the perfection of the heavenly state consists in a perfect conformity to God. That the perfection of the heavenly state does consist in a perfect conformity to God, is abundantly evident, from the representations which the scriptures give us of that state. "Behold, says the apostle John, now are we the sons of God; and it doth not yet appear what

we shall be; but *we know* that when he shall appear we shall be *like him*, for we shall see him as he is." " Then shall I be satisfied, says the Psalmist, when I awake with thy likeness." A perfect and entire conformity to God, in all the views and exercises of their souls, is that which constitutes the endless and inconceivable felicity of the celestial inhabitants. To view things in the same light, in which God views them; to feel towards every thing as God does; and to act as God acts, so far as the creature is capable; this constitutes the perfection and the happiness of heaven. Hence, it is clearly evident, that true religion must consist in a conformity of heart to God; or in having the same holy and benevolent exercises which God has. And in proportion as we are conformed to the moral image of God, in the same proportion we are truly religious, and no farther.

SERMON VI.

Conformity to God the Essence of True Religion.

MATTHEW, v. 48.

Be ye therefore perfect, even as your Father which is in heaven is perfect.

OF all the vast variety of creatures that inhabit this world, whether on the earth, in the earth, in the air, or in the seas, man alone was made after the image of God. And as he alone is capable of bearing the moral image of his Maker, so he alone is capable of true religion; which consists in a conformity of heart to the Deity; in a resemblance of him, in the inward temper and disposition of the mind, or in the moral exercises of the heart. This important truth we attempted to illustrate and confirm in the preceding discourse, by a variety of considerations, which we supposed made it evident, that true religion does essentially consist in a conformity of heart to God. But it may

may be considered as an objection to this, that there are certain duties enjoined on us, which require such exercises of heart, as it is impossible that God should ever feel; and therefore religion in the creature must, in many respects, be essentially different from a conformity of heart to God. But, from a careful attention to the various duties enjoined upon us in the word of God, it will appear, that they all naturally arise and flow from a heart conformed to the moral image of God, or from a spirit and temper like that which God possesses. Hence I would further add,

9. That true religion essentially consists in a conformity of heart to God, appears from attending to the duties, which God has particularly inculcated on us in his word. Any one, who pays a careful attention to his Bible, must be convinced, that the religion there taught and inculcated, essentially consists in those holy exercises of heart, which God himself feels, and which constitute the perfection and glory of the divine character. But, before we attend to any particular duties, it may not be amiss to observe, that there are some general and comprehensive injunctions, inclusive of all religion, which particularly require a conformity of heart to God. Thus in the text; "Be ye therefore perfect, even as your Father which is in heaven is perfect." Without mentioning any one attribute or perfection of the Deity, which we are to copy after, the injunction is, to resemble God in all

all the moral attributes and perfections of his nature, so far as human nature will admit. Or if any thing in particular be intended, in which we are to imitate and resemble God, it is unquestionably in that universal and disinterested love and benevolence, mentioned in some preceding verses; or that love to our enemies, which God manifests towards his enemies.

We have also this general injunction: " Ye shall be holy: For I the Lord your God am holy." Here the holiness of God is given as a reason why we should be holy; and we are required to be conformed to God in the holiness of his nature. Holiness is essentially the same in all beings; in God, in angels, in saints in heaven, and in saints on earth. Holiness is moral rectitude, a conformity to perfect goodness; or, in other words, it is the perfection of benevolence or love. To be holy, therefore, as God is holy, is to be wholly under the influence of real love. All the moral exercises of heart, which God has enjoined upon us, are either directly such as God himself has; or they are the natural fruit and effect of such exercises, in such creatures as we are. Let us now pay a particular attention to some of the principal duties, or moral exercises of heart, which God has enjoined upon us.

And here I may well begin where God himself begins, and say, " The first of all the commandments is, Thou shalt love the Lord thy God with all

SERMON VI.

all thy heart," &c. Nothing is more evident, than that this command directly and immediately requires a conformity of heart to God. God is love; his nature, his essence is love—all his ways and works are ways and works of love. Love, as we have repeatedly observed, is the perfection of God's moral character; it is this which makes him holy; it is this which renders him infinitely glorious. And because he is such an infinitely glorious and perfect being, therefore he loves himself infinitely more than every thing else. And he thus loves himself, not because, (if I may be allowed the expression) not because it is himself; but because it is infinite perfection, infinite goodness, that he loves. Hence he loves every other being as he loves himself, so far forth as that being resembles himself, or is perfect, holy, and good. And was it possible that there should be any other being equally perfect with himself, he would love that being as himself, or *equally* with himself. And, therefore, when he requires us to love him with all the heart, he requires us to feel, as far as our nature will admit, as he himself does; or to love supreme excellence with supreme affection. He does not require us to love him from selfish, mercenary motives, because we imagine he loves us, or because he has been good and kind to us; but to love him for what he is in himself. This love to God arises and flows from a clear view and lively sense of the infinite glory and perfection of the divine nature. And when we love

F   God

God, because he is supremely good, or because he is absolutely perfect, then we are conformed to God, and love him as he loves himself.

Hence we see the propriety of Christ's saying, that the second commandment is like to the first, viz. "Thou shalt love thy neighbor as thyself." For this love of our neighbor flows from the same benevolent source from which love to God flows. When we love our neighbor as ourselves, we then only act as God does, who loves all his creatures, and that in proportion to their moral excellence, and real importance. We are to love our neighbor as ourselves, because he is of the same nature with us, and with us shares in the same love of God. "On these two commandments, says Christ, hang all the law and the prophets." And Paul says, that "love is the fulfilling of the law." All the requirements of the law, and even all gospel duties, are comprised in such love as we have considered. An heart under the perfect influence of this love, will feel all those other exercises, and perform all those other duties, which the word of God inculcates. Thus the heart, possessed of this true love and disinterested affection, will love its enemies. For the good man loves God, not for what he is to him in particular, but for what he is in himself. He loves his neighbor, not for the good which he receives from him, but because he is a fellow creature, and shares with him the love of God. And he loves his

his enemy, not as an enemy, but as a man, as a fellow candidate for eternity. In all these instances, he resembles the Deity. Hence St. John says, "He that loveth is born of God; and he that loveth him that begat, loveth him also that is begotten of him: He that dwelleth in love dwelleth in God, and God in him." It is evident, therefore, that a conformity of heart to God in love, is the highest perfection of human nature, and therefore must be the sum of all religion. When the soul is thus conformed to the moral image of God, and loves him with a supreme and ardent affection, then it will naturally and necessarily deny itself; its own interests and concerns will appear to be nothing, in comparison with the interests of God's kingdom; it will sink into nothing before God, and desire to live only to him, and for his honor and glory. When the christian feels such a spirit and temper as this, it is evident, that he is then conformed to the moral image of God, and acts in some measure as God does, who prefers and seeks his own glory as the ultimate end of all his conduct. It will be difficult to attend particularly to every duty enjoined upon us by God in his word, and show how they are all only a conformity of heart and life to God. However, I cannot omit just mentioning a number.

Does God require of us universal righteousness? This is but to be conformed to God, who is holy in all his ways, and righteous in all his works. Does

God require of us strict justice, in all our dealings with each other? This is but an expression of real love and benevolence, and a conformity to him, who is a just God and Savior, and the habitation of whose throne is justice and judgment. Does God enjoin truth and faithfulness upon us? This is but an expression of love, and a resemblance of him, whose character is that of faithful and true. Does God require us to do good to all, as we have opportunity? This is only to act out benevolence, and to imitate him, who is good unto all, and whose tender mercies are over all his works. Does God require us to love our enemies, to bless them that curse us, and to do good to them that hate us? This is only the fruit and effect of a benevolent heart, and a conformity to him, who is slow to anger, who waits to be gracious, and who is ready to forgive. I might proceed to mention all the christian graces and virtues, and show that they are all but so many particulars of conformity to God, that infinitely perfect and glorious being.

But it may still be said, are there not some duties inculcated, which do not imply, or which are not expressive of a conformity of heart to God? e. g. Repentance is an important duty for such guilty creatures as we are. But what conformity is there in this, to God? Surely God does not repent of his conduct. True, God can never exercise or feel repentance; and yet repentance for sin,

SERMON VI.

fin, in the truly good man, arises and flows from his present conformity to God in the temper of his heart; and never yet did any man exercise true repentance for sin, until his heart was renewed after the image of God, and filled with love to him. Repentance for sin flows not from fear, but from love; not from a dread of divine wrath, but from a view of the infinite glory and perfection of God, and a sense of the exceeding evil of sin, as committed against such a being. In the exercise of true repentance, the soul has, in some measure, the same views of the evil of sin, that God has, and hates it, in some measure, as God does; and therefore the more humble and penitent the heart is, the more it is conformed to God in love; in love of him, of his law and government. Hence, the true penitent always loves a holy God, and desires to see his law magnified, his government supported, and his character displayed. And all his exercises of holy desires; his ascriptions of praise to God; his confessions and humiliations; his petitions and requests; and his intercessions for mankind, for the church of Christ, and for the advancement of the Redeemer's kingdom, as far as they partake of the nature of true religion, and are real acts of duty, so far they flow from a heart conformed to God, from love to him, and a desire of his honor and glory. And when the soul feels most entirely resigned and submissive to the will of God, and does as it were go entirely out of itself

itself, and refer every thing to the sovereign disposal of the Deity; then it is most of all conformed to the moral image of God. Then it feels as Christ did, who was the brightness of his Father's glory, and the express image of his person. He said, "I delight to do thy will, O my God; yea, thy law is within my heart." And again he said, in a time of the greatest possible trial, "Father, not my will but thine be done." On the whole, is it not abundantly evident, that true religion consists in a conformity of heart to God? In the same moral exercises; in the same holy and benevolent feelings which God has? In the same proportion as we are conformed to God, and feel and act like him; in the same proportion we are truly religious, and perfect as our Father which is in heaven is perfect.

I now proceed to improve the subject.

1. If true religion consists in a conformity of heart to God; if it consists in the heart's being united to him, and having the same holy exercises which God has; then we learn the nature and importance of that change, which the scriptures make necessary, in order to the enjoyment of God in heaven; or the nature and importance of regeneration. Much has been said, and various have been the opinions of mankind, respecting the nature and importance of regeneration; but without attending to these, it is evident, that regeneration consists in the change of the sinner's heart, from a state of enmity and opposition to God, to a state of love.

SERMON VI.

love and friendship for him; or, it is the recovery of the soul to the moral image of God, which was lost by the fall. And the importance of this change is obvious; for there can be no true religion without this change, and previously to its being wrought. If regeneration does consist in the recovery of the soul to the moral image of God, then the soul is naturally destitute of this moral image of the Deity; and must remain so, until a work of regeneration is wrought in it. There may be, indeed, many external acts of duty, as they are commonly called, many outward acts which religion requires, and yet no religion in them, so long as the heart is destitute of the moral image of God. Conformity to God does not consist in outward actions, but in inward moral exercises. Hence there is no true religion without these inward exercises, which are real conformity to God. There are many, we have reason to fear, in a gospel land, who are so entirely ignorant of the nature of true religion, as to think that all religion consists in certain external actions, that proceed from no higher than selfish affections, which are not only not conformed, but really opposed to God. True religion is a divine and heavenly principle, which leads the heart to God, and forms it into a resemblance of the divine character. Hence it is that Christ says, "Except a man be born again, he cannot see the kingdom of God." And hence it is, that the apostle says, that "they that are in the flesh,

F 4

that

that is, in a state of unrenewed nature, cannot please God.

2. If true religion consists in a conformity of heart to God; then there is a real, an inward, and essential difference, between saints and sinners, or between those who are christians and those who are not. And this difference does not consist in the former's performing certain external actions, which the latter might; but it especially consists in the different temper and disposition of their hearts, and the different motives from which they act. The real christian acts from a principle of supreme love to God, in his external obedience to the divine commands; while **the sinner,** in all his external obedience to God, acts only from love to himself, or from a supreme regard to his own happiness. A man may be very strict and exact in the performance of every outward duty; he may read and pray, attend public worship and divine ordinances—he may be morally honest and upright in his dealings —he may be kind and charitable to the poor— yea, he may be greatly engaged in his religion; and yet he may do all these things without any love to God, and consequently without having the least degree of true religion. The difference between such an one and the real christian is, that the former is actuated by a primary and ultimate regard to himself; while the latter, or the real christian, is actuated by a supreme regard to God, and aims at his glory in all his religious duties; at least,

he

he does this so far as he is really religious. It is indeed a truth, that the real christian is sanctified but in part—he is but in part conformed to God—there is much sin and imperfection in him at all times, and he often feels and acts too much like the wicked man—but yet there is a real difference between them; the good man has something of the moral image of God on his heart, and is growing into a greater conformity to him, while the sinner has nothing of this, but is more and more alienated from God.

3. We learn from this discourse, why it is, that God loves the saint, and takes pleasure in him, while he is angry with the wicked, and condemns all his conduct. The reason is, because the saint bears his own moral image, and is in some measure conformed to him; whereas the sinner is opposed to God in the exercises of his heart, and will not become reconciled to his character. God cannot but love his own image, wherever he finds it. As a being of infinite benevolence and love, he must be pleased with the same benevolence and love in any of his intelligent creatures. He must be pleased with all their truly religious and benevolent exercises and actions. He must be pleased with their holy services, so far as they are holy. But as there is much sin and imperfection in them, it is only through Christ that they can be accepted. But as the wicked man is wholly destitute of the moral image of God, and utterly opposed to him;

him; so God cannot be pleased with him, nor accept his pretended services, but must be angry with him every day. As a being of infinite benevolence, he may love him as a creature capable of moral purity and holiness, and yet hate him as a sinner opposed to himself.

4. We further learn why holiness of heart and life is required of all moral agents, and why this is required of believers under the gospel, as much as ever it was under the law. The infinite perfection of God will not suffer him to allow and approve of sin, in any creature capable of holiness, capable of a conformity to his moral image. He must require all to love him with supreme affection: Not to do this would be to deny himself. Hence all rational creatures, angels, men, and devils, must be required, and must be under obligation, to love God, and be conformed to him. The christian under the gospel must, therefore, be under the same obligation to love God with all his heart, to be wholly conformed to God (which is holiness of heart and life) as he would have been under the law. And though Christ has died to make atonement for sin, to purchase pardon and eternal life for the believer; yet he is under no less obligation to be perfectly holy, than he would have been, if there had been no Savior provided.

5. We learn what is the best and only sure evidence of our being christians indeed, and so of our title to eternal life. It is finding and feeling in our

SERMON VI.

our hearts a conformity to God. Without a conformity to God, we cannot be admitted to heaven; we cannot enjoy God; we cannot be happy with him. The great inquiry then, is, am I conformed to God? Is my heart renewed after the image of God? Is the love of God shed abroad in my heart? Can I truly say, that I love God above every thing? That I love him for his own sake; for his own infinite perfection, and not particularly for what he is to me, or has done for me? Do I prefer his honor and glory, to my own ease, comfort, or happiness? Do I delight to do his will, and place my happiness in adoring, praising, and serving him? These are important inquiries, and may determine our character and state. It is undoubtedly true, that, upon inquiring, every one will find much opposition to God, much pride, selfishness and wickedness in his heart, and even in his best services; but yet, any real christian may, perhaps, know, that he does love God supremely, and does desire to live to his glory. And whoever knows this, may know, that he is a child of God, and an heir to the inheritance of the saints in light.

SERMON VII.

The Benefit and Delight of drawing near to God.

PSALM lxxiii. 28.

But it is good for me to draw near to God.

IN the former part of this pfalm, David gives an account of the fore temptation which he met with, to envy the profperity of wicked men; to think hard of the ways of providence; and particularly to think, that there was no benefit or advantage to be derived from religion, from the fear and fervice of God. He then proceeds to fay how he overcame the temptation, and got rid of that fevere conflict, which he had in his own mind; and that was by going into the houfe of God, by attending upon the public and inftituted duties of the fanctuary. " There, he fays, he underftood their end; then he faw, that, notwithftanding their outward profperity, they were in a truly wretched and miferable condition; that they were ftanding on flippery places, on the very

brink

brink of destruction, and in a moment ready to plunge into eternal misery. Upon this just view of their case, he was surprised at his own stupidity and folly, in envying their condition. "So foolish was I, and ignorant, says he to God; I was as a beast before thee." But having overcome the temptation, and gotten deliverance from the sore trial, he comes out of it like gold from the furnace, more purified and refined thereby. His love to God, and his resolutions to adhere only to him, were more confirmed and established than ever before. Among other sensible benefits, which he derived from the trial, this full conviction of heart was one: "It is good for me to draw near to God." Though once, in my haste, I was ready to say, that there was no good to be gotten from religion, that I had cleansed my heart in vain, and washed my hands in innocency; yet now I am of a different opinion; I know that it is good for me to draw near to God, and to live a life of communion with him. It is for my present comfort, and it will be for my everlasting benefit. I am resolved, whatever others may do, that I will keep near my God. And in this, every good man, who has once tasted that the Lord is gracious, will fully join with him, and say, "It is good for me to draw near to God." In treating the subject before us, I shall endeavor,

I. To show what is intended, or implied, in drawing near to God.

II. Why it is good, or in what sense, and on what account, it is good thus to draw near to God.

I. Our first inquiry is, what is intended, or implied, in the expression, *drawing near to God.*

Need I here observe, that drawing near to God is not a bodily, but a mental or spiritual exercise? Bodies may draw near to each other, by the power of gravitation or attraction; but nearness and distance, in such cases, have respect only to place. Whereas God is a spirit, and, in reference to place, is not far from every one of us; for in him we live, and move, and have our being. He fills all places, and knows all things. As he is a spirit, so it is only the spirit or soul of man, that draws near to, or removes far from him. In the psalm preceding the text, the Psalmist says, " Lo, they that are far from thee shall perish." By those that are far from God, he undoubtedly means those, whose affections are alienated from God; who have no love for God, no desires after him, no delight in him, and no real acquaintance with him. Hence it is evident, that those who are near to God, are those who have placed their affections upon him, delight in him, and desire to know and enjoy him. It is, therefore, only in and by the exercises of the heart, that we draw near to God. But as these inward affections or exercises of heart, are not only expressed by certain outward acts and duties, but many times awakened, quickened and excited thereby; so these outward or bodily acts and exercises

ercises are sometimes called drawing near to God. Hence we find God saying, "This people draw near me with their mouth, and with their lips do honor me, but have removed their heart far from me." Accordingly, attending upon the worship and ordinances, which God has appointed as means or mediums, in and by which his people may draw near to him, and the performance of prayer and other external duties, are considered and spoken of as drawing near unto God, and waiting upon him. Nor do I question whether the Psalmist, in the text, by the expression of drawing near to God, may intend waiting on God in his house, and attending upon the services of the sanctuary. And I am the more convinced that he means this *in particular*, from his mentioning the benefit that he had found from going into the sanctuary, where he learned the miserable end of those prosperous sinners, whose state he had so lately and so greatly envied. Drawing near to God may, therefore, imply,

1. Attending on the public worship and ordinances of God, and performing all those devotional exercises of prayer, praise, reading, hearing, and meditating on the word of God, which he has instituted and appointed, as means or mediums of communion with him.

Though God fills all places, and is excluded from none, yet he is said, in a special and peculiar sense, to dwell in his house or sanctuary, and to be
present

present in the public assembly of his saints. Hence, the place of public worship is usually called the house of the Lord, or God's house. God says, "he loveth the *gates of Zion*, more than all the dwellings of Jacob." And of the sanctuary he says, "This is my rest, here will I dwell, for I have desired it." And Christ has promised, that where but two or three are gathered together in his name, there he will be in the midst of them. The divine presence, therefore, in those passages, means something different from that essential presence of God, which fills all places; it intends some special tokens or manifestations of himself. Hence the Psalmist speaks of the goings of God in his sanctuary; as having seen him in that holy place. Now, as God is considered as being in a peculiar sense present in his house, in public and solemn assemblies; so attending upon the public worship and ordinances of his house, is spoken of as drawing near to God. And it is in the serious and devout attendance upon the public worship and ordinances of his house, that pious souls do indeed draw near to God. These are the instituted and appointed mediums of the soul's drawing near to him; therefore serve to awaken and excite, as well as to express, those holy exercises of heart, in which the soul has communion with God. For the same reason also, private meditation, prayer, and praise, may be called drawing near to God; for in these private and secret devotions, the soul often has access to God

with

with confidence, and finds sweet communion with him. But it is undoubtedly true, that many attend upon the worship and ordinances of God's house, and perform the external acts of prayer and praise in public, in private, and in secret, without ever really drawing near to God. Or, at most, they only draw near unto him with their mouth, and honor him with their lips, while their hearts are far from him. Such persons must, of necessity, be strangers to God, and to that delightful converse and communion with him, which the saints enjoy. They know not what it is to have God drawing nigh to them, in reviving manifestations of himself, and communications of his grace to them. For this reason, they can hardly say, " It is good for me to draw near to God." Drawing near to God, therefore, must further imply,

2. The going forth of the heart in holy and devout exercises towards him; in love to him, delight in him, and desires after him : Or, in the exercise of faith in him, repentance and humiliation before him, a hope in his mercy, an ardent, longing desire after the enjoyment of him : Or, in a sweet sense of his love, in a lively sense of his adorable attributes and perfections, in the delightful contemplation of them, and adoring and praising him for them : In the exercise of some one or more of these affections of the soul, the essence and excellency of drawing near to God consists.

It is not always, perhaps not commonly the case, that *all* these affections are exercised, when the soul draws near to God, and has communion with him. At one time, one particular grace may be in the most lively and vigorous exercise, and may seem to swallow up the whole soul; at another time, another grace may have the ascendency. At one time, when the good man draws near to God, his heart may be so deeply affected with a sense of his sins, and of the evil of them, that he can hardly do, or say, or feel any thing, but lament and bewail his sins before God, and lie in sackcloth and ashes before him; he can only pour out his heart in most humble and penitent confessions. At another time, he feels so sensibly his need of the influences of the Divine Spirit, to direct him in duty, to lead and guide him, to strengthen and assist him, that his devotional exercises consist especially in fervent supplications and entreaties. At another time, his heart is swallowed up with delightful transporting views of the glory of God, and he scarcely does any thing but admire and adore him: Or with a sense of his love shed abroad in his heart, and then his most delightful exercise is thanksgiving and praise. Now, in all these pious and devotional exercises, the heart draws near to God. In the book of Psalms in particular, we find all these various acts and exercises expressed, sometimes one and sometimes another of them. The book of Psalms is different from all the other books of the Bible, being wholly

SERMON VII.

wholly made up of devotional acts and exercises, which express the feelings of the writers, at one time and another, and on various occasions. But, to return to our subject; drawing near to God is the soul's converse and communion with him. It is something between God and the soul, that resembles the intimate and endearing society and converse of particular friends, whose hearts are knit together in love, and who do, as it were, mutually interchange affections and hearts, with one another. In order, indeed, to this communion with God, it is necessary, not only that the soul draw near to God in those religious acts and exercises, mentioned above, but God also must draw near to such a soul, by the influences of his Holy Spirit. And this God is ever ready to do; for he is never backward to meet the soul; he has said, "Draw nigh to me, and I will draw nigh to you." Yea, when the holy soul does draw near to God, it is because God has prevented it by his goodness, or because God has first drawn near to the soul and drawn it unto him. "No man, says Christ, can come unto me, except the Father, which hath sent me, draw him." The pious soul, sensible of its need of the drawings of the Spirit of God, says, "Draw me, we will run after thee?" The soul may, indeed, draw near to God, and yet not sensibly feel the sweet and refreshing presence of God; but, on the contrary, may complain with Job, "Behold, I go forward, but he is not there; and backward, but I cannot

cannot perceive him ; on the left hand, where he doth work, but I cannot behold him ; he hideth himself on the right hand, that I cannot see him." And many a soul has complained of the hidings of his face, that is, of the want of sensible evidence and manifestation of the love of God ; yet, at the same time, that soul does really enjoy the love and grace of God, in those desires after God, and those exercises of heart towards him, which are excited by God himself. The soul may sometimes be near to God, when it is mourning its distance from him, and in the midst of its mournful complaints, its tears of sorrow may be turned into songs of praise, by the unexpected manifestation of God's gracious presence. When this is the case, surely such a soul will be ready to say, " It is good for me to draw near to God." We proceed, then,

II. To consider why, or in what sense, or on what account, it is good thus to draw near to God.

The psalmist says, " It is good for me to draw near to God." He was convinced, that it was not only in general a good thing to draw near to God, but that is was good for himself personally to do it. Many are convinced, that religion is a good thing in general ; it is good for the world, it is good for society, and it is good for every one but themselves. As for them, they have no relish for it, nor, at present, at least, any desire to practise it. But this was not the case with the psalmist. He was

convinced,

convinced, not only of its being a good thing in general, to draw near to God, but of its being good for him, in particular, to do it. He seems to speak feelingly and experimentally, as one personally acquainted with it ; *q. d.* Whatever others may think, and however they may act, though they may imagine that it is for their good to depart from God, and live a life of alienation from God ; yet, for myself, I know that it is good *for me* to draw near to God, to wait upon him in his instituted worship and ordinances, and to maintain a constant communion with him. This was the opinion of the Psalmist, and this is the opinion of every good man. But why is it good to draw near to God? I answer,

1. Because there is a moral fitness, propriety, and beauty, in doing it.

It was not only the happiness of man in his original state, that he was allowed to draw near to God, and hold the most endearing and intimate communion with him ; but the moral beauty and excellency of his soul consisted in its conformity to the image of God, in those holy exercises of heart, which assimilated him to God, and brought him near to him. It is, therefore, an evidence, that the soul is renewed after the image of God, when it loves to draw near to him, and longs for intercourse and communion with him. And there is a real goodness, a moral excellency, in drawing near to God ; there is a beauty in it, pleasing in the view of angels, yea, pleasing to God himself. Nothing can be more amiable than the soul's returning to God, exercising holy affections towards him, and resting sweetly on him. But as the Psalmist said, "It is good for me to draw near to God," he undoubtedly meant to express the pleasure and delight, which he took in doing this, and the benefit and advantage, which he derived from it. Therefore I observe,

2. It is pleasing and delightful.

It affords the sweetest joy, delight, and satisfaction, to the gracious soul. There is no pleasure to be compared with this in this life. The nearer the soul gets to God, the greater and the sweeter its joy and pleasure. Nearness to God is what essentially constitutes the happiness of heaven; to be in the immediate presence of God, to behold the brightest displays of his glory, to enjoy the greatest communications of his love, to have the soul wholly conformed to God, to be always full of holy affections towards God, and to be constantly employed in praising him; these things constitute the felicity of heaven, and in these things consist a nearness to God. In proportion as these are found in the heart of a good man, in the same proportion is he near to God; and in the same proportion he is happy. It was this that made the Psalmist say, "Blessed is the man whom thou choosest, and causest to approach unto thee, that he may dwell in thy house." Hence, while many were inquiring,

Who

Who will shew us any good? he cries, "Lord, lift thou up the light of thy countenance upon us. Thou hast put gladness in my heart, more than in the time that their corn and their wine increased." The delight, which he found in drawing near to God, made him love the house of God so much, that he could say, in a rapture of joy, "How amiable are thy tabernacles, O Lord of hosts! My soul longeth, yea, even fainteth for the courts of the Lord; my heart and my flesh crieth out for the living God." And again, "I was glad when they said unto me, Let us go into the house of the Lord." And the reason why he had such a love to the worship of God was, because in it his soul drew near to God; he had communion with God, and this afforded him the greatest pleasure. Every one loves those places and those employments most, that afford him the greatest pleasure and delight. But the sweetest moments, and the divinest pleasures, which the holy soul ever enjoys, are those which it finds in drawing near to God. Hence it will ever say, "It is good for me to draw near to God." I might proceed to point out the advantages to be derived from drawing near to God; but as these are many and great, I cannot attend to them, in this discourse, and, reserving them for another opportunity, shall conclude, at present, with one reflection.

Does drawing near to God consist, not in a bare attendance upon the worship and ordinances of God,

God, not in the bodily exercises of prayer and praise, but in the inward exercises of heart, expressed in and excited by those outward acts and exercises? Then let none of us content ourselves with a bare attendance upon, or performance of, those external acts and exercises, but see that our hearts draw near to God in them. The outward acts and exercises of religion are, by no means, to be despised or neglected; they are instituted by God, to serve valuable and important purposes; they often serve as means to lead the soul to communion with God. Hence they never will nor can be despised, by a gracious soul, but will be highly prized, greatly esteemed, and devoutly improved. But to rest in them, and to think, because we have observed the bare form of public, private, or secret prayer and praise, that we have done our duty, is a gross perversion of sacred things. It is not improving, but abusing the means of grace. It is not drawing near to God, in the proper sense; but abusing those sacred rights, which were designed to bring us near to God, not to satisfy and content us while estranged from him. But how often do men satisfy themselves with this! Are there not many, who know nothing about drawing near to God, only with their bodily presence? Are there not many, who wish or desire nothing more than this? And yet will not such profess to hope, yea, even to believe, that they shall be admitted into the immediate presence of God in heaven, and to a holy near-

nefs

ness to him, when they leave this world? Vain hope! groundless faith! But can such, indeed, hope for that heaven and that happiness, which consists in nearness to God, when they have no desires after God now? No, it is not such a heaven, it is not such happiness, that they desire; and yet this is the only heaven, the only happiness, prepared for rational and immortal souls. And the soul must be wrought to a fitness for heaven, before it can be admitted there; and in order to this, it must be formed to a love of God, to a delight in him, to a desire of nearness to him. How, then, can you quiet yourselves with mere bodily exercises, which profit nothing?

But is it not still more strange, that those, who have ever tasted the pleasure of drawing near to God, should at any time quiet themselves with attending upon, and performing external duties, without drawing near to God? And yet is not this sometimes almost, if not wholly, the case, with many, if not all of us? How cold, lifeless, and formal, are many of our prayers, and other religious exercises! Do we not sometimes come to, and go from the house of God, almost without any desire of drawing near to him, in his worship and ordinances? Alas! my christian friends! how unworthy is this of the character of those, who have chosen God for their portion, and who place their happiness in being near to him? Let us, then, more highly prize the means of drawing near to God; let us improve

prove them better, and let us ſtir up our ſlothful ſouls to greater activity and fervor. Let us ſeek after a greater and more holy nearneſs to God, in his worſhip here, that we may be the better prepared to dwell in his preſence, and delight in his ſervice, hereafter.

SERMON

SERMON VIII.

The Benefit and Delight of drawing near to God.

PSALM lxxiii. 28.

It is good for me to draw near to God.

HAPPY is the man, who, having found the supreme good, which he ought to seek after in this life, does cheerfully and steadily pursue it! Such an one may indeed obtain and enjoy great felicity. But it is unhappily the case, that most men overlook their own good, or mistake the means of securing it. They vainly imagine, that happiness is to be had from those objects and enjoyments, which can never afford it ; though they are eager in the pursuit of it, yet they take the wrong road, and can never overtake it ; they weary themselves in vain ; they spend their money for that which is not bread, and their labor for that which satisfieth not. To such, Wisdom crieth aloud, she crieth without, she uttereth her voice in the streets; she crieth in the chief place of concourse, in the

opening

openings of the gate; in the city she uttereth her words, saying, How long, ye simple ones, will ye love simplicity; and the scorners delight in scorning, and fools hate knowledge? Turn ye at my reproof. He, then, is truly wise, who hearkens to the voice of Wisdom, and follows her guidance and direction; for she will lead him, not into the enchanted fields of sensual pleasure, but into the narrow way that leads to life. She will lead him unto God, even unto God his exceeding joy. And then shall he find, with the Psalmist, that it is good for him to draw near to God.

What is implied in drawing near to God, we have particularly and largely considered, in the preceding discourse. We began also to consider, in what sense, or on what account, it is good to draw near to God. We observed, in the first place, that it is good to draw near to God, because there is a moral fitness, beauty, and propriety, in doing it: And, in the second place, because it affords the greatest joy and delight, the sweetest and noblest pleasure. I proceed now to say,

3. It is good to draw near to God, because it naturally produces the most desirable effects upon the mind.

The benefits and advantages, which accrue to the soul, from drawing near to God, are many and great; they are almost too numerous to be particularly considered; but some of the most important, and which, perhaps, comprehend and include all others, are such as these: It cures an envious spirit; it quiets

SERMON VIII.

quiets a murmuring spirit; it relieves the burden of an accusing conscience; it gives comfort and hope in adversity; it adds to the joys of prosperity, and guards the heart against the danger of it; it produces calmness and serenity of mind at all times, particularly in the view and near approach of death; and it prepares the soul for heaven. Suffer me a little to illustrate each of these particulars, in order to excite you the more to a life of holy nearness to God.

First, One particular benefit and advantage, arising from drawing near to God, is, that it cures an envious spirit.

I mention this first, because it is particularly suggested by the text, and the occasion of the Psalmist's expressing himself thus in it. He particularly mentions his envious spirit, when he saw the prosperity of the wicked; and he tells us too how this spirit was cured, even by going into the sanctuary of God, by drawing near to him in holy and devout exercises of religious worship. Then he saw how foolish and sinful such a spirit was, and condemned it, and himself for it, and resolved in future to live near to God. The same benefit and advantage will every good man find from the same holy exercise. Envious feelings are too apt to arise in the hearts of the best of men, when they behold a wicked world in blooming prosperity around them. But at such a time, a recourse to God, a near and intimate communion with him, will immediately

diately subdue these envious feelings, and cause the heart to feel the vanity of the world, and its own infinitely superior portion in God, and to say as the Psalmist does immediately after resisting his temptations: " Whom have I in heaven but thee? and there is none on the earth that I desire besides thee!" When the soul does, indeed, draw near to God, and, especially, if at the same time, God draws near to it, and gives it some lively manifestation of his love, it feels it has no reason to envy the richest monarch on earth, his crown, or his kingdom; for it has that, which far surpasses all that the world can bestow. And as drawing near to God cures an envious spirit, so, for the same reason,

Secondly, It stills a murmuring, discontented spirit.

This is a spirit and temper very nearly resembling the former, but it does not always arise from the same cause. An envious spirit may always imply or include a murmuring spirit; but a murmuring spirit does not always imply an envious spirit. Good men are many times apt to feel a murmuring, discontented spirit, **not only** from the view of the apparent greater prosperity of others, but also from troubles and difficulties which they feel, or apprehend, are coming on themselves. They may be ready to think hard of the dispensations of Providence towards themselves, and say, all these things are against them. But if, when hard thoughts arise in the mind, the soul betakes itself to God, and makes him its refuge, its murmurs are hushed in silence.

SERMON VIII.

filence. Shall a man complain, a living man, for the punifhment of his fins? I will leave my complaint on myfelf, fays fuch an one, and with the pfalmift fay, That thou mayeft be juftified when thou fpeakeft, and clear when thou judgeft.

Thirdly, Drawing near to God relieves a guilty confcience, and quiets its painful accufations.

A guilty, accufing confcience is one of the greateft and heavieft burdens, that can be borne in this life; yea, it is fometimes quite infupportable. Hence Solomon has faid, "The fpirit of a man will fuftain his infirmity; but a wounded fpirit who can bear?" In what a lamentable and piteous cafe does the Pfalmift reprefent himfelf to be, on this account? "Thine arrows ftick faft in me, and thine hand prefleth me fore. There is no foundnefs in my flefh, becaufe of thine anger; neither is there any foundnefs in my bones, becaufe of my fin. Mine iniquities are gone over my head; as a heavy burden they are too heavy for me." And in another place, he fays, "When I kept filence, my bones waxed old through my roaring all the day long. For day and night thy hand was heavy upon me; my moifture is turned into the drought of fummer." The method which he took to gain relief in this deplorable condition, and the relief he gained, he informs us in the words following: "I acknowledged my fin unto thee, and mine iniquities have I not hid; I faid, I will confefs my tranfgreffions unto the Lord; and thou forgaveft the iniquity of

my

my sins. For this shall every one that is godly pray unto thee, in a time when thou mayest be found." And what the Psalmist here records of himself, has been experienced by most, if not all, good men. Nothing gives such relief to a guilty conscience, as drawing near to God, and pouring out the heart in humble, penitent confession; drawing near in a way of true repentance, and faith in the blood of Christ. And as the good man is daily sinning, he will find daily occasion of drawing near to God, and derive daily relief from it. Indeed, nothing will keep the soul from sin, like living near to God; and nothing will afford it relief, when it has departed from God, but returning to him again.

Fourthly, Drawing near to God gives comfort and hope in adversity.

Adversity is more or less the lot of all mankind in this life; good men are no more exempted from it, than others; for our Lord says to such, " In the world ye shall have tribulation." The good man has many dark and gloomy days to experience, many and various temptations, trials, and troubles to endure; and had he not a God to go to, and was he not a God at hand, to whom he may at all times repair, he would be miserable indeed. But in the midst of the most gloomy and distressing scenes, let him, with faith and love, and holy confidence, go to God, and he finds hope, joy, comfort, and peace, beaming upon his soul. To the upright

SERMON VIII.

right there ariseth light in darkness. How do such triumph in God in the most distressing day! "God is our refuge and strength, a very present help in trouble. Therefore will not we fear, though the earth be removed, and though the mountains are carried into the sea." Nor is this a presumptuous hope and confidence; for God has said to every one that trusts in him, "Thou shalt not be afraid for the terror by night, nor for the arrow that flieth by day; nor for the pestilence that walketh in darkness, nor for the destruction that wasteth at noon day." As long as the soul keeps near to God, it can triumph over all opposition, it can conquer every enemy, it can endure every trial, it can rejoice even in tribulation, and sing praise in the dungeon, though confined in the stocks, and loaded with irons. Again,

5. Another benefit and advantage of drawing near to God, and living near to him, is, that it adds to the joys of prosperity, and guards the heart against the dangers of it.

Prosperity is more dangerous to the soul than adversity. The prosperity of fools shall destroy them. Hence the many cautions given to those in prosperity. It particularly exposes us to set our affections on the world, to grow unmindful of God, to neglect our souls; it tends to feed the pride of our hearts, and lead us to treat the poor with scorn and contempt; it is very apt to feed our lusts, and inflame our vanity. To prevent these things, nothing will do but to keep the heart near to God. The soul that daily draws near to God, and has communion with him, will see the vanity of all these things, and therefore will not put confidence in them; but esteem them as loss and dung, in comparison with the excellency of the knowledge of God in Christ. And while nearness to God takes off the heart from the world, it will add to the comfort of earthly enjoyments, as it will lead us to view them as the gifts of our heavenly Father. We often esteem gifts, not according to their real intrinsic value, but in proportion to our love of the giver, and as an evidence or expression of his affection for us. So the pious soul receives the good things of this life, as evidences of God's peculiar love, and therefore enjoys the giver in the gift, which greatly increases all his outward prosperity. But not to enlarge here, I proceed to say,

6. Another benefit arising from drawing near to God is, that it produces calmness and serenity of mind at all times, and especially in the near view and approach of death.

So long as the soul keeps near to God, it must enjoy rest and peace. This, indeed, is implied in what has already been said, and therefore need not be repeated. But it may be worth while to consider the benefit of this, in the immediate view and near approach of death. This is a trying hour, which shall come upon and try all flesh; it is an hour, when the world and all its enjoyments can afford

afford no support or comfort; when even the flesh and the heart will fail us. But the soul that has lived near to God, and that can now draw near to him, will remain calm and unmoved. Death will be stripped of its terrors, and the soul triumphantly say, "Though I walk through the valley of the shadow of death, I will fear no evil, for thou, Lord, art with me. O death! where is thy sting? O grave! where is thy victory?" Mark the perfect man, and behold the upright; for the end of that man is peace. I may add,

7. Drawing near to God in his worship and service here, and in those holy exercises of heart, in which communion with him consists, will fit the soul for heaven.

The happiness of heaven, we know, consists in being near to God, and in those holy exercises of heart, which are put forth, in worshipping him in spirit and truth. Now, it is evident, that the soul which truly draws near to God in this life, is in some measure wrought to a fitness for heaven. Hence says the apostle, " He who hath wrought us for the self same thing is God, who hath also given us the earnest of the spirit;" that is, the first fruits of the heavenly Canaan. It is true, indeed, that the nearness to God, which any enjoy in this life, is at best very imperfect and often interrupted. But he who has begun a good work in any soul, will carry it on until, and complete it at, the day of Christ. And the nearer we live to God in this world, the greater will be our preparation to dwell with him forever, in the world to come.

What now remains is to improve the subject.

1. Is it a thing so good in itself, so pleasing and advantageous to the soul, to draw near to God? then what reason, what encouragement have we to draw near to God, and live in communion with him!

Surely the psalmist might well say, "It is good for me to draw near to God;" and with equal propriety may we say the same. But, alas! how few are there, who are at all acquainted with this happiness? The generality of the world choose to be at a distance from God, and desire not the knowledge of him or of his ways. They have never tasted that the Lord is gracious. But even those, who have known something of what it is, to draw near to God, are not careful, as they ought to be, to live near him. Alas! my christian friends, how shamefully, how criminally negligent and indifferent are we in this respect. Are we not too indifferent about the means of drawing near to God? Do we not many times feel cold and indifferent about the public worship and ordinances of God, which he has instituted and appointed, as mediums, by and through which, we may draw near to him? And when we attend upon these means of grace, are we not too indifferent, whether we get near to God and enjoy him, or not? Do our souls hunger and thirst after God, and after the times and seasons of drawing near to him, in public and private worship,

as

SERMON VIII.

as our bodies do for their daily meals? Or as we do to converse with our best friends? Surely if we prized the happy privilege as we ought, we should often be impatient for the time of drawing near to God. God condescends, not only to allow us, but even to invite us, to draw near to him. And Christ speaks of manifesting himself to his friends, as he does not to the world; and says, " If any man love me, he will keep my words; and my Father will love him, and we will come unto him, and make our abode with him!" Happy soul! in whom God and Christ dwell! And should we not desire, should we not seek after God, when the pleasure and delight, when the benefits and advantages, are so many and so great? And when God and Christ encourage and invite us to it? Could we always keep near to God, what a source of delight should we enjoy! It would not be in the power of earth or hell to disturb our peace and rest. If through the infirmity of the flesh, we sometimes depart from God, let us think on our ways, and make haste, and delay not to return to him. Let us remember, that we are daily drawing nearer to that heavenly rest, where our souls hope and expect ever to live near to God, to dwell forever with him, to behold his face in righteousness, and to be satisfied with his likeness. Let us be concerned, then, to live nearer to him now, that we may be the better prepared for heaven, and have clearer and stronger evidence of our right and title to it.

2. If

2. If there be so much pleasure and delight in drawing near to God in his worship and ordinances now, and such benefit and advantages from it here, how great must the happiness of heaven be!

There are some favored and happy moments, when the real christian enjoys heavenly delight; when he gets so near to God, and has such pleasing views of his character, such near and intimate communion with him, and such lively manifestations and communications of his grace, that he even longs to be absent from the body, that he may be present with the Lord. But these are short and momentary seasons; they are soon interrupted. But the happiness of heaven is far superior, and it is constant and durable. In this life, our enjoyment of God is imperfect at best, and of very short and uncertain continuance; but there it is perfect and everlasting. Here we see as through a glass darkly; but there face to face! Here we see but in part, and know but in part; but there we shall see as we are seen, and know as we are known! As it is happy to be near God in this life; so it will be unspeakably happier to be near him in heaven. It is more than probable, that this is what constitutes the perfection of the soul there; that this is the reason, why there is no sin and no temptation there; that this is the reason, why the soul is perfect in every grace, in every virtue, and excellence. It is filled with God. God has, indeed, taken up his everlasting abode in it, and he constantly imparts of his infinite fulness to it. O! how happy muſt heaven be! and how truly bleſſed are thoſe who poſſeſs it!

3. If the greateſt happineſs that can be enjoyed on earth, and all the happineſs of heaven, conſiſts in being near to God; then how far from happineſs muſt thoſe be, who are far from God!

The pſalmiſt ſaid, in the verſe immediately preceding the text, "Lo! they that are far from God ſhall periſh;" and then adds, "but it is good for me to draw near to God." Man was happy in his original ſtate, when he was near to God; but as ſoon as he forſook God, he was plunged into a ſtate of miſery. Forſaking God is the cauſe of all the miſery that is found in the world; and this world would have been but little better than a hell of miſery, if Chriſt had not come to recover us to God. The only reaſon, why wicked men, who are far from God, are no more miſerable now, is, becauſe the things of the world take up their attention, and pleaſe their bodily ſenſes. But how completely miſerable will they be, when ſtripped of all their worldly enjoyments, and baniſhed forever from God! Let thoſe, then, who are now ſtrangers to God, and who chooſe to remain far from him, who, in their hearts and conduct, ſay unto God, "Depart from us"—let ſuch remember how dreadful it will be, to be baniſhed forever from God, by thoſe awful words, "Depart from me, ye curſed, into everlaſting fire, prepared for the devil and his angels."

SERMON IX.

The restless Soul resting in God.

PSALM cxvi. 7.

Return unto thy rest, O my soul.

THERE is, in every man, a certain something, which we usually call the soul. This we know, we feel, to be different from these gross, these fleshly bodies, which we carry about with us. It is something, which animates the body, which has a commanding influence over all the bodily organs, and which constantly prompts us to seek after objects, superior to all earthly enjoyments, to satisfy its boundless desires. This soul of ours is evidently and essentially different from that spirit, which actuates brutes. Their desires are few, they are easily satisfied, and they are satisfied with present enjoyments. But the soul of man is ever restless and uneasy, never satisfied with present enjoyments, but ever on the wing, ever in pursuit of something new. Even the most pleasing and promising prospects deceive us, and fail

of

of that satisfaction in the enjoyment, which we expected. When disappointed of the satisfaction, in the enjoyment of any object, which pleased us in expectation; instead of being convinced, that it is not in the power of any earthly enjoyment to satisfy the desires of the soul, we fly as eagerly as ever to some other object, promising ourselves, that we shall find that satisfaction *in this*, which every former enjoyment failed of affording us. And thus the mind wanders, from object to object, from one enjoyment to another, in pursuit of what it can never obtain, from all the enjoyments of this world.

"We try new pleasures, but we feel
"The inward thirst and torment still."

There may, indeed, be some short lived and momentary satisfaction, from the enjoyment of some favorite object; but it is, at best, but short lived and momentary; like the morning cloud and early dew, it soon passes away. For the truth of these observations, I dare appeal to the experience of every one present, as well as to the history of mankind, in every age and in every part of the world. Sometimes, indeed, we may find those, who, for the present moment, may be disposed to question, if not deny, this truth. They seem to imagine, that they have found the happiness, the rest, the satisfaction, that they have been in pursuit of: But tarry with them a few days, and you will find, that their sunshine of happiness begins to be obscured

scured by intervening clouds, and they still look forward to a brighter day, which they expect from new, not from present, acquisitions. Thus are mankind in general, be their present enjoyments what they may, like the rich man in the parable, whose ground brought forth plentifully, so that he had not where to bestow his goods. He thought within himself what to do; and at length resolves, I will pull down my barns and build greater, and there will I bestow my goods. And what then? Why, then I will say to my soul, Soul, thou hast much goods laid up for many years; take thine ease, &c. Observe, notwithstanding all his present wealth, notwithstanding all his present possessions, he could not be happy now; but when this and the other object is obtained, *then* he shall be happy. So it is with all mankind. But, what shall we say to these things? Was man made to be the sport of fancy? Was he made only to be deceived with the prospect of happiness, which can never be realized? To be constantly led about by an *ignis fatuus*, which can never be overtaken, and which will finally plunge him in the ditch? No, certainly. This would be a reflection on his Maker. This would be a state less desirable than that of a brute, whose desires indeed are fewer, and of a much lower nature, and much more easily and perfectly satisfied. Some, perhaps, may imagine, that it is no matter whether a man's happiness consists in present enjoyments, or in the pleasing expectation

SERMON IX.

pectation of future good, which he shall never find; but can this be just? Though it is true, that a man may enjoy great present pleasure, from the anticipation of future good; yet will not the pain and the mortification, which arises from blasted hopes and disappointed expectations, nearly equal, if not overbalance, his delusive happiness? Must it not fill him with regret, to think he has been all the time pursuing a shadow, and catching at a phantom? Surely, truth is more eligible than falsehood. It would be more eligible to desire less, and enjoy all that we desire; than to desire more, and enjoy nothing. It cannot be, therefore, that God has made the soul of man capable of such vast desires, and yet put it absolutely out of his power, ever to obtain that which will satisfy it. There is a rest that remaineth to the people of God; there is that which will fully satisfy the desires of an immortal soul; there is a hope, which maketh not ashamed, and which shall be as an anchor to the soul, sure and steadfast. God himself has said, "Open thy mouth wide, and I will fill it;" that is, Extend your desires as far as you please, and I will satisfy them. But, in order to this, our desires must be fixed on the right object; we must choose the better part; we must set our affections on things above; we must look not at things seen and temporal; but at those which are not seen, and which are eternal. We ought not to conclude, that, because worldly objects and enjoyments

joyments never satisfy, never afford that happiness, which we promised ourselves from them, but have always disappointed our expectations; I say, we ought not from hence to conclude, that nothing can satisfy the desires of the soul. When we find ourselves disappointed in our expectations from the world, and when we have roved, from object to object, and from one enjoyment to another, in the pursuit of rest, let us then say with the psalmist, " Return unto thy rest, O my soul." Here, then, we may,

I. More particularly consider, that there is an object, on which the soul may rest, or in the enjoyment of which it may find satisfaction and happiness, equal to its highest expectation.

II. Shew what this object is.

III. Shew what is implied in the soul's returning to this rest, or how it may do this.

I. Let us now particularly consider, that there is an object, on which the soul may rest, or in the enjoyment of which it may find satisfaction and happiness, equal to its highest expectation.

And if it be true, that there is such an object, on which the soul may rest, and in the enjoyment of which it can find full satisfaction, must it not be a pleasing, a delightful thought, to the weary and heavy laden soul, that has been long on the wing, flying from object to object, in the pursuit of rest, and yet finding none? Surely it must. But, alas! how few are there, who are yet convinced,

vinced, that they can find no rest on worldly enjoyments? Though they have been a thousand times disappointed in their expectations from the world, they will yet think, that they shall finally find what they have so long been in the pursuit of. But, if there are any, who are wearied with the pursuit of worldly happiness, and convinced that real satisfaction cannot be had in any of the enjoyments of this life, *they* will rejoice to hear, that there is an object, on which the soul may rest, and in the enjoyment of which they may find real happiness. He, who has formed the soul of man within him, and filled it with vast and boundless desires of happiness, has also formed a happiness adequate to its desires. He has set this happiness before us. He has appointed and revealed the way, in which we may seek and find it. He has said, " Ask, and it shall be given you; seek, and ye shall find; knock, and it shall be opened unto you. Come unto me, all ye that are heavy laden, and I will give you rest. Learn of me, and ye shall find rest unto your souls." But, the great difficulty is, vain man would be wise, though born like the wild ass's colt. Being wise in his own conceit, he refuses to hearken to the voice of God; he chooses to walk in his own ways, and to follow his own devices; to walk in the sight of his own eyes, and after the desire of his own heart. He vainly imagines, that his own wisdom is sufficient to direct him, and that he can obtain the object of his wishes, by following

his

his own inclinations. The great reason, therefore, why mankind are not happy, are not satisfied, and their souls at rest, is not because there is no rest for the soul; it is not because God has formed desires which cannot be satisfied, and hedged up the way to happiness, on purpose that we might never find it; but, it is owing to our own perverseness and obstinacy; to our rejecting the counsel of God against ourselves, and placing our happiness in things, which can never profit, which can never afford, and which were never *designed* to afford, happiness. Ever since the fatal apostasy of mankind from God, the hearts of the sons of men have been fully set in them to do evil. Our first parents learned discontentment with the happy station, which Divine Providence assigned them; they aspired after independence and a rivalship with God; they wandered from the path of duty, in which God had placed them; and not only lost the greater happiness and rest, which they were in pursuit of, but they lost all that they before possessed. And all their posterity possess the same spirit and temper, and pursue the wandering steps of their first parents; hereby plainly proving, that they are the children of those, who, at first, revolted from God, and deserve the same curse. Like the prodigal son, we are uneasy in our Father's house; we dislike his authority and government; we cannot bear the restraint of his laws; we sigh and long to be released. Like the prodigal, too, we forsake

the

SERMON IX.

the fulness of good, the rest, the peace, the joy of our Father's house, and wander in pursuit of forbidden pleasures; we try all the pleasures of sin; we even endeavor to fill our bellies with the husks, which swine do eat. Wretched condition! piteous state! But, when, like the prodigal, we come to ourselves, when we awake from our vain and delusive dreams, to see our true state, and feel our wretchedness and misery, and can say with him, "In my father's house is bread enough and to spare, and I perish with hunger;" that is, when we are led to reflect, that in God there is enough, and more than enough, to satisfy all our wants; and, therefore, with him, resolve, "I will return to my father, and will say, Father, I have sinned against heaven and before thee, and am no more worthy to be called thy son;" then we shall find, as he did, a Father coming forth to meet us, ready, with open arms, to receive us to the bosom of his love, and making ample provision for our future joy, rest, honor, and perfect felicity. This leads us, in the next place, more particularly,

II. To consider what that object is, on which the weary soul, tired with the pursuit of happiness, in the delusive pleasures of this life, may rest, and in the enjoyment of which it may be happy.

And what object, what enjoyment is there, that can satisfy the boundless desires of an immortal soul, but that which is as boundless as those desires? And where is this object to be found? The depth, that is, the depth of the earth, saith, It is not in me. The sea saith, It is not in me! Every created object saith, It is not in me! These are all finite, limited objects. God alone is able to fill the soul of man; he only can give it rest, and satisfy all its desires. It is his infinite fulness, that fills all in all. He has formed the soul of man to find rest and happiness in the enjoyment of himself; and it is vain to expect it in the enjoyment of any other object. Every object must fail of affording rest and peace to the soul, in the same proportion as it is foreign from God. And the soul that has once truly found rest in God, will very feelingly adopt the language of the psalmist, and say, " Whom have I in heaven but thee? and there is none upon earth, that I desire besides thee. Thou art my portion, O Lord. O God, thou art my God, early will I seek thee: My soul thirsteth for thee, my flesh longeth in a dry and thirsty land, where no water is. As the hart panteth after the water brooks, so my soul panteth after thee, O God. My soul thirsteth for God, for the living God: When shall I come and appear before God?" Wearied with the delusions of a vain world, the soul returns to God, and finds rest in him. This undoubtedly is what the psalmist intends by his rest, when he says, in our text, " Return unto thy rest, O my soul;" for he adds, " The Lord hath dealt bountifully with thee." He had experienced the power, the goodness, and the allsufficiency of God; and, therefore, would

renewedly

renewedly repair to him, and rest his soul on him. But you may ask, Does not the expression of the psalmist in the text, "Return unto thy rest," imply, that he had wandered from this rest, or that he did not, at all times, enjoy rest and peace, joy and happiness, in God? I answer, It undoubtedly does. The good man, who has chosen God for his portion, and who has often found great rest and comfort in God, is at best but a very imperfect creature; he is sanctified but in part; his flesh lusteth against his spirit; **he often** wanders from God, his supreme object; the world, with its delusive charms, for the present moment, captivate his too thoughtless heart, and he sets his affections on earthly enjoyments, and forgets that he cannot find rest in himself. But, soon he perceives, that he has wandered from his rest, and is impatient until he returns. He will, therefore, often find occasion to say, "Return unto thy rest, O my soul." This is owing, not to any insufficiency in God, the object on which his soul rests, to afford him perfect, perpetual, and undisturbed rest and felicity; but to his own imperfection, to his wandering, roving heart. In God, there is enough to satisfy every desire of every restless soul; and of his fulness we may all receive, even grace for grace. He is a fountain open, not shut up and sealed; he is a never failing good, to all that trust in him; he is a sure foundation. Hence we read, "They that wait upon the Lord shall be as mount Zion, which can never be moved."

moved." And again, " Thou wilt keep him in *perfect* peace, whose mind is stayed on thee." In proportion as the affections of the heart are placed on God, in the same proportion does the soul find rest and peace in him. But it is far otherwise with respect to earthly things; for, in proportion as our affections are placed on them, the greater our anxiety and uneasiness will be. He, who rests his soul on God, will find all peace, joy and comfort. It was this that made the psalmist resolve ever to wait on God; at all times to trust in him. It was this that calmed all his fears, that stilled the tumult of his ruffled mind, that filled him with such undaunted confidence and courage, and that made him express himself in such language as this: " The Lord is my light and my salvation; whom shall I fear? The Lord is the strength of my life; of whom shall I be afraid? Though an host encamp against me, yet will I not fear. God is our refuge and strength, a very present help in trouble; therefore will we not fear, though the earth be removed, and though the mountains be carried into the sea. Yea, though I walk through the valley of the shadow of death, I will fear no evil, for thou art with me." Thus may the soul, that truly rests on God, make her boast in the Lord; for God himself speaks peace to such a soul. " Fear thou not, saith God, for I am with thee; be not dismayed, I am thy God. My grace is sufficient for thee; my strength is made perfect in weakness.

SERMON IX.

All things are yours, whether Paul, or Apollos, or Cephas, or the world, or life, or death, or things present, or things to come, all are yours, and ye are Chrift's, and Chrift is God's." Is it not, then, abundantly evident, that the weary foul may at all times reft on God ? And that he is the only object, which can afford perfect reft and peace to the foul ?

SERMON X.

The restless Soul resting on God.

PSALM cxvi. 7.

Return unto thy rest, O my soul.

SHOULD I be so happy, in this discourse, as to find any restless, weary, heavy laden soul, which longs to find rest, to find something on which it can safely and calmly repose itself; I may be sure of the attention of such an one, to what I have yet to offer on this subject. And may I not also expect the attention of such as have already returned to God, and found rest in him? Such, I am sure, will feel a satisfaction in being confirmed in that rest and peace, which they enjoy; yea, they will often find it necessary to call home their wandering affections, and to say with the psalmist, " Return unto thy rest, O my soul."

We have already considered, that there is an object (and O! remember that there is but one) on which the soul may rest, and in the enjoyment

of

of which, it may find satisfaction and happiness, equal to its most enlarged desires and highest expectations. We have also considered, that this object is God; that he who formed the soul, who made it to be happy in the enjoyment of himself, that he alone, can satisfy its desires and give it rest. Are you convinced of the truth of these observations? And are you desirous of inquiring how you shall go to God, in such a way and manner, as to find rest and peace, joy and comfort in him? It shall be my endeavor to answer your inquiry, while I proceed to the *third* thing proposed from the subject, which was,

III. To show what is implied in the soul's returning to this rest, or how it may do this.

The inquiry is important; and the more so, because many quiet themselves with a false rest, and peace, which will fail them, at a time when they most of all will need it. Many imagine, that they have rest in God, while they are indeed resting on other objects. Let us beware, that we do not deceive ourselves with a vain hope. If I am not deceived, the subject, which we have already been considering, or what was said in the last discourse, will help us to answer this important inquiry. The soul of man, we have observed, is full of restless desires; it flies from object to object, in pursuit of satisfaction, comfort, or happiness. This, I think, every one will readily acknowledge from his own experience. And he must, at the same time,

time, as readily acknowledge, that that object, or enjoyment, to which the soul flies for comfort, has the affections of the heart, or has its love. It is only by the affections, that the soul flies to any object. In the exercise of hope, desire, love, confidence, &c. the soul rests on an object; and in proportion as these exercises centre in, or are fixed upon, any object, in the same proportion does the soul fly to, or rest upon, that object. This being allowed (which certainly cannot be denied) it is evident,

1. That the soul's returning to God, as its rest, must imply, that the affections of the soul, its desire, hope, love, joy, and confidence, are placed on him.

Love is, indeed, the leading and governing affection of the soul; it necessarily carries all the affections of the heart along with it, to the object on which it rests. The object, which we love, is certainly the object of our desire; we never desire what we do not love. Hope, also, attends on love; for what we love, that we hope for; nor do we ever rejoice, or put confidence in any object, which we do not love. Indeed, all these exercises of hope, desire, joy, and confidence, are but modifications of love, or love variously expressed. So that love and affection are commonly used to signify the same thing. Love, also, commands those exercises of the heart, which are opposed to it, such as fear, dread, abhorrence, &c. For the only reason why we fear, is because we
love

love; not because we love and fear the same object; but because, when we love any object, then we are afraid of every thing, that will rob us of, or prevent our obtaining or enjoying that object. We never fear losing any thing, which we do not love; nor dread any thing, but what is opposed to the object, on which our love is placed. In proportion to our love of any object, in the same proportion will be our fear, our dread, our abhorrence of every thing, that opposes that object. Love, therefore, is the leading, governing affection of the soul; it is in the exercise of this affection, properly speaking, that the soul rests on any object. Hence it is evident, that in order to the soul's resting on God, its supreme love must be placed on him. In the same proportion as we love God, we shall rest on him, we shall place our hopes, desires, joys, and confidence in him. Hence pious men made those warm, pathetic expressions of love to God, which we mentioned, in the last discourse: " Whom have I in heaven, but God?" &c. &c. The soul can never return to God, as its rest, can never find real joy and comfort, peace and happiness in God, whilst it loves other objects and enjoyments more than God. Hence it is, that God has said, " There is no peace to the wicked; the wicked are like the troubled sea, when it cannot rest, whose waters cast up mire and dirt." Before the soul can ever return to God, and rest on him, it must, like the returning prodigal, be brought to a sense of its wretchedness and misery; it must see itself reduced to the greatest extremity; must see that it has been seeking for rest and happiness, where it can never be found; it must feel its affections returning home to its long forsaken Father, and rejoicing in his perfection and government. Then, and then only, can the soul rest on God. In this way, whosoever cometh to him shall find rest.

2. Returning to God, as our rest, must imply a free, full, entire, and cheerful submission to his will.

The soul can never rest itself on God, until it cheerfully acquiesces in his will. Rest must necessarily imply a calm, quiet, peaceable state; but this is certainly inconsistent with an uneasy, discontented, troubled mind. There can be no rest in God, or in any thing else, while the heart feels a disposition to murmur or complain, or to be in any measure unwilling to submit to the will of God. The moment such a disposition arises in the heart, the rest of the soul is disturbed. This is the great cause of all that sinful departure of mankind from God, An unwillingness to submit to his authority and government. When, therefore, the soul returns to God, as its rest, it comes and makes a cheerful and entire submission of itself, and its all, to the will of God. It rejoices in the universal dominion and government of the Diety; it is pleased with the thought of being resigned to his will. There can be no true love to God, without a love of submission

to

to his will, his authority, and superintendency. In proportion as we are uneasy and discontented with the will of God, our love to him abates. It is undoubtedly true, that the best of men, even those who enjoy the greatest rest in God, do sometimes feel a degree of reluctance at complying with the will of God; murmuring thoughts may arise; the passions not subdued may rebel. But when this is the case, their rest and peace are disturbed, nor can they become calm and quiet, and enjoy rest, until they return to God, in a way of unfeigned submission to his all perfect will, and give up all to his disposal. I may add,

3. Returning to God, as our rest, further implies faith in the Lord Jesus Christ, which is the only way of reconciliation between God and man.

It is only through Christ, and by faith in him, that the soul can rest in God. He is the way, the truth, and the life, and no man cometh unto the Father, but by him. He is our peace, who hath made peace for us. Through the all atoning merits of his blood, God is willing to receive returning prodigals. And in the belief of this, the soul returns to God, and rests on him. This faith, also, includes a belief of the divine promises to the penitent sinner; a reliance and confidence in God, that he will fulfil his word, on which he has caused him to hope. In this way, the word and promises of God lead the soul to rest. But when the christian suffers his faith to fail, when he becomes slow

of

of heart to believe; his rest is interrupted and disturbed, nor can he recover it, until his faith is confirmed and established, and he exercises a lively and unshaken confidence in God.

Because of the imperfection of the best of men, in this life, on account of the remainders of sin within them, and the lusting of the flesh against the spirit, there is no such thing as settled rest, in the present state; the best of men will frequently have occasion to call home their wandering affections, and say, "Return unto thy rest, O my soul." But the more our hearts are filled with love to God, and the more we are resigned to the will of God, the greater our rest and peace will be, and nothing but a departure from God can disturb this rest. There is, therefore, every inducement to return unto God, as our rest, that there could be, if perfect, undisturbed rest was the consequence; for it will really be so, in proportion to our love and subjection to God. And in this way only can the soul be trained up to a fitness for that state of perfect, uninterrupted, never ceasing rest and felicity, which is reserved for the saints in Zion above, and which certainly consists in the most ardent love to God, and the most perfect and entire subjection to his will. The nearer we resemble the blessed spirits above, in the temper and disposition of our hearts, the more we shall partake of their rest and felicity; the greater will be our evidence of our right and title to their joys; the more shall we rejoice

joice in the hope of the glory of God; and the more fensibly shall we feel and say with the psalmist, "I shall be satisfied, when I awake in thy likeness."

IMPROVEMENT.

1. The subject naturally leads us to reflect, how wisely God has ordered it, that men should find so little happiness, and meet with so many disappointments, troubles and afflictions, in this world.

We are ready, many times, to wonder, why there is so little happiness, and so many troubles, in this life. We are too often ready to complain of the little comfort, and of the many trials, troubles, and afflictions, which we here meet with; and when our most pleasing hopes are disappointed, and our most flattering expectations are blasted, we are too apt to think that ours is a hard lot. But, what are these hopes and expectations, which we complain of as disappointed? What are these troubles and afflictions, which are so hard and tedious to be borne? Are they not all worldly? And why have these things been such troubles and disappointments to us? Was it not because we set our affections too much upon them, and promised ourselves more from them than, in the nature of things, they could afford? The truth is, notwithstanding all the disappointments, troubles, and afflictions, which we meet with, in this life; notwithstanding our experience

of

of the infufficiency of all worldly enjoyments, to afford us reft and happinefs, yet we do fly to them for reft, and endeavor to repofe ourfelves on them. It is wife, therefore, it is kind in God, to order that thefe things fhould difappoint us, that thereby we might be led to feek for that reft and that happinefs, which he defigned and fitted us for; and that we might feek it now, while there is an opportunity to obtain it. Indeed, it is impoffible, in the nature of things, that earthly objects fhould fatisfy the defires of a rational and immortal foul, which is formed to enjoy reft in God. To complain, therefore, becaufe the world does not make us happy, or becaufe we cannot derive happinefs from it, is to complain, that we were made men, that we were not made brutes. Could the world deceive us, could it difappoint our hopes and expectations, if we did not fet our affections too much upon it? Should we complain of it, if our fouls fought for reft only in God? No, certainly. Is it not then wifely ordered of God, that we fhould find fo little happinefs, and meet with fo many difappointments, troubles, and even vexations, from the world, that fo we might be led to reft in God only? If men could find reft and peace, joy and felicity, in this world, they never would feek the heavenly reft. What then muft become of the foul, when ftripped of all its worldly enjoyments; when it quitted the prefent ftate, and entered the world of fpirits? Let us, then, inftead instead of complaining, that the world is full of trouble, disappointment, and sorrow, be thankful to God, that he is, in this way, weaning us from the world; and let us be concerned so to improve these things, as that we may thereby be led to God, and rest ourselves on him.

2. Let us learn the true and only proper use of worldly enjoyments, namely, to lead us to God, the supreme Source of rest and blessedness.

As comforts and conveniences here, we should receive them as evidences of the goodness of God. They may serve, in this way, to lead our hearts to the Fountain of all good. They may help us the better to serve God, and prepare us for the heavenly rest. But they should never have our hearts; we should never place our happiness in them, or attempt to rest our souls upon them. It is our own flattering expectations, which deceive and disappoint us. The fault is not in the world, or the things of it; they answer all the ends for which they were designed. The fault is in ourselves; we deceive ourselves; we prepare disappointments and sorrows, troubles and afflictions, for ourselves, by overvaluing the world, and promising ourselves that from it, which it was never designed to give us, and which it never can afford.

3. Let none blame God, if they are not happy, if they do not enjoy rest and peace.

This men are disposed to do; but it is infinitely unreasonable. " The foolishness of man perverteth his way, and his heart fretteth against the Lord." God has formed the soul of man, not only with desires of happiness, but with a capacity of obtaining and enjoying happiness; and this a happiness not mean, low, and contemptible, like that of brutes; but a happiness divine and Godlike, truly worthy of a rational and immortal mind. He has also kindly and plainly told us what this happiness is, and wherein it consists. And he has opened a way for our attainment and enjoyment of it. When we had forfeited and lost it, and might justly have been left to perish in our misery, he sent his own Son to recover it for us, and his Holy Spirit to lead and guide us to it; and he uses every argument and motive with us, to persuade us to seek after it. If, therefore, we finally miss of it, it must be owing to our own wilful, perverse and obstinate refusal of it. It must be because we seek it in wrong objects, and in such a way as it can never be obtained. It concerns all, therefore, *now* to make a wise and happy choice. Wherefore,

4. Let every soul be persuaded to rest in God.

Let us return to him as our only rest. We have, like prodigals, forsaken our heavenly Father, in whom alone we can enjoy rest. We have tried the world, its enjoyments and pleasures, enough to convince us, if we will act like rational beings, that there is no rest to be found in these things. Let each of us, then, seriously and solemnly call upon our souls, and say, " Return unto thy rest, O my soul."

foul." Let us return to God, as our only rest; and let us carefully remember what is implied in doing this. There are many, who seem to be convinced of the necessity of returning to God for rest; and yet they stop short of him. They rest upon religious duties; they betake themselves to prayer, and other devotional exercises, and here they rest, here they stop. But, methinks some may be ready to say, Is not this the way to return to God, in the performance of religious duties? I say, that barely to perform the external duties of religion is not returning to God; yet the pious soul does often return to God in the performance of these duties. But then it does not rest upon the duty, but upon God, to whom it draws near in duty. Hypocrites rest upon the religious duties, which they perform, not on God; but the truly gracious soul rests on God, in the exercise of holy love, and unfeigned submission, and lively faith; and these exercises are not only expressed, but many times awakened, excited, and stirred up, by the performance of religious duties. In order, therefore, to our returning to God, it is not enough that we set ourselves to perform the external duties of religion; but the soul must go to God in them, or they are all nothing.

Not only is it important for those, who have never yet returned to God, as their rest, now to do it; lest God, provoked by their revolt, should swear in his wrath, that they shall not enter into his
rest:

rest: But the real christian, who has heretofore fled for refuge to lay hold on the hope set before him, will find occasion renewedly to do it. The psalmist, no doubt, was a good man, before he expressed himself in the words of the text. How often will the good man find himself disturbed by fears some evil to come upon himself, his family, his friends, or the church of God; and perhaps his soul will be greatly overwhelmed and cast down within him! How important then will it be for him to calm his fears, by saying, "Return unto thy rest, O my soul!" How often is the good man in trouble, on account of some worldly losses, afflictions, or bereavements, and is ready to give up himself to grief, and say with Jacob, "All these things are against me!" What a happy effect will it have for him truly to say, "Return unto thy rest, O my soul!" How often does he find his heart going out in unreasonable desires after the world! And then what rest will he find in saying, "Return unto thy rest, O my soul!" How often does he find himself cold, remiss, and negligent in religion! And then his most certain remedy is, to say, "Return unto thy rest, O my soul." And in that last, that greatest, and most important trial in this world, when death shall lay its cold hand upon him, when his flesh and his heart shall fail him, then let him say, "Return unto thy rest, O my soul;" and his soul shall be immediately admitted to that rest, which remaineth for the people of God.

SERMON XI.

The Friend of God.

JAMES ii. 23.

And he was called the friend of God.

To be esteemed by great and good men, to have their love and friendship, is an honor and happiness, worthy of the desire and pursuit of every one. But to obtain the friendship of God, how much more honorable is it! How much more to be desired and sought after! This is what some men have obtained, and what all might obtain, if they would only seek it aright. Abraham obtained this honorable character, **that he was called** *the friend of God.* He was not **only called so** by men, who knew the intimacy that there was between God and him; but he was called so by God himself. Hear the divine declaration concerning him. " But thou, Israel, art my servant, Jacob, whom I have chosen, the seed of Abraham *my friend."* Friendship is love; it is almost more than love; it is more than that cold and lifeless affection, which

most

most men feel for one another; it is a warm and benevolent affection, which subsists between hearts mutually united, where there is an intimacy of union, where there is a mutual interchange of love and endearing benevolent actions. Such friendship can subsist only between kindred souls; can be found no where, but in hearts formed for love. There is something, which, in many respects, resembles this friendship, in a selfish and wicked person, but it is influenced and restricted by mercenary motives; and whenever it appears to be for the personal safety or advantage of such a man, he will desert and forsake, and sometimes betray his friend. True friendship, therefore, is founded in really disinterested love; it cannot exist without virtuous affection; it is found only in the gracious heart; it is an exercise of true Godlike love and benevolence. Abraham was the friend of God, and God was the friend of Abraham. The expression, " and he was called the friend of God", may be designed to denote either the love and affection, which God had for Abraham, or that which Abraham had for God; in both these respects, Abraham was the friend of God. There was a mutual affection and endearing intimacy between God and Abraham, as there is between near and intimate friends on earth. Here, then, let us consider,

I. How God manifested his friendship to Abraham: And then,

II. How Abraham manifested his friendship to God.
I. Let

SERMON XI.

I. Let us consider how God manifested his friendship to Abraham.

It may be said, in general, that all God's conduct towards Abraham was kind and benevolent; but there were some particular instances of his conduct, which were more peculiarly expressive of friendship, and which deserve to be distinctly mentioned. Here then;

1. The first particular mark or token of God's friendship for Abraham, was his calling him from Ur of the Chaldees into the land of Canaan, and giving that land for an inheritance to himself, and to his seed after him. This is the first instance of God's particular favor to Abraham, which we find mentioned in sacred history. Before this, he is only mentioned in the genealogy of his family, without any mark of distinction. But though nothing is said of any peculiar intimacy between God and Abraham, before this call to leave his country; yet we must suppose, that Abraham was acquainted with God before; for, when he received this call, he knew it came from God, and he had so much love to him, so much faith in him, and such an obedient heart, that he cheerfully went out, not knowing whither he went. This calling of Abraham, by God, was a very peculiar mark of the divine affection and favor towards him. Abraham was singled out, not only from among his brethren, his nation and people; but he only was thus called and chosen of God from all the inhabitants

of the world. And why was he thus called and chosen? Was it not because he was the friend of God, the favorite of heaven? This clearly appears from what God said to him at this time. Hear his endearing expressions of friendship. "Now the Lord said unto Abram, Get thee out of thy country, and from thy kindred, and from thy father's house, unto a land that I will shew thee: And I will make of thee a great nation, and I will bless thee, and make thy name great: And thou shalt be a blessing. And I will bless them that bless thee, and curse them that curse thee: And in thee shall all the families of the earth be blessed." It is true, these blessings look further than to Abraham and his immediate family, even to the whole nation of the Jews that descended from him, and to all believers, even among the Gentile nations. And the design of God, in calling Abraham, and separating him from the rest of the world, was not merely for the sake of manifesting his love to Abraham, but for the support of his church and people in the world. But that Abraham should be the man, whom God should choose; that he should be the man, in whom all the families of the earth should be blessed; this was an honor peculiar to Abraham, and shows him to be the friend of God. How dear to God must he be, to whom God says, "I will bless them that bless thee, and I will curse them that curse thee!" God would, in every thing, take the part of his friend, and interest himself

self in his welfare and happiness. Surely, then, God was the friend of Abraham.

2. Another mark of God's special regard and friendship for Abraham, was his entering into covenant with him, and thereby, as it were, making over to him all that he had.

It was an evidence of God's peculiar friendship for Abraham, that he took him and his posterity into a particular covenant relation to him, and gave him an outward seal or token of this covenant. By this covenant, the seal of which he had in his flesh, God engaged to be his God; he engaged to keep him, and to bless him; to give him temporal favors, and to bestow upon him eternal life. Never had God before entered into such a particular and formal covenant with any of the fallen sons of Adam. Abraham was the first, with whom God thus visibly covenanted, and to whom he gave a seal of his covenant. But you may inquire, what evidence was this of peculiar friendship for Abraham? Had not all his natural seed the same covenant, and the same seal of it? And has not God's visible church and people ever since been his covenant people, and enjoyed the seal of his covenant? Grant it to be so; still this does not prove, but that this was a peculiar token of God's friendship to Abraham. Was it not an honor to Abraham, and has it not been to his honor in every age of the world, that he was God's covenant friend, and that blessings were derived to all his seed through

through him, agreeably to the promise, "In thee shall all the families of the earth be blessed?" Was it not, and is it not now, the honor of Abraham, that he was called the father of believers? Besides, the covenant was sure to Abraham in a different sense, from what it was to all his natural seed; many of whom, notwithstanding they had the seal of the covenant in their flesh, never were really partakers of the spiritual blessings of the covenant. But Abraham was not only insured by this covenant, that he should have outward favors, a numerous seed, who should certainly possess the land of Canaan; but God did, as it were, make over himself to Abraham; for he expressly says, " I will be a God to thee." Abraham had every spiritual blessing, which is contained in the covenant of grace, absolutely confirmed to him; and this certainly must prove, that God was the friend of Abraham. Again,

3. Another thing, which evidences that God was a friend to Abraham, or another mark of his friendship, was, that he frequently visited Abraham, or made visible and sensible manifestations of himself to him.

Abraham was not, indeed, the only person, to whom God appeared, in the patriarchal age. Divine appearances were then frequent; many others were favored with them, as well as Abraham. But none but the friends of God, none but eminently pious and good men, were favored with such

such divine visits. We never read of God's appearing, or manifesting himself, to wicked men. Abraham was not only favored by God with a visible appearance, when God at first commanded him to leave his native country; but he was honored with frequent and repeated visits, with kind and endearing manifestations, and with gracious and solemn promises. The first appearance of God to Abraham was, as we have observed, when he was called to leave his country, which we have an account of in the 12th chapter of Genesis. What promises did God then make to him! How rich and full! The next particular and sensible visit, which Abraham had from God, was when Lot and he parted, and Abraham, to prevent all difficulty and controversy, had given liberty to Lot to choose any part of the land, and engaged himself to go another way. Then God appeared to him, and renewed the promise to give to him, and to his seed, all that land, and to make his posterity numerous as the dust of the earth. This is recorded in the 13th chapter. The 15th chapter is entirely taken up with an interview, shall I call it? or with a dialogue between God and Abraham, in which Abraham, who hitherto had no child, has the promise of a son, and of a seed as numerous as the stars of heaven; and in which he receives a renewed promise of Canaan, and a visible token and pledge of his enjoying it. In the 17th chapter, God again appears to Abraham, enters into a

particular

particular covenant with him, appoints the seal of the covenant to be circumcision, and promises him another son, from Sarai, whose name is, by divine appointment, altered to Sarah. There are repeated accounts, after these, of God's appearing to Abraham, and conversing with him, renewing his promises, and encouraging his hope and confidence in him, and his obedience to him; but as these, which have been mentioned, are sufficient to shew how, in this view, God was the friend of Abraham, I shall omit noticing them, and proceed to say,

4. It appears that God was the friend of Abraham, from his revealing his purposes and designs to Abraham, and thereby making him, as it were, the man of his council, his secret confidant, in whom he could confide.

In the 15th chapter, God informs Abraham, very particularly, what the state of his posterity should be; that they should be in bondage and servitude four hundred years, in a strange land; that after that, they should be brought out with great substance, and be put in possession of the land of Canaan; and that these things should take place after he was peaceably laid in his grave. "And thou shalt go to thy fathers in peace; thou shalt be buried in a good old age." But that which most of all discovers the friendship of God for Abraham, is his revealing to him what he designed respecting Sodom. The manner in which this account is given is indeed very remarkable. "And the

Lord said, Shall I hide from Abraham that thing which I do; seeing that Abraham shall surely become a great and mighty nation, and all the nations of the earth shall be blessed in him? For I know him, that he will command his children, and his houshold after him, and they shall keep the way of the Lord, to do justice and judgment; that the Lord may bring upon Abraham that which he hath spoken of him." Never could any thing more clearly discover God's friendship for any one, than this passage, which I have read, does God's friendly regard to Abraham. *And the Lord said,* he said to himself, he did as it were argue and reason the case with himself, *Shall I hide from Abraham that thing which I do?* or, as some read it, *Am I hiding from Abraham that thing which I do?* Can I go about such a thing, and not tell Abraham of it? Thus God is pleased to express himself in the language of men, who often reveal to some very near and intimate friend those purposes and resolutions of their hearts, which they keep concealed from every one else. And the reason which he gives, why he would reveal this to Abraham, is not only greatly to Abraham's honor, but is further evidential of his friendship for him. "For I know him," says God; I am fully acquainted with him; he is my friend and favorite; he interests himself in my cause; and he is one for whom I have great things in view; he shall become a great nation. Abraham must know, for

he

he will teach his houshold, he will take care to improve this knowledge aright, to give counsel and warning to his children after him, that they may learn to do justice and judgment: Abraham must know, because he will make a good use of his knowledge.

5. It appears that God was the friend of Abraham, or that he esteemed and loved him, from his hearkening to the voice of his supplication, and regarding his intercession; or from the influence and efficacy of his fervent prayers.

The apostle tells us, that the effectual fervent prayer of a righteous man avails much; and how is this verified in the instance of Abraham's intercession for Sodom! No sooner had God revealed to Abraham his purpose respecting Sodom, than he undertakes to intercede for that city. As God had said to himself, Shall I hide from Abraham that thing which I do? Shall I destroy Sodom, and not tell Abraham of it? So it seems as if Abraham said to himself, Shall Sodom be destroyed, and I offer not one petition for its preservation? After this, we have an account of his prayer, and the efficacy of it. Abraham drew near to God, in order to pour out his heart before him. And in his prayer he discovers great humility, great reverence of God, great faith in the justice and goodness of God, great pity and compassion towards sinners; and yet great boldness and confidence in his address to God. And we find, that, by his prayer,

he

he obtained all that he really asked for. God promised him, that he would spare the wicked for the sake of the righteous; that, if he found fifty, or forty five, or thirty, or even ten, righteous persons in the city, he would spare it. God continued granting his petitions, so long as Abraham continued to ask; and though Abraham gave up his request to have the city spared, if these could not be found; yet God granted his request, that the righteous might not be destroyed with the wicked; and therefore he delivered just Lot from the destruction. Can any thing be more evidential of real friendship, of real love, affection, and esteem, than this, to regard the petitions and grant the requests which are offered; especially for God to regard and grant the requests, even all the requests of such creatures as we are? Surely God was the friend of Abraham. I shall add only once more,

6. That God was the friend of Abraham, appears from the kindness, which God all along manifested towards him.

From the day that Abraham forsook his native land, to the last day of his life, God never left nor forsook him, but followed him with loving kindness and tender mercies. He continually protected and defended him; gave him peace from all the enemies which surrounded him; gave him favor with those, among whom he at any time resided; blessed him with riches and honor; gave him joy and happiness in his children, more especially in

his

his son Isaac; lengthened out his days to a good old age; gathered him to his fathers in peace; and received his departing spirit to the bosom of his love, where he has ever since remained, and where he shall remain, to enjoy the smiles, and sing the praises, of God and the Redeemer, through eternal ages.

Happy Abraham! happy wast thou, when once thou dwelt on earth. Though afflicted with inward weakness and infirmity, and though surrounded with outward trials and temptations; yet even then wast thou happy in the friendship of thy God, in the sweet manifestations of his love. But O! how happy, how inconceivably happy, art thou now! Now thou art free from sin, free from all imperfection, free from even painful trial, free from every kind and degree of temptation! Thou now enjoyest the full and complete friendship of thy Father God!

Would we, my brethren, be also called the friends of God; would we enjoy the tokens of his friendship? The way is as open to us as it was to him. We must be followers of them, who, through faith and patience, inherit the promises. We must become the children of Abraham: We must exercise the same faith, the same love, the same obedience, the same selfdenial, the same confidence in God; and keep up the same communion with God, that Abraham did; then shall we, like him, be called *the friends of God*.

SERMON

SERMON XII.

The Friend of God.

JAMES ii. 23.

And he was called the friend of God.

ABRAHAM is one of the most illustrious personages, which we find in sacred history. His character and conduct shine with a superior lustre. Few, if any, of mankind, deserve to be more admired than he. His example is, in many respects, and on many accounts, worthy of our most careful imitation. Since Abraham was a mere man, a sinful, imperfect creature, as we are, and since he enjoyed no external privileges and advantages for improvement in virtue and piety, superior to those we enjoy; why may we not equal him in every grace, and become as eminently the friends of God as he was? I observed, in the preceding discourse, that the expression, " he was called the friend of God," may be designed to denote either the love and affection which God had for Abraham, or that which Abraham had for God; in both

these

these respects it is true, that Abraham was the friend of God; though perhaps it is the former of these that is particularly intended. It was, however, proposed to consider the words in each of those views. In the former discourse, we considered how God manifested his friendship to Abraham, or discovered that he was his friend. We may now consider,

II. How Abraham manifested his friendship to God.

You will still retain this idea of friendship, that it is love, pure, genuine, unfeigned love, real affection and esteem, for a person or being. It is the cordial agreement, harmony, or union of souls. To say, then, that Abraham manifested his friendship to God, by his love to him, is only saying, that he manifested his love by his love, his friendship by his friendship, or that he was a friend to God.

The apostle James will answer the question before us in short, and tell us how it was that Abraham manifested his friendship for God, and how he obtained the honorable character, which is given to him in the text. He says, " Was not Abraham our father justified by works, when he had offered Isaac his son upon the altar? Seest thou how faith wrought with his works, and by works was faith made perfect? And the scripture was fulfilled which saith, Abraham believed God, and it was imputed to him for righteousness: And he

was

was called the friend of God." It seems, then, that in the view of St. James, Abraham manifested his friendship to God, and that he obtained this honorable character, to be called the friend of God, by his faith, or by his faith and obedience; by a faith which wrought with his works, and was made perfect by it. The only particular act of obedience which he mentions, is that of offering up his son, and so the only particular act or exercise of faith which he refers to, is that of his believing in the divine promise, that, "in him and in his seed, all nations shall be blessed;" or perhaps more particularly in that promise, "In Isaac shall thy seed be called;" accounting that God was able to raise him up from the dead, and that he would do this, rather than his promise should fail. But we are not to imagine, that it was only one exercise of faith, or one act of obedience, that gave Abraham this character of being the friend of God. His whole life, or his general conduct, proved that he was the friend of God. We may, therefore, derive advantage to ourselves, from a more particular survey of those things in the life and conduct of Abraham, which manifested that he was a friend to God, that he really loved and esteemed God, and that he valued his favor and friendship above every thing else. There are many things in the life and conduct of Abraham, which deserve particular notice. Here then we may observe, in the first place,

1. That

1. That Abraham manifested his love to God, or his affection and friendship for him, by a cheerful obedience to his commands.

Abraham had the same general commands to obey, and the same common duties to perform, that we and all others have. These he performed, we may suppose, with carefulness and fidelity, and with uncommon alacrity, which was one reason, why God put his obedience to such peculiar trials, that so he might stand upon record, as an eminent and illustrious example of obedience to all future generations. The particular and remarkable instances of his cheerful obedience to the divine command, which are recorded in the word of God, are two: That of leaving his native land, and that of offering up his beloved son a sacrifice to God.

The first of these was a proof of his readiness to obey the divine will. God said to him, while dwelling with his friends and kindred, " Get thee out from thy country, and from thy kindred, and from thy father's house, unto a land which I shall shew thee." This was the command; and what made it peculiarly trying was, that he was not only required to leave the only country with which he was acquainted, and all his kindred and friends, except such as would accompany him; but to go he knew not where, nor how far. He must wholly give up himself to the divine guidance and direction, and follow wherever God should lead. St. Paul says, " He went out, not knowing whither he went."

SERMON XII.

went." But Abraham obeyed the divine command, becaufe he knew God was acquainted with his true character, and was a real friend to him. He knew that God would not direct him to do any thing, which was not wife and good. He knew that God was his friend, that God would not banifh him from himfelf, if he did from his earthly friends; and he was willing to go to any place, where God would go with him. By this, therefore, he manifefted himfelf to be the friend of God.

The other inftance of obedience required and performed was ftill more fingular and furprifing. "Take now thy fon, thine only fon Ifaac, whom thou loveft, and get thee into the land of Moriah; and offer him there for a burnt offering, upon one of the mountains which I will tell thee of."

How painful is this precept! Every word which God makes ufe of is enough to cut him to the heart. *Take now thy fon*—not thy bullock, not thy lamb, not thy fheep, not thoufands of rams; but take *thy fon*; and this not Ifhmael, who had been caft out and cut off from the family; but thine only fon that is left, he on whom all thy hopes are built, in whom all the promifes centre—that fon whom *thou loveft*, whom thou preferreft to every earthly friend. And what is to be done with him? Why he muft be offered up for a burnt offering; not barely fent off and banifhed from the family, which would have been painful indeed, though eafy in comparifon with this; for then hope might have had fomething to

reft

rest upon. But this is not the order—no, he must die, and not only die, but he must be offered up for a burnt offering, he must be consumed to ashes. Well, if it must be so, may not Abraham be allowed to commit him to some one as the executioner? No; the father must put him to death with his own hand; and he must do it after full deliberation and reflection; for he must go three days' journey with him, before he can reach the place of execution. Does he appear to hesitate whether to obey or not? No; he knew it was the command of God; he knew that he ought to obey, and he delays not a moment to execute the divine injunction. He rises early in the morning after he had received the command, and steadily pursues the journey, with an unalterable and fixed resolution to obey, until, on the third day, he comes in sight of the place where the fatal scene was to be acted. Then, leaving his servants, he takes his son along with him to the destined spot; there he builds his altar, lays the wood in order, binds his son, lays him on the funeral pile. Now he stretches out his hand and takes the knife. Still his heart does not fail him, nor his hand refuse to perform the painful task—he is fixed in his resolution to obey God, whatever it may cost him. God accepts the will for the deed; he sees his willing and obedient heart, he stays his hand, and presents him with a ram, to be offered in the place of his son. The command was given to make trial of his obedience, the trial was made, and

and his obedience proved. It now appeared, that Abraham was indeed the friend of God, seeing he withheld not his son, his only son from him. Again,

2. Abraham manifested his friendship to God, by his faith and confidence in him.

Faith and confidence in another, is many times as strong a proof of love and affection as any thing can be. Abraham was a true believer in God, and put the most implicit confidence in every thing which God said. He believed that God was invariably faithful to his word; he believed that heaven and earth should pass away, and the whole course of nature change, sooner than God's word should fail. This faith and confidence in God Abraham discovered on all occasions, however unlikely, or even impossible to human view it seemed, that his word should be accomplished. It was this faith and confidence in God, which induced him to leave his native land. So says the apostle to the Hebrews. " By faith Abraham, when he was called to go out into a place which he should after receive for an inheritance, obeyed; and went out, not knowing whither he went." Though God, when he called him, did not particularly tell what land he would give him; yet it seems he had made some promise to him of an inheritance, and he believed that God would give it, confiding in his goodness as well as faithfulness. By faith he sojourned in the land of promise, as in a strange country, dwelling in tabernacles with Isaac and Jacob, the heirs with him of the same promise ; for he looked for a city which hath foundations whose builder and maker is God." Abraham not only believed the promise, that his seed should inherit the land of Canaan ; but he considered this land as a type of heaven, and believed that he should inherit this also. His faith was again tried in the promise of a son by Sarah in his old age. This, according to the common course of nature, was impossible ; but he knew and believed the power and faithfulness of God. And we are told, " being not weak in faith, he considered not his own body now dead, when he was about an hundred years old, neither yet the deadness of Sarah's womb : He staggered not at the promise of God through unbelief; but was strong in faith, giving glory to God."

But the greatest trial of his faith was that which was the greatest trial of his obedience. " By faith, says the apostle, Abraham, when he was tried, offered up Isaac : And he that had received the promises, offered up his only begotten son ; of whom it was said, that in Isaac shall thy seed be called." This was indeed a trial of his faith. How was it possible, that all the promises which God had made him of a numerous posterity should be fulfilled ? And especially how was it possible, that this promise in particular should be fulfilled in Isaac, if he were put to death in his youth ? Where would

SERMON XII.

would be any room for faith? On what could faith be founded? Would it not be folly, presumption, and even madness, to expect that a numerous posterity should spring from a dead child? But Abraham knew that the promise was absolute, and he was equally certain that God was faithful; he therefore believed God, accounting that God was able to raise him up from the dead, even from the ashes of a burnt offering; and that he would do it, sooner than his promise should fail. Abraham's faith, therefore, proved him to be a friend to God—one that relied on his power and goodness, his truth and faithfulness; one who would confide in God, and against hope believe in hope.

3. Abraham's friendship to God was manifested, by a course of cheerful submission and selfdenial.

Nothing was too dear to him to be parted with for God. He was willing to part with father and mother, kindred and friends, and even with his beloved son, who was dear to him as his own soul, whenever God required it. Did he ever murmur and complain at the will of God? Did he ever manifest a reluctance at parting with any thing, which God called for? No; he appeared to be all submission: Not my will, but thine be done, was the language of all his conduct! What painful trials did he meet with! and with what meekness and humble submission, did he bear them! By such conduct, he made it appear, that he regarded the divine will more than his own private good, and that he was a true, sincere, disinterested friend to God.

4. Abraham manifested his friendship to God, by his daily and intimate converse and communion with him.

Friends love to meet and converse together; and they take every convenient opportunity to visit each other. As God manifested his friendship for Abraham, by frequent visits, by repeated promises, and by endearing communications; so Abraham manifested his friendship for God, by his frequent and intimate converse with him. It is true, there is no particular mention made how often Abraham was employed in prayer and praise, and other religious devotions, in which the pious soul has communion with God, and keeps up an intimacy with him; yet there is enough said to make it evident, that Abraham was a man of prayer, and that he was no stranger to communion with God. We find him engaged in this duty himself, and enjoining it upon others. At his first entrance into the promised land, he came to the place called Sichem, and there the Lord appeared unto him, and said, " Unto thy seed will I give this land;" and there he builded an altar unto the Lord, who appeared unto him. And he removed from thence unto a mountain on the east of Bethel, and there he builded an altar, and called upon the name of the Lord. From this place he went down into Egypt, because of a famine in the land; but he soon returned to

Bethel,

Bethel, where he had before built an altar; and there, we are told, he again called on the name of the Lord. At length, he removed his tent, and came and dwelt in the plain of Mamre, which is in Hebron, and built an altar there unto the Lord. In every place where he dwelt, he built an altar, and called on the name of the Lord. It is clearly evident, therefore, that he was a man of real piety and devotion; a man of prayer; one who kept up a constant communion with God. Several of his prayers are mentioned; and there is one in particular, which you can never forget, his fervent intercession for Sodom. Such faith, obedience, and submission, as he often exercised, could not be maintained, without prayer. And his prayers and devotions proved him to be the sincere and intimate friend of God.

5. Abraham clearly manifested his friendship to God, by his faithful endeavors to promote his cause among men.

It is the part of true friends to espouse each other's cause, to make the interest of each other their own. As God manifested his friendship to Abraham, by taking his part, and espousing his cause; so Abraham manifested his friendship to God, by professing and promoting true religion among men.

Abraham not only paid a sacred regard to the commands and laws of God himself, but he endeavored to bring others to do the same. Hence,

God says of him, "I know him, that he will command his children, and his houshold after him, and they shall keep the way of the Lord, to do justice and judgment." Abraham not only took pains to teach his children and servants the knowledge of God and his ways; but he exerted all his authority over his houshold, to oblige them to do justice and judgment. This was a bright part of Abraham's character; it was greatly to his honor, and very evidential of his friendship to God. Thus did Abraham in every way manifest his love to God, and his regard for his honor and interest in the world. It is true, that Abraham's love, notwithstanding the great trials it endured, and the astonishing acts, which it led him to perform, was imperfect. Abraham was guilty of some great sins. " There is not a just man upon earth, that doeth good, and sinneth not." But still he is an eminent and illustrious example to saints in every age; and in him we learn, not only what is our duty, and how we ought to conduct towards God; but how, like him, we may obtain the honorable character of being the friends of God, and how we may secure the blessing of that glorious and all perfect Being.

And now, let me ask you, my brethren, whether you are the friends or the enemies of God? Whether you are in heart reconciled to God, to his laws and providence? And whether you manifest your friendship to him, as Abraham did?

Does

Does your love to God, and your friendship for him, appear in your cheerful obedience to all the intimations of his will? You have not been called to such painful and trying acts of obedience as Abraham was; the strength of your love has not been tried by a command, to forsake every thing for God; yet you have met with many things in the course of life to try you, whether you would submit to God and obey his will. Have you then been obedient? Have you been ready to perform the most self denying duties? Have you had respect to all the divine commands, and been disposed to say, All that the Lord our God requires, we will do, and be obedient? You may have sometimes transgressed. Abraham did. But do you feel a heart to obey? Have you an obediential temper? Is it the desire of your heart, and the endeavor of your life, to obey the will of God?

Have you manifested, and do you manifest, your love and friendship to God, by your faith and confidence in him? Do you rely and depend, with the most implicit confidence, on his word, believing all that he has said, and looking for the accomplishment and fulfilment of all his promises, and of all his threatenings? Do you believe in the Son of God, the Savior of sinners, and rely upon him for pardon and eternal life; and in the belief of God's word, do you live in the hope of eternal life, which God, who cannot lie, has promised?

Do

Do you, like Abraham, discover your friendship to God, by a cheerful and entire submission to his providence? Have you given up yourselves, and your all, to his absolute disposal? Are you willing that God should order all your circumstances in life, and can you part with your dearest friends and comforts, at his call, without murmuring or repining?

Do you manifest your love to God, your friendship for him, and your delight in him, by a daily and frequent intercourse and communion with him? There is nothing, perhaps, more evidential of love and friendship, than a pleasing and endearing converse and communion. It is in this way, that friends do, as it were, interchange hearts, and give each other the strongest expressions of mutual confidence, love, and esteem. Have you this evidence of friendship to God? Do you draw near to God? Do you delight in coming into his presence? Do you keep up a daily and delightful intercourse and communion with him? Have you your altar for morning and evening sacrifice in your houses? Are your families witnesses of your devotions, and called to join in them? And do you find communion with God in your devotions? How can you think, that you are the friends of God, if you neglect prayer; if you do not converse with God; or if you live as without God in the world? Do you thus neglect your earthly friends? Be not deceived, God is not mocked;

he

he cannot be deceived by your empty professions. He knows the heart; he knows whether the desire of your soul be towards him, and whether you really delight in maintaining a friendly intercourse and communion with him. Once more: Do you manifest your friendship to God, by endeavoring to promote his cause and interest in the world? Are you careful to teach and command your families to keep the commands of God, and to do justice and judgment? Do you wish that the cause of God might flourish; and do you endeavor to promote it, by your prayers, your example, your counsels and instructions, and, as far as your influence extends, by your authority? These questions may help you to determine, whether you are the real friends of God, or hearty enemies to him. If you are the friends of God, you are, and you will be happy. God is your friend. And how happy are those, who have God for their friend, and exceeding great reward! But how dreadful is the condition of those, who are enemies to God! God is as awful and terrible to his enemies, as he is amiable and kind to his friends. As though, therefore, God did beseech you by us, we pray you, in Christ's stead, be ye reconciled to God.

SERMON

SERMON XIII.

Self Knowledge, or Acquaintance with our own Hearts

PSALM iv. 4.

Commune with your own heart.

WE find ourselves this moment in the house of God! Yet, such strange, inconsiderate creatures are we, that, it is more than probable, there are some here present, who have not once seriously thought of their being in the house of God. Though some serious, solemn duties have been already performed, yet some may have paid no real attention to them, nor once have considered, whether they had any concern in them, or not. It is certain, therefore, that some men do not really know, at certain times, what is done, or said, or what takes place, in their immediate presence. We commonly say, that they are inattentive—the truth is, they are attending to something else. The eye often calls up the mind to some object, which presents itself to view, and which so entirely engrosses the attention, that, although the ear hears the
sound

SERMON XIII.

found of a voice speaking, yet it conveys no idea to the mind. At another time, the ear engages the attention of the mind so absolutely, that the eye can make no impression on it. The eye and the ear convey to us most of our ideas of material objects. But there is another way, by which the mind furnishes itself with many important ideas, that is, by meditation, or reflection; when the mind does, as it were, shut itself up, and pay no attention to the objects which the eye beholds, or which the ear hears. Hence, we are sometimes surprised to find a man in such a deep study, as we call it, or so much engaged in thinking upon some subject, that he seems not to see the objects that are immediately before him, nor to hear the words that are immediately addressed to him. But when this is the case, the mind is either attending to some object or enjoyment, which the eye has before seen, or which the ear has before heard of; or attending to some mere creature of the imagination. But there is another (I had almost said, divine) power, which the mind has, of shutting out from itself all the objects and enjoyments, which the bodily senses have ever presented to it, and of turning its attention inward upon itself, and contemplating its own powers, capacities, and exercises, or, in the language of the text, " communing with itself." When the psalmist directs us to commune with our own hearts, the direction is, to turn off our attention from every other object and enjoyment, and

fix

fix it wholly upon what passes within us. This excellent capacity man has, and it is peculiar to man; that is, in this, man is distinguished from all the other creatures, that inhabit this earth, with which only we are acquainted. A very little attention to ourselves will convince us, that we are different beings from the beasts, birds, fishes, worms, and insects, of this earth, not only in the form and fashion of our bodies; but still more in the powers and capacities of our minds, or in that spirit which dwells in and animates the body. Though the most of these creatures appear to have a kind and degree of knowledge, and thought; yet it is very evident, that their knowledge is vastly different in nature and kind, as well as degree, from ours.

To have our whole attention, therefore, fixed on external objects and enjoyments, is to act unworthy our character, as rational and accountable creatures. Nothing so much demands our attention, as our own hearts; and yet, I presume, nothing is so greatly and generally neglected. Hence it is, that mankind in general are not only strangers to their own hearts, but strangers to human nature. For there is really no such thing as knowing human nature, but by becoming intimately acquainted with our own hearts. Human nature is not learned, by seeing men's bodies, or hearing their voices; (for these do not constitute human nature) but by knowing the heart of man; for it is the heart

that

that makes the man, or determines what he is. But how can we know the hearts of others? I answer, by knowing our own hearts; for, as in water face anfwers to face, fo the heart of man to man. All mankind have the fame nature; and it may be faid, in one fenfe, that the hearts of all men are the fame; that is, by nature all are equally corrupt and finful. It is true, that one man is naturally more inclined to one particular fin, or to one particular way of manifefting or acting out the wickednefs of his heart, and another, to another; but ftill they all poffefs the fame corrupt heart, until, by the power and grace of God, it is renewed. This, I know, many are unwilling to allow; but the only reafon is, they are ftrangers to their own hearts. I do not mean, that all men are equally wicked, though it be equally true of all, that their hearts are corrupt and finful; for it is an undoubted truth, that fome men increafe in wickednefs much fafter than others; fome are under much greater reftraints than others; and fome difcover their wickednefs by overt acts of fin, while others conceal it within themfelves. But the word of God, which certainly is true, reprefents all mankind as, by nature, the fame fallen, corrupt, and finful creatures. And this every man would fee and feel to be the truth, if he was really acquainted with his own heart: And this acquaintance with his own heart he might have, if he would really and faithfully commune with it. We become acquainted with others, by

frequent

frequent and intimate communion with them, by seeing and observing them in different situations and circumstances, and by carefully attending to their words and actions. A man may be frequently in company with another, may see and hear him converse often; yet, if he be not particularly attentive to him, if he does not carefully observe him, if he is not disposed to look as it were into him, and find out what he is, he will be a stranger to his real temper and disposition. The same may be said with respect to ourselves. It is not a very easy matter to gain a real and intimate acquaintance with our own hearts: And few people are really disposed to get this acquaintance. There is nothing more generally neglected by mankind, than their own hearts. In this sense, they are seldom, if ever, at home. Their attention is taken up with the world and the things of it. Their thoughts are employed, even when their hands are idle, about the riches, the honors, or pleasures of this life. Present objects and enjoyments swallow up their whole time. In consequence of this, they remain ignorant of themselves, and unacquainted with their own hearts. In order to become acquainted with our own hearts, we must commune with them, that is, we must carefully attend to them, at all times and under all circumstances. We must watch them carefully, examine them critically, and judge of them impartially, by the unerring rule of God's word. This is the only sure rule, the only infallible

standard,

standard, and this will never deceive us. Men certainly may become acquainted with themselves; they may know their own hearts; they may know what passes within them, as well as what passes without them. They can always find their hearts, for they are always at hand.

But it may be objected, that the prophet Jeremiah says, " The heart is deceitful above all things, and desperately wicked; who can know it?" It is true, the heart is wicked, exceedingly so, and it is also deceitful, and men are often deceived by it; but this is principally owing to their inattention to it, to their quick and hasty determinations respecting it. Men are strangers to their own hearts, and therefore are continually liable to be deceived by them: But the man who daily watches his own heart, carefully observes what passes there, and tries his thoughts and feelings by the word of God, will soon become acquainted with the treachery of his heart, and will not be deceived by it. The more corrupt and wicked the heart is, and the more deceitful it is, the more need there is of paying a constant attention to it, keeping the strictest watch over it, and attentively observing all its motions. If we know a man to be deceitful, and have any concern with him, we always suppose it is proper and necessary to watch him more critically, and observe him more narrowly, on that account. This certainly ought to be the case with respect to our own hearts; for deceit here is infinitely more haz-

ardous

ardous than in any other case. For man to deceive himself with respect to himself is, of all evils, the greatest; since such an one can never really know what he is, how he does act, nor in reality how he ought to act. Hence it is, that among all the creatures that exist, none act so absurdly, so inconsistently, and so unworthily as man. These may appear to some to be harsh expressions, and hard reflections on human nature ; but commune with your own hearts, and, I am persuaded, you will find them to be true respecting yourselves. Let me then recommend to you this self acquaintance, this attention to and communion with your own hearts, from the following considerations.

Without this attention to your own hearts, you never can know what creatures you are ; how you ought to act ; how you do act ; or what will be the consequence of your actions.

1. Without this attention to and communion with your own heart, you can never know what creatures you are. We have already observed, and a little attention will prove the observation just, that it is the heart, which makes the man, or forms his just and true character. It is not the form and shape of his body ; it is not his bodily beauty or deformity ; it is not the softness and sweetness, or harshness of his voice ; it is not his saying little or much ; it is not his worldly poverty or wealth ; it is not his being in or out of office among men ; it is not his learning, or ignorance ; that forms a man's

moral,

moral, which is his real character: But it is his heart, or the inward temper and disposition of his mind. This must be evident to every one, who views mankind, in the light in which God views them, which is undoubtedly a just light; that is, rational and moral agents, accountable creatures. Hence it appears, that he who is a stranger to his own heart, must be a stranger to his own character; he does not know himself, he does not know what a creature or being he is. He knows, indeed, that he is a rational creature; he knows what kind of body he has, and what his outward circumstances are; and he may be so foolish as to think, that these things form his character. And, in truth, these things do form all the character that some men have in the view of others like themselves, who forget that men have hearts, because they have never attended to their own moral exercises. But if a man's real character depends on his heart, or is as his heart is, then he cannot know what a creature he is, without knowing what his heart is. Without attending to his own heart, he cannot know whether he has a sinful heart, or a holy heart; whether he has an honest heart, or a deceitful heart, and yet upon this his true moral character depends. But it may be thought, that every man knows so much of himself, as to know he has a sinful heart. I question it. Every man may know, that he has been guilty of some sins, that he has done those things which the law of God forbids; but in viewing these sins, he looks not to his heart, but to the outward conduct only; he knows nothing about his heart. Hence it is, that so many deny the natural sinfulness of the heart. And for the same reason, they entirely overlook the greatest part of their guilt, which lies in the inward exercises of their hearts. Men are guilty, perhaps, of a thousand sins in the heart, to one in their outward conduct; and for want of attention to their hearts, they are ignorant of themselves, and blind to the real criminality and turpitude of their characters. Hence it is, that many men think themselves to be very different creatures from what they really are. This was the case of the Laodiceans, to whom Christ says, "Thou sayest, I am rich, and increased with goods, and have need of nothing; and knowest not that thou art wretched, and miserable, and poor, and blind, and naked." It is, therefore, absolutely necessary, that we commune with our own hearts, in order to our knowing what creatures we are.

2. Without knowing our own hearts, we cannot know how we ought to act.

No man can know how he ought to act, and what he ought to be, who does not know what sort of a creature he is, and what situation he is in. The man, who views himself as having existence in this world only, and thinks nothing of his connection with another, will act only with respect to this world; and if, in fact, he was made only for this world, he would act right and consistently with his

real

real character. But if man is made for immortality, if he has entered upon an endless existence, if this world is only a state of trial and probation for an unchangeable and eternal state, then certainly all his conduct ought to be directed to that state; and he who acts only for this world acts out of character, acts inconsistently.

Furthermore; if we allow that every man does know, that he is made for immortality, and ought to live for another world, without any great attention to or examination of his own heart; yet it is certain, that many do not live and act for eternity, that is, as they ought to; nor can they, without a particular acquaintance with their own hearts. For, without this knowledge of their own hearts, they cannot know what those duties are, which they ought to perform. He who is ignorant what manner of person he is, cannot know how such a person as he is ought to act. He who is unacquainted with his own sinful heart, cannot feel his obligation to repent of all his sins, and turn from them unto God. A man can never feel his obligations to repent of sins, which he is not conscious of committing. He must see and feel his guilt, before he will ever cast himself at the foot of an offended God, and own that he deserves his wrath and curse forever. He must see his own heart, before he can feel his need of Christ; for " the whole need not a physician, but they that are sick." It is owing to this ignorance or unacquaintedness with their own hearts, that most men are so entirely unacquainted with the nature of religion, and think that all they have to do is, to attend to some external acts of duty, in which the heart is never engaged. But let them once become acquainted with their own hearts, and they will immediately see what they have to do, and how they ought to act. They will then see what now they cannot perceive, that they have much to do with their own hearts; that every thing depends on the heart, and that nothing is of any avail, unless the heart be in it. It is therefore impossible, that any one should know how he ought to act, and what he has to do, without an acquaintance with his own heart. Nor,

3. Can he know how he does act, without knowing his own heart.

As a man's character depends upon his heart, and is as his heart is; and as duty primarily and essentially respects the heart; so he can never know what his conduct is, or how he really acts, without knowing what are the exercises of his heart. An action is morally good or evil, duty or sin, according to the temper and disposition of the heart from which it proceeds. How then can any man know whether he has done duty in any action, unless he knows the temper and disposition of his heart, with which the action is performed, or from which it proceeds? Many are ignorant what their conduct is, because ignorant of their own hearts. Indeed, very few know what their actions are.

And,

And, perhaps, thofe who are the leaft attentive to their own hearts, and the leaft acquainted with themfelves, are the moft confident of the goodnefs of their own actions. It is for want of an acquaintance with their own hearts, and the real temper and difpofition with which they act, that a great part of mankind think they are doing God fervice, when they are acting very wickedly. Hence many deceive themfelves with the thought, that they are acting well, and going in the way of life, while they are walking in the broad road to deftruction. This leads me to add,

4. That without knowing our own hearts, we cannot know what will be the confequence of our actions.

If we knew our own hearts, and knew the nature of our actions, we might know the final confequence of our conduct. God has plainly told us in his word, what the confequence of every action will be; that is, he has told us, that "the wages of fin is death," and that fin, unrepented of and unforfaken, will be punifhed in "the lake which burneth with fire and brimftone." And he has plainly and certainly told us, that "he that believeth fhall be faved," and whoever "is born again fhall fee the kingdom of heaven." If, therefore, we can fo far know our own hearts, as to know that we are in a ftate of fin, then we may know that we are in a ftate of condemnation, and that the wrath of God abideth on us. But if, on the contrary, we know that we are renewed after the image of God, and have the spirit of the gospel, then we may know that we are heirs of God, and joint heirs with Christ, and be assured of our present good estate, and of our final salvation.

How important, then, is the direction in the text: " Commune with your own heart." Would you know what you are—how you ought to act—how you do act—and what will be the consequence of all your conduct, commune with your own hearts; examine them critically and impartially; compare them with the word of God; and look to Him, who knows them perfectly, and fervently pray, " Search me, O God, and know my heart; try me, and know my thoughts; and see if there be any wicked way in me, and lead me in the way everlasting."

SERMON XIV.

Joy for the Happiness of Others.

LUKE xv. 9.

And when she hath found it, she calleth her friends and neighbors together, saying, Rejoice with me; for I have found the piece which I had lost.

THE parable of the lost piece of money, and the preceding one of the lost sheep, were both (you will probably recollect) spoken by our Lord, as a reproof of the Scribes and Pharisees, for their murmuring and complaining at his conduct, in receiving sinners, and eating with them. Both these parables are designed to teach us, not only that there is joy in heaven for the conversion of a sinner; but that it is our duty also to rejoice in such an event; yea, that it is our duty to rejoice in all the comfort and happiness of others. He, who found the sheep which he had lost, called together his friends and neighbors, and said unto them, "Rejoice with me, for I have found my sheep which was lost." And the woman, who had

lost

lost and found her piece of money, did the same. It is an addition to the joy of any one, to have others share with him in his joy. And those who had found their lost goods seem to take it for granted, that their friends and neighbors would rejoice with them. This, you may say, was naturally to be expected; for who would not rejoice with his neighbor, that had found any thing which he had lost? But let me ask, in my turn, Does every one do this? Does every one rejoice in the good of his neighbor? Far from it! There are many, who seem to grieve at the good of others; who envy them their comfort and happiness; and who seem to be unhappy themselves, merely because others enjoy more than they. But our text, in connection with the parable, and our Saviour's exposition of it, clearly teaches us this important truth:

That it is the duty of every one to rejoice in all the good and happiness of others.

Reason and revelation will both conspire to establish the truth of this observation, however repugnant it may be to the selfish feelings of those, whose hearts know *no joy*, but what arises from personal good.

It is abundantly evident, that the angels of heaven, those perfectly holy and benevolent beings, do not only rejoice in the glory and felicity, which they themselves enjoy in the immediate presence of God; but also in all that happiness, which is diffused through heaven and earth. Their highest pleasure, their greatest joy is that, which arises

from

SERMON XIV.

from the honor and glory of God; next to this, they rejoice most in the greatest good and happiness of his creatures. Hence it was, that when God laid the foundations of the earth, and began the creation of this world, these morning stars sang together, and all the sons of God shouted for joy. They rejoiced that the scale of happiness was enlarged, and a new and extensive source of good opened. So again, when the Savior of the world was born, and a particular angel was sent to inform the shepherds of this most auspicious and happy event, not only did this particular angel exult with joy in being the happy messenger of such good tidings, saying, "Fear not, behold I bring you good tidings of great joy, which shall be to all people;" but a vast multitude of the heavenly host, transported with the most lively joy on this happy event, came to shew their most cordial congratulations, and with a glowing ardor joined in a general song of praise, saying, with united voices, " Glory to God in the highest, and on earth peace, good will toward men." These are not the only instances which prove, that angels rejoice in the good of others. Our Lord assures us, in our context, that there is joy in heaven, joy among the angels of heaven, over one sinner that repenteth; that not a single sinner can be converted from the error of his ways, and brought home to God, and to an interest in the benefits of the Redeemer's death, but those amiable spirits rejoice in it. Their

joy

joy is increased, their happiness is enlarged, by the increase of good to a single individual! And for the same reason, notwithstanding their high and glorious exaltation, they are pleased with being ministering spirits to mankind, and are happy in being the instruments of good to those, who are the heirs of salvation. Now, if such be the disposition of these dignified spirits, if such be their joy and pleasure, and such their gratitude and *praise* to God for the good and happiness of others; surely it must be our duty to feel and express the same benevolent disposition. It will certainly be an honor to us to imitate and resemble these blessed spirits.

And if we attend to the character of the best of men, as it is delineated in the sacred scriptures, we shall find, that they always rejoiced more in public, than in private, blessings; and that they dreaded and deprecated public judgments and calamities far more, than those which were private and personal. Thus Moses, when God was angry with his people, and threatened to blot out their name from under heaven, and to make of him and of his family a favorite people for himself, fervently prays, that God would rather spare them, and blot him out of his book. So David, when God was visiting his people with judgments, prays that God would spare them, and let his judgments fall on him and on his house. St. Paul says, that he could wish himself accursed from Christ, for his brethren

his

his kinsmen according to the flesh; and that he had great heaviness and continual sorrow in his heart for their unbelief. He expresses the same spirit in all his epistles; for he every where gives thanks to God for all the spiritual gifts and graces bestowed, either on the churches in general, or on particular members. And it was this love to the happiness of others, which made the apostle, and which makes every good man, willing to deny himself, and suffer personal inconvenience, pain, and trouble, in order to relieve the distresses and promote the happiness of his fellow creatures. In a word, so universally amiable is the man, who interests himself in the good and happiness of others; who rejoices in all the happiness of the world around him; and who is willing to do any thing, or to suffer any thing, for the public good; I say, so universally amiable is such a man, that even the writers of novels and romances, who would delineate the most perfect characters, find it necessary to make their Hero possess and display this benevolent disposition. Every man, however different his own character may be, is always pleased and delighted with one, who rejoices with those that rejoice, and who weeps with those that weep—who enters into the feelings of others, and partakes with them in their joys and sorrows. Every man would have others feel and do so towards him; and is not the plain language of all this, " Go thou, and do likewise." What one maxim, what one direction

tion is there, that comes more home to the confcience of every man, and carries more conviction with it than this; "What ye would that others fhould do to you, do ye even the fame to them?" Hence it muft be the duty of every one to rejoice in the good of others.

But in order, if poffible, to fet the truth of this obfervation in a clear, familiar, and convincing light, it may not be amifs to confider the reafonablenefs of one perfon's rejoicing in the good of another. Here then let it be obferved,

1. That happinefs is in itfelf defirable to all, and therefore we ought to rejoice in the happinefs of all.

That happinefs is in itfelf defirable, we need no other proof than that which every man finds and feels in his own breaft. It is a felf evident truth; and to offer any labored arguments to prove it, would be an affront to common fenfe. But if happinefs be defirable in its own nature, and we all defire it for ourfelves, why fhould we not defire it for others? Or if we rejoice in our own happinefs, why fhould we not rejoice in the happinefs of others? For,

2. The happinefs of others is as important as our own happinefs.

If every man does not feel the truth and importance of this obfervation, it is not becaufe it is not as true as the former, but becaufe he is too much fwallowed up in himfelf to feel any thing, which

does

SERMON XIV.

does not immediately respect himself. His reason and conscience, however, will convince him, if he will but attend to their dictates, that the happiness of another is as important as his own. Happiness is not desirable merely because *it is mine;* but because it is, in itself considered, a good, a desirable object. Self, therefore, has nothing to do with the real nature of an object or enjoyment; that is, self does not increase or diminish the real worth and excellency of it, though it often does our joy or complacency in it. The happiness of another, is as truly happiness, as if I enjoyed it; and the greatness of this happiness is the same, whether I enjoy it, or another.

It is one perfection of the Deity, that he is no respecter of persons; that he has an invariable regard to the general and greatest good of his creatures. Who can wish to be the only object of divine favor, to enjoy every thing himself, to engross all good ? Is it not suitable, that God should confer happiness and bestow favors upon others as well as upon us ? If others are capable of enjoying happiness as well as we, why should not their happiness be as important as our own, and why should not we rejoice in their happiness as truly as in our own ? It is possible that the happiness of another may be more important than our own; and therefore we ought to rejoice in it more than our own. When I say, the happiness of another *may be* more important than our own; it may perhaps appear a

strange

strange assertion; but, consider a moment; is not the happiness of a man of more importance than the happiness of a beast? Yes, certainly; for a man is of more value than many beasts or sparrows. The happiness of a man is a rational happiness, but that of a beast is merely animal—the happiness of a man is much greater than that of a beast, and therefore the happiness of a man is a much greater cause of joy, than that of a beast. Ought we not then to rejoice more in the happiness of a man, than in that of a beast? Yes, certainly; and why? Because it is of more worth and value; not because of any personal interest in either. For the same reason, the happiness of one man may be of more consequence and importance, than that of another man; his happiness may be more rational, as well as greater in degree, than that of another; and therefore ought to be more rejoiced in. Every man is capable of feeling happiness; but every man is not capable of feeling an equal degree of happiness. But in proportion as men are capable of feeling and enjoying happiness, and in proportion to the nature and kind of their happiness, in the same proportion is their happiness to be rejoiced in. We all know, that one particular object or enjoyment will contribute more to the happiness of another, than it will to our own; therefore we ought to rejoice more that another possesses it, than if we possessed it ourselves, because hereby the general good is increased. Hence it is, that benevolent minds rejoice in the happiness of others; yea, that they are willing, in many instances, to suffer for their good. And hence it is, that we are required to give to him that needeth; to feed the hungry; and to clothe the naked. What we impart of our good things to such, will more increase their comfort and happiness, than it will diminish our own; yea, if we are truly benevolent, it will augment our own personal happiness. This leads me to observe,

3. That another reason, why we should rejoice in the good and happiness of others, is, that in this way we become partakers with others in their happiness.

The good man, whose heart rejoices in the good and happiness of others, has a perpetual source of the most pure and refined felicity. He can at all times look around him, and see happiness and rejoice in it. If he has not himself every enjoyment that he could wish, yet he finds one and another possessing some desirable enjoyments, and rejoicing in them; and when he considers that they are as dear and important to others as they would be to himself, his soul enters into the joys of others, and he rejoices with them in all their happiness. In the exercise of such a benevolent temper, the good man does, as it were, participate the joys of saints and angels in heaven. When he reflects upon the pure and sublime pleasures and enjoyments of those holy beings above, his heart rejoices with them,

them, in all their felicity and blessedness. For the same reason, and in the same way, he participates the joys of the world around him, and shares in all the happiness which they possess. He is pleased with the thought of that goodness, which fills heaven and earth; and his benevolent heart gives thanks to God for all the happiness bestowed upon his creatures. The sacred Scripture, and in particular the Book of Psalms, is full of praise, not only for personal favors, but for God's goodness to all. And St. Paul in all his epistles gives thanks to God, for all spiritual blessings, in particular, bestowed on all the saints. Now, these things prove that the **benevolent soul not only** rejoices in the good and happiness of others, but does also, as it were, partake of the blessings which others enjoy, merely because they are happy. The more our hearts rejoice in the good and happiness of others, the more happy we must necessarily be. It is not the possession or enjoyment of this or the other object, that makes men happy; but it is the heart that rejoices in universal happiness. I may add,

4. It is our duty to rejoice in the good of others, because herein we resemble God himself.

The infinite goodness and love of the Deity causes him to delight in the good and happiness of his creatures. It was this, that caused him to create so many beings capable of enjoying happiness, and to make such ample provision for their enjoyment of it. And he does, undoubtedly, in the course of his

his providence, confult the greateft good, not of an individual, but of the whole fyftem. He is not partial of his favors to me, or to another man; but he is good unto all, and his tender mercies are over all his works. And fo far as any one refembles God, he will rejoice, not only in favors conferred upon him, but in thofe that are conferred upon others. He will rejoice in the greateft good of the whole intelligent fyftem. Let us then cultivate this benevolent fpirit, and learn to rejoice in the happinefs of all around us.

IMPROVEMENT.

1. From the fubject we infer, that true love is difinterefted; or, in other words, that the religion of the gofpel requires difinterefted affection.

Mankind in general are almoft entirely fwallowed up in felf. They are concerned about only their own intereft and happinefs. They know little of any other joy, than that which arifes from perfonal good. They are greatly indifferent about the good and happinefs of others, if they can but enjoy happinefs themfelves; yea, many would be willing that others fhould be miferable, if their mifery would but turn to their own perfonal advantage. For this reafon it is, that many will fteal, cheat, defraud, and opprefs others, to increafe their own wealth. And for this alfo it is, that many are difpofed to injure and abufe, afflict and diftrefs others, to procure some personal benefit to themselves. But this is directly contrary to the spirit and genius of that gospel, which teaches us to love our neighbors as ourselves, and to do to others as we would that they should do to us. He, who is possessed of this spirit, will be as truly concerned for his neighbor as for himself; and he will rejoice in his neighbor's good, as sincerely as in his own. This is disenterested love—this is the religion of the gospel.

2. The subject teaches us the evil of envying the happiness of others, and of murmuring and complaining because others enjoy more than we do, or because they possess things which we do not possess.

This is the spirit and temper of many. They look round them, and see others in the possession and enjoyment of things which they have not; and instead of rejoicing in their happiness, they are the more miserable on this account. They would, perhaps, be tolerably contented, with what they have, if no one were in a better situation; but because others are more happy, they feel themselves more miserable. But why should the happiness of another make me more miserable? Why should I envy another those enjoyments which contribute to his comfort? His happiness is as important as mine, and perhaps more so; and his happiness cannot diminish mine, unless I please to turn it into an object of envy, instead of joy. So far ought we to be from envying the prosperity of others, that we ought to rejoice

joice in it. If we are miserable, we ought to rejoice that others are happy. It is, indeed, an old and common observation, "That misery loves company." But, if this be true, it is a melancholy truth, and affords a striking evidence of the corruption of the human heart. To love misery is a diabolical temper; it is the same that prompted the devil to seduce mankind, because he himself had lost his honor, dignity, and happiness. But is there not too much of this spirit and temper to be found in all our hearts? Do we not often feel a disposition to complain, when we look round and see others happier than ourselves? This is far from a christian spirit. We ought rather to rejoice in all the happiness, which we see a kind and bountiful Providence is pouring into the bosoms of our fellow men.

Suffer me to ask, whether Lazarus ought not to have rejoiced, when he lay in poverty and pain, that all men were not in his wretched condition; and even that the rich man was able to fare sumptuously every day? Suppose a number of malefactors are condemned to die; but at length, they are all pardoned but one, and he must suffer a painful and ignominious death. Shall he complain, because others are pardoned, and he is not? Shall he wish them to suffer, merely because he must? No, if he possesses a good heart, he will say, "I rejoice, that you have obtained a pardon; that your lives are spared; that you are restored to your friends;

friends; and that their hearts will be filled with joy on your account. I too could have wished for a pardon; but, though I must die, I rejoice that you can live. Your death could be of no advantage to me; it could not ease me of one of my pains, nor in the least degree lessen the anguish of my heart. Live, then, and rejoice; and let all rejoice with you." Would not such a character and conduct be amiable? Go, then, and do likewise. Rejoice with them that rejoice.

SERMON

SERMON XV.

The Hypocrite.

JOB, xxxvi. 13.

But the hypocrites in heart heap up wrath.

THERE is no character more odious in the view of God and man, than that of a hypocrite; none against which there are more woes denounced in the word of God. It is true, a man may put on the mask, and so constantly wear it and act under it, as never to be really discovered to be what he in fact is; that is, men may never discover him to be a hypocrite, and therefore may never despise him in this world. But no mask can deceive God; no profession can hide the heart from him. For the Lord seeth not as man seeth; for man looketh on the outward appearance, but the Lord looketh on the heart. Men may not only be deceived by the conduct of others, so as to think those to be real saints, who are but painted hypocrites; but they may also think those to be hypocrites, who are not, as Job's friends did with respect to him.

him. They accused Job of hypocrisy, and thought he was guilty of it, merely on account of the outward evils and calamities in which he was involved. They were as ignorant of the true character of God, as they were of Job's. They thought it inconsistent with the character of God, to bring a good man into such troubles as they saw Job in, and therefore concluded that he must be a hypocrite. But they were deceived. Job was a good man, notwithstanding all the evils that surrounded him. Elihu evidently supposes, that good men may meet with afflictions; but that these will do them good, will humble and reform them, and that then they will be removed; while those who are not benefited by afflictions will be destroyed. Hence he says, " But the hypocrites in heart heap up wrath." —" See, says one, the nature of hypocrisy. It lies in the heart, that is for the world and the flesh, when the outside seems to be for God and religion. Many that are saints in shew, and saints in word, are hypocrites in heart. That spring is corrupt, and there is an evil treasure there. See also the mischievousness of it. Hypocrites heap up wrath. They are doing that every day which is provoking to God, and they will be reckoned with for it altogether in the great day. They treasure up wrath against the day of wrath; their sins are laid up in store with God among his treasures." Since, then, the sin of hypocrisy is so great, and the end of it so awful, the subject demands the particular attention

of

SERMON XV.

of every one, and more especially of those, who profess friendship to God and his ways. And though it belongs not to us to determine whether this, or the other man, is an hypocrite; yet it belongs to every one of us to determine for himself, whether this be his own character. It will, therefore, be proper for us, in this discourse, more particularly to point out the nature of hypocrisy, or to show wherein it consists; and also the evil of it. Accordingly, I shall endeavor,

I. To delineate the character of an hypocrite, or show in what hypocrisy consists.

II. To shew the evil of it, or the awful and aggravated condemnation of hypocrites—"they heap up warth."

I. I am to delineate the character of an hypocrite, or shew wherein hypocrisy consists.

And here I wish, if it were possible, so to describe the character of an hypocrite, as that those who are such may see what they are; and no longer build a hope upon a sandy foundation, which the floods of divine wrath will finally sweep away; and so as likewise to afford comfort to the sound believer. But how shall I do this? Not by making the religious experiences of any man the standard; but by carefully attending to the character, as it is represented in the word of God. Here then we may observe,

1. That an hypocrite is one who professes to be what he really and in fact is not. This is a short

and

and juft definition of an hypocrite; and is no doubt what is generally, if not univerfally, underftood to be the meaning of the word. There are hypocrites in things of this life, as well as in religion. When any one makes particular profeffion of friendfhip for another, and yet in heart is not his friend; he is an hypocrite. But a hypocrite, in a religious fenfe, is one who makes profeffion or outward fhow of religion, of love to God, of obedience to his will; and yet in heart is an enemy to God, and his ways. From whence it appears, that one who makes no profeffion or pretence to religion, one who pays no regard to the external parts of religion, and does not pretend to do any religious duties, but indulges himfelf in fins of omiffion and commiffion, and that in the view of the world; fuch an one cannot, with propriety, be called a hypocrite; for he is an open and avowed enemy of God; he lives in the moft open and daring rebellion againft the Majefty of heaven. Though all mankind are in fact divided into two effentially different claffes, and are all either faints or finners, friends or enemies of God; yet finners or enemies of God, may again be divided into two other claffes, namely, his *fecret* and his *open* enemies. Thofe are the *fecret* enemies of God, who, under the mafk of friendfhip, under the external covering of religious profeffions and outward duties, are heartily oppofed to his character and government. And thofe are his *open* enemies, who

act

act out the wickedness of their hearts, and discover it in the wickedness of their lives. The former of these two kinds of sinners are hypocrites, whose character we are more especially to attend to in this discourse. An hypocrite, then, is one who makes public profession, or outward show and appearance of religion, or who, at least, performs some external duties, which God requires, but yet is not a real christian at heart. Therefore,

2. An hypocrite is one, who, under the profession of religion, or outward show and appearance of it, is actuated, not by supreme love to God, but by some selfish and sinister views and motives. The real christian is one, whose heart is for God, one who loves God with supreme affection; who loves God more than the world and all things in it, more than his own life, yea, more than his own soul. And all the duties which he performs proceed from this principle of supreme love to God. He professes religion, because he feels it. He says openly that he loves God, because the love of God is shed abroad in his heart. He devotes himself to the service of God, because he loves his service; he feels in his heart that he loves his Master, and would not go out free. He obeys the divine commands, because he delights in the law of God after the inward man. He has respect to all God's precepts, he esteems them all to be right, and hates every false way. But the hypocrite,
notwithstanding

notwithstanding all his fair professions and formal duties, is corrupt at heart; his heart is not right with God, nor is he governed and actuated in what he does, by love to God, but by love to himself. All his professions and performances proceed from some selfish principle. Some make a profession of religion, and perform external duties, merely that they may be seen of men. This Christ said was the case with the Pharisees, whom he calls hypocrites. They prayed standing in the corners of the streets, that they might be seen of men. They also gave alms from the same motive and in the same manner. And it has often been the case, that men have made profession of religion, and performed many outward acts of duty, merely to recommend themselves to others, that they might be thought to be good men, or that others might have the better opinion of them. Now such are hypocrites in heart, whatever they may be in the view of the world. So are all those, who make a profession, or perform any outward duties of religion, because it is the custom or fashion of the people among whom they live, or who do it to gain advantage to themselves, or to their families. He also is an hypocrite, who makes a profession of religion, and sets himself to perform religious duties, merely out of fear of divine wrath, or to obtain heaven by his duties; for it is evident that his religion is merely selfish and mercenary. Instead of being actuated by supreme love to God, he is governed ernedentirely by love to himself. This, it is abundantly evident, is only hypocrisy. This was the religion of the people of Israel, when they were terrified by the thunders of mount Sinai. Though they unanimously said, all that the Lord commanded them, they would do, and be obedient; yet, in less than forty days, they made a calf and worshipped it, and said, "These be thy gods, O Israel." So when they smarted under divine judgments, then they were full of promises and professions. "When he slew them, then they sought him; and they returned and inquired early after God. And they remembered that God was their rock, and the high God their redeemer. Nevertheless, they did flatter him with their mouth, and they lied unto him with their tongues. For their heart was not right with God, neither were they stedfast in his covenant." Satan insinuated, that the religion of Job was of this kind, merely selfish; but he was deceived with respect to the matter. It is to be feared, however, that the religion of many, if not of most, arises from no better source, than the hope of the divine favor, or the fear of the divine wrath. If this be the case with any, their religion is not the service of God, but of themselves; they are only hypocrites. I doubt not but there are many, who are wholly actuated by this principle of self love, and who are destitute of true love to God, that yet think they are no hypocrites. Some really suppose, if they are sincere in seeking heaven in

the

the way of outward duty, which God has enjoined, they are acting right, though they are influenced altogether by felf love. But they are in reality mere hypocrites; they are not the friends of God, but lovers of themfelves. It is certain, that not only thofe who mean to deceive others, by their profeffion and external religious performances, are hypocrites; but thofe alfo who deceive themfelves. Hence it is, that we find fuch expreffions as thefe refpecting hypocrites : " The hypocrite's hope fhall perifh. The joy of the hypocrite is but for a moment. What is the hope of the hypocrite, though he hath gained, when God taketh away his foul ?" From whence it appears, that hypocrites may have great and confident hopes of future happinefs, and great joys arifing from thofe hopes ; and yet find themfelves awfully difapppointed. " There is a generation, fays Solomon, that are pure in their own eyes, and yet are not wafhed from their filthinefs." According to the word of God, therefore, all thofe perfons are hypocrites, who affume the profeffion, and put on the outward garb and appearance of religion, and yet are not in heart friends to God. Hence Chrift fays of fuch, " They make clean the outfide of the cup, and of the platter, but within are full of extortion and excefs." They are like unto whited fepulchres, which indeed appear beautiful outward. Outwardly they appear righteous unto men, but within are full of hypocrify. They honor God with their lips, but their hearts are far

from

from him." Hence it is evident, that hypocrify confifts in profeffing or pretending friendfhip to God, when the heart is not fincere and upright with him. Or he is an hypocrite, who makes an outward fhow of religion, and yet is not in heart a real chriftian, or true friend to God.

But fome may ftill be difpofed to inquire, How fhall I know whether I am an hypocrite or not? How fhall I determine whether I am actuated by a fupreme regard to God, or by love to myfelf? If men may not only deceive others, by a profeffion of religion and the performance of external duties, but may deceive themfelves too; how fhall I know whether this is not the cafe with me? This queftion is important, and deferves a ferious and careful anfwer. And in anfwering it, I fhall have further opportunity to give you the character of the hypocrite. Among others, we may mention the following marks of hypocrify.

1. Hypocrites are more concerned to gain the approbation of men, than the approbation of God. The real chriftian feels himfelf in the view of God, and realizes his all feeing and heart fearching eye, in all his religious performances. Hence he is ever concerned about his heart in duty, and folicitous to have that right with God. He is not fo much concerned about his words and actions, as about his thoughts and affections. He is not fo much concerned about the expreffions which he makes ufe of in prayer, as about the exercifes of
his

his heart. He is as careful to watch over his most secret thoughts and actions, as over his most public conduct. But the hypocrite is not so much afraid of secret sin, as he is of that which is open, and exposed to the view of men. He would not do any thing that the world can find fault with, he is afraid of the reproach of his fellow mortals, but he often indulges secret sins. He is much concerned about what the world thinks and says of him, though but a little concerned about his heart, and what God thinks of it. But it is a small thing to be judged of man's judgment. It is infinitely more important to secure the approbation of God than of man. And therefore it is a dark mark of hypocrisy, to be more concerned to approve ourselves to men than to God.

2. Hypocrites are more concerned to perform public duties than private, and more concerned about the manner of duty than the matter. Hypocrites often neglect secret prayer, when they will not neglect to pray in public. They are concerned to pray well before men, when any thing will satisfy them in private. They can easily quiet themselves with running over a mere form of prayer in secret, and saying a few words in haste; when they would be ashamed to pray in such a manner before their family, or any of their fellow men. Nor is this all; they often feel much more engaged, much more lively in their public, than in their secret devotions. And for this reason, because they are

are more concerned about the honor that cometh from men, than that which cometh from God only.

3. Hypocrites are often very exact in little matters, when they are careless about more important things. This Christ remarks in the conduct of the scribes and pharisees, who were hypocrites. "Wo unto you scribes and pharisees, hypocrites! for ye pay tithe of mint, and anise, and cummin, and have omitted the weightier matters of the law, judgment, mercy, and faith; these ought ye to have done, and not to leave the other undone. Ye blind guides, which strain at a gnat, and swallow a camel." Hypocrites are apt to attend to external duties, to the modes and forms of religion, while they neglect the power and life of religion. They may be stated and constant in their morning and evening prayers, but scarcely think of God, the rest of the day. They may very punctually attend public worship on the Sabbath, but neither retain nor practise the duties which they hear solemnly and plainly inculcated. And though they confess their sins before God, yet they are much more affected with a sense of guilt, on account of particular external sins, than on account of the corruption and wickedness of their hearts. They are like a cake not turned. They are uneven and inconsistent in their views, and feelings, and conduct.

4. Hypocrites are more influenced by fear than by love. They are more apt to be engaged in religious duties, when their fears are alarmed, and they

they question their title to heaven, than when their hopes are bright and strong. This is very different from the conduct of the real christian. He is more influenced by love than by fear. Hence the greater his love, the more engaged he is in the duties of devotion. Love is a more constant principle than fear. This makes the sincere christian more steady and uniform in his religion, than the hypocrite. When the latter enjoys hope, and sees no danger, he is cold, remiss, and negligent in his religious duties, and often casts off fear, and restrains prayer before God. Hence that demand of Job concerning the hypocrite, "Will he delight himself in the Almighty? Will he *always* call upon God?" This question plainly supposes, that hypocrites are not disposed to call upon God steadily and uniformly, but are moved to do it, by fear, or some other constraining motive.

5. Hypocrites are apt to have an high opinion of their own goodness, and to be full of self confidence. The language of their hearts and lips is, "Stand by thyself, come not near me; for I am holier than thou." And our Savior spake a parable to certain, "that trusted in themselves that they were righteous, and despised others." The hypocritical scribes and pharisees looked down upon all others, with the greatest contempt, and thanked God, that they were not as other men. But the sincere christian has a low and abasing view of himself, and is ready to think others better than

than himself. The psalmist said, "I am more brutish than any man." And Paul said, "I am less than the least of all saints." Hence it is a mark of hypocrisy, for men to have a high opinion of their own attainments in grace, and to look upon themselves better than common christians. I may add,

6. Hypocrites often fall away. This was often the case with the false hearted Israelites. They were almost constantly declining in their religion. God says, "They were bent to backsliding." Though they made high professions of love and obedience, yet their love soon waxed cold. Though they sang God's praise with raptures, when they experienced his mercy; yet they soon forgat his works. And we find by observation, that some, who make the highest pretences to religion, and express the highest joy, and warmest zeal, soon lose their raised affections, become cold and indifferent in religion, and at length fall into open vice and total apostasy. To this Job seems to have an eye, when he says of the hypocrite, "Will he delight himself in the Almighty? Will he always call upon God?" This not only expresses the inconstancy of the hypocrite; but seems to intimate his proneness to backslide from God, and forsake his ways. These are some of the marks of hypocrisy, some of the particular and prominent features of the hypocrite. And they ought to be attended to by all; especially by those, who profess to be the

true disciples of Christ. Many have been deceived, and probably many more will be in time to come. When our Lord mentioned the hypocrisy of one of his disciples, every one of the rest cried out with solicitude for himself, " Lord, is it I ?" If our heart condemn us ; God is greater than our heart, and knoweth all things. But if our heart condemn us not, then have we confidence toward God.

SERMON

SERMON XVI.

The Hypocrite.

JOB, xxxvi. 13.

But the hypocrites in heart heap up wrath.

THE nature of hypocrisy, or the character of an hypocrite, I endeavored to describe in my last discourse. In which it was made to appear, that hypocrisy is a profession of, or pretence to religion, when the heart is not in it. It is assuming the christian name and character, and attending to and performing the external duties of religion, from selfish views and motives, either to gain the esteem of men, or the approbation of God, without any regard to his honor and glory. A man is a hypocrite in religion, if, in his religious professions and practices, he is aiming only at his own interest. Yet this is the very end which hypocrites have in view. For this cause they put on the outward garb of religion. But how far will they fall short of their end? How different will be the event and issue of their religion from what they expect?

SERMON XVI.

Instead of laying up for themselves treasures in heaven, as they expect, our text tells us, " they heap up wrath." An hypocritical profession of religion may answer their purpose in this world; it may gain them a christian name; it may procure them the applause of men; but it will not avail them after death : " For what is the hope of the hypocrite when God taketh away his soul ?" This will more clearly appear from attending to the second proposition, which is,

II. To show the evil of hypocrisy, or the awful end and aggravated condemnation of hypocrites— " they heap up wrath."

The evil of hypocrisy may appear from the view which men naturally have of an hypocrite; from considering how odious and despicable the character is in the view of every one, in the things of this life. Every one despises in his heart the man, who acts the hypocrite towards his neighbor; who speaks fair to his face, but reproaches him behind his back; who professes great friendship and esteem for him, when, at the same time, he is an enemy to him in his heart. The man, who professes great love to his neighbor, a readiness to serve him, and to do him all the good in his power; and yet, at the same time, is only seeking to serve himself, to promote his own private advantage, such an one, I say, is despised by every one. And is hypocrisy and deceit less odious, when exercised towards God, than when it is exercised towards man ? Is it a less crime

SERMON XVI.

crime to pretend friendship to God, when the heart is not in the profession, than it is to make the same false pretence to man? No, this cannot be imagined. Hence God every where expresses his displeasure against hypocrites. And Christ often denounced his woes against such; he calls them "whited sepulchres," and says to them, "ye serpents, ye generation of vipers; how can ye escape the damnation of hell?" It is certain that hypocrites cannot deceive God, by all their solemn professions of religion; for he knows their thoughts, searches their hearts, and tries their reins. And as he cannot be deceived, so he will not be mocked. He requires truth in the inward part; he has pleasure in uprightness; he hateth lying and deceit; he has no delight in mere external services. Accordingly, he declares, that in the judgment of the great day, when many shall plead what services they had done for him; how they had eaten and drank in his presence, cast out devils in his name, and in his name had done many wonderful works; he will then profess unto them, I never knew you; and will say, Depart from me, ye workers of iniquity. It is abundantly evident from the whole tenor of sacred scripture, that none but the real friends of God, none but those whose hearts have been renewed by the power and grace of God, will be finally admitted to the enjoyment of him.

But hypocrites shall not only lose their labor in religion, or miss of heaven, which they seek after;

but as they now heap up wrath, so they shall hereafter meet a most awful and aggravated condemnation. There is something peculiarly criminal in known and allowed hypocrisy; it is solemn falsehood; it is devout deceit; it is injuring under the pretence of friendship. Secret enemies are the worst kind of enemies; by them Christ is wounded in the house of his friends. Like Judas, they say, Hail, Master, and kiss him, that they may betray him. Hypocrites, especially those who deceive themselves, are the least likely to obtain salvation; for they feel secure from conviction, they think themselves safe from the wrath to come, and are not alarmed at all the threatenings of God's word against sinners. They think themselves rich and increased in goods, and have need of nothing. The means of grace, therefore, only serve to harden their hearts, and blind their minds, and stupify their consciences, and make them ripe for ruin.

But furthermore; hypocrites heap up wrath to themselves, as their own consciences will forever condemn them in the world to come, for professing what they never felt, and what they never practised; for satisfying themselves with only a name to live, while they were dead; for acting a deceitful part, and deceiving themselves as well as others, with an empty show. Their own hearts will condemn them, for abusing the means of grace, and using them only to ripen themselves for destruction. They will feel the folly of toiling in external duties, ries, in which their hearts were never engaged. Hypocrites, therefore, are spoken of as some of the vilest and most wretched of sinners; for it is represented as an aggravation of the punishment of the finally impenitent, that they shall be doomed to have their portion with *hypocrites* and unbelievers. We now pass to improve the subject.

1. If the character of the hypocrite has been justly described in these discourses—if it consists in professing religion, when the heart does not feel it; in professing friendship to God, when the heart is at enmity with him; or in acting from love to self, instead of aiming at the glory of God; then we learn, that true religion does not at all consist in outward professions or practices, but in the inward exercises of the heart, in the temper and disposition of the mind. It is true, external professions and outward duties are required, and the good man will as naturally perform them, as the good tree will produce good fruit; but yet, in themselves considered, or separate from an upright heart, they are nothing. But you may ask, Does not God require us to perform external duties, to read, pray, attend public worship, and the like? I say, Yes, I said it before; but does God require men to be hypocrites? Does he require them to profess what is not true? Does he require them to profess themselves to be his friends, when they are his enemies? Does he require them to pray, or to do any other external action, with a wicked heart?

No;

No; David says, "If I regard iniquity in my heart, the Lord will not hear me." And Solomon says, "The sacrifices of the wicked are an abomination to the Lord." A man may live all his life time in the profession of religion, and in the performance of external services, and yet do no part of his duty, but remain an hypocrite, and only heap up wrath to himself against the day of wrath. Hence it clearly appears, that true religion consists in the pure and upright intentions of the heart, and not in mere external services.

2. We infer that many persons are deceived, not only with respect to their real character, but deceived with respect to their religious services. Multitudes dare not make a public profession of religion, lest they should be hypocrites; but yet they perform many external acts of duty, and think there is something really good and acceptable to God in what they do. But they deceive themselves; for there is some kind of profession in these external religious duties, and if their hearts be not right with God, in the performance of them, they are only hypocritical services. And what of duty is there in hypocrisy? Can God be pleased with such services? No; if we do not act from love to God, if we do not aim at his glory and honor in our religious duties, we act the part of real hypocrites.

3. From the subject we infer, that it is the heart which determines every one's character, or that every one is in reality as his heart is. If in his heart

he

he loves God, if he is cordially reconciled to his law and government, if he is actuated by a regard to his honor and glory, then he is a chriftian. But if his heart be unrenewed, if it be under the power and dominion of fin; if he be actuated only by a regard to himfelf; then, notwithftanding all his reformations of life, notwithftanding all his religious profeffions and pretences, and notwithftanding all his outward acts of duty, he muft be confidered as an enemy to God. So fays Solomon, " As a man thinketh in his heart, fo is he;" as the temper and difpofition of his heart is, fuch is he in reality. A man may be very diligent and careful in the performance of outward duties, and be thought by the world in general to be a very good man, and yet be only an hypocrite; for hypocrify lies in the heart, and therefore out of the view of the world. We can judge only from what is outward, from what appears to us, and therefore if a man appear to us to act well, if his outward conduct and behavior be good, we may and ought to hope that he is a good man; but God looketh at the heart, and will judge according to that; for that determines his real character.

4. We learn of what importance it is, that every one look to his heart. It is for want of looking to our own hearts, for want of knowing our own hearts, that we are fo ignorant of ourfelves. Moft men are ftrangers to their own hearts. Few look to their hearts at all; they pay fome attention to their outward conduct, and from this determine

their

their character. Sinners look to their outward conduct, and most of them think that they are not very bad. They do not commit many sins; they do not steal, nor lie, nor get drunk, nor swear, nor cheat, nor commit adultery, nor fornication; they mean to be honest and upright in their dealings, and injure no man's person or property; and therefore they think that they are very good kind of folks: And, indeed, for this world they are good sort of folks; it is well for the world, it is for the benefit of society, that they are such. But what is this in the view of God, who searches the heart? Is not all this consistent with a heart at enmity against God? a heart under the power and dominion of sin? Do not such live every day, every hour and moment, destitute of that love to God and love to man, which is the fulfilling of the law, and the whole of duty? Sin does not consist so much in those outward acts of wickedness, from which they refrain, as it does in a corrupt and wicked heart. This they have every moment; and yet being insensible of it, they can live in peace and quietness in sin. I have often been surprised to find sick and dying persons, when complaining of their wickedness, mentioning that they had done this or that act of wickedness, and that they had omitted this or the other outward act of duty; as though all their sin and wickedness consisted in these things, while they say nothing about the wickedness of their heart, in which all criminality consists.

fists. For the same reason, or for want of attending to and knowing the wickedness of their own hearts, it is, that the very worst of men do not think themselves very bad. It is true, they have sometimes got drunk, or they have sometimes stolen, defrauded, committed adultery, and the like; but they are free from other crimes which other men commit; and it is but a few times that they have done these things, and therefore they cannot think themselves very criminal. So, because they have not done every wicked action that ever was done, they are not very wicked; though they have in many instances acted out the wickedness of their hearts, and at all times possessed a heart fully set in them to do evil, and as corrupt and vile as can be conceived of. From the same cause, that is, from ignorance of their own hearts, others, who have kept themselves from gross acts of wickedness, who have performed many outward acts of duty, who have lived in the practice of attending public worship, and family and secret prayer, are ready to imagine, that they are really very good christians; when, at the same time, they are only hypocrites, and under the power and dominion of sin. How important is it, then, that we should attend to our own heart, and examine it very critically and impartially; especially since the heart is deceitful above all things and desperately wicked. Men are universally fond of thinking well of themselves; and because we wish to have a good opinion of ourselves, we

easily

easily entertain it. But how dreadful will it be to remain blind to our own character, until death undeceive us, and we open our eyes in a world of misery, where there will be no remedy! Let us, then, feel the importance of having a right heart, of acting from a real regard to God, and of aiming sincerely at his glory in all our conduct. Since this is the only right motive, since if we are destitute of this we are, at best, no better than hypocrites, let us see to it, that our hearts be right with God.

5. From this subject we infer, that true religion is infinitely important to all mankind. Nor is this inference unnatural; for even the hypocrisy of men proves it to be true. If religion were of no importance, their would be no hypocrites. It is only that which is good that is counterfeited. Men feel the importance of religion; at least, that it is of some importance, otherwise no one would make pretensions to it. But we find mankind all over the world making pretensions to some kind of religion, and this shows that there is a general belief among all nations, that religion is really important. All false religion, and all false pretensions to religion, afford a clear and strong proof of the importance of true religion. If any religion be important, it must be that which is true, or that which consists in love to God, in friendship to him, in a heart devoted to his service, and not in any thing selfish; for selfishness is the sum and substance of all sin, and the source of all the hypocrisy in the world.

6. What

6. What little reason have sinners to quiet themselves with the thought, that they are no hypocrites? With this many seem to quiet themselves. How often may we hear one and another say, that they are no hypocrites? Has not this thought occurred to some of you today, while we have been treating on this subject? Has not one and another said, "Well, I am not an hypocrite?" What are you then? Are you a real christian? Are you the hearty friend of God? If this be your character, you are no hypocrite. But when you say, that you are no hypocrite, do you mean to say, that you make no pretensions to any religion, that you do not pretend to have any love to God, or any regard to his law? Do you mean to declare yourself to be an open, avowed enemy to God? Are you willing to own this character? This must be your character, if you are neither a christian, nor an hypocrite. But is this an amiable character? Will this procure the love and esteem of any of your fellow men? However, if this be the character which you are willing to own, let me entreat you to consider, a moment, what it is to be of such a character. It is to be an enemy to God, the greatest and best of beings, who is your Creator, Preserver, and Benefactor, who has given his Son to suffer and die for your eternal good, who has invited you to accept salvation, who has waited upon you to be gracious to you, who now invites you to return to him and live, and who has power and authority to

send

send you, in a moment, to eternal perdition! As an ambassador of Christ, I pray you in his stead to become reconciled to God. Knowing the terror of the Lord, I would persuade you to flee from the wrath to come, and lay hold on eternal life: Remember that you are, this moment, in the hands of that God, who is angry with the wicked every day, who has bent his bow and made it ready, and prepared his instruments of death. And remember, that God has said, his spirit shall not always strive with sinners. Behold, now is the accepted time, behold, now is the day of salvation. Wherefore, today if ye will hear his voice, harden not your hearts; but if you refuse and rebel, know that their remaineth no more sacrifice for sins, but a certain fearful looking for of judgment, and fiery indignation, which shall devour the adversaries.

SERMON XVII.

The unchanging Goodness and Mercy of God an everlasting Source of Gratitude and Praise.

[A Thanksgiving Sermon.]

PSALM cxxxvi. 1.

O give thanks unto the Lord, for he is good; for his mercy endureth forever.

PRAISING God is not the duty of a thanksgiving day only, but of every other day. This is the duty of all rational creatures; and will remain to be their duty, as long as God continues unchangeably good and merciful. And since his goodness and mercy will endure forever, it will forever be the duty of reasonable creatures, to pay him this reasonable service. Gratitude and praise, or praise flowing from a grateful heart, will be the employment of saints and angels, in the ceaseless ages of eternity. The exhortations to gratitude and

and praife in the word of God are almoft innumerable; and the examples of good men, in this refpect, are very frequent. We often find thofe who poffeffed a grateful heart, celebrating the praifes of Jehovah, and giving thanks to God, for innumerable mercies and favors received. The book of Pfalms, in particular, is almoft entirely made up of fongs of praife. And we often find the pious pfalmift fo deeply impreffed with a lively fenfe of the infinite goodnefs of God, and his worthinefs to be praifed, that he calls upon all mankind, yea, upon all creation, to praife the Lord. Though the pious foul often fenfibly feels its perfonal obligation to gratitude for perfonal favors, and is difpofed to recite particular inftances of divine goodnefs to itfelf; yet all its gratitude and praife does not flow from a fenfe of perfonal good enjoyed. It is led, by the ftreams of divine goodnefs, which flow to itfelf, up to the Source and Fountain of all the good which flows to the univerfe, and of which all creatures partake; and therefore feels its obligation, and the obligation of all creatures, to praife the Lord; becaufe "he is good, and his mercy endureth forever." The truly pious and grateful heart is not felfifh in its gratitude, is not thankful merely for thofe favors which itfelf enjoys; but feels grateful for all that goodnefs which fills heaven and earth.

This was evidently the fpirit and temper of the pious pfalmift, when he compofed this pfalm, which has

has this peculiarity in it, that every verse in the psalm ends with these words, "for his mercy endureth forever;" which are emphatically repeated twenty six times. In enumerating the acts of divine goodness and mercy, the psalmist takes notice, not only of particular instances of God's goodness to the church, but of his wrath to their enemies; because those instances of his wrath were real instances of his mercy to his people. Hence he mentions it as an instance of God's goodness, that he not only made his people pass safely through the Red Sea, but also that he overthrew Pharaoh and his host. And for the same reason, saints and angels are represented, in the Revelation of St. John, as rejoicing and praising God, for the judgments executed upon spiritual Babylon. "And after these things I heard a great voice of much people in heaven, saying, Alleluia : Salvation, and glory, and honor, and power unto the Lord our God : For true and righteous are his judgments ; for he hath judged the great whore, which did corrupt the earth with her fornications, and hath avenged the blood of his servants at her hand. And again they said, Alleluia. And her smoke rose up forever and ever. And the four and twenty elders and the four beasts fell down and worshipped God that sat on the throne, saying, Amen ; Alleluia." Thus heaven and earth join to give thanks to God, for his righteous judgments upon his and his church's enemies, because these judgments flow from his essential goodness, and are as expressive of his mercy, as the bestowment of good. He is the same kind and benevolent Being, when he inflicts wrath upon his enemies, that he is when he confers favors upon his friends; " for his mercy endureth forever." Hence this observation naturally comes into view, from the words of our text, namely,

That the everlasting and unchanging goodness and mercy of God, are an everlasting source of gratitude and praise.

This is indeed the spirit of the text. The psalmist here calls upon all to give thanks unto the Lord, for this reason, that his goodness, and that his **mercy**, endureth forever. And this is the great reason, why we should give thanks to God, not merely because we receive particular and personal favors from him, but because he is unchangeably good and merciful. I would not, however, be understood to say, that we are not obliged to give thanks to God for particular and personal favors, for it is certain that we are; and the real christian will feel his heart most sensibly and gratefully affected, with the innumerable mercies which God confers upon him. The divine goodness will appear *great indeed*, in conferring so many and such undeserved favors upon one so greatly unworthy. Hence he will feelingly adopt the words of David, " Who am I, O Lord God, and what is my house, that thou hast brought me hitherto?" But it is evident, that it is not *merely*, or *especially*, the personal favors received,

received, that are the cause of gratitude; but these favors conferred on one so unworthy give him a more lively and animating sense of the infinite goodness of that Being, from whom such favors flow.

But that the goodness and mercy of God are an everlasting source of gratitude and praise, will appear, with additional evidence, from considering,

1. That the goodness and mercy of God are infinite in their nature and degree.

God is not only good and merciful, but his goodness and mercy are perfect. In all creatures goodness is limited and finite. Angels are good; they are possessed of real benevolence and love; they always feel benevolent; they always rejoice in benevolence, they are always disposed to express benevolence, and to promote the happiness of all God's creatures; but still their goodness is nothing in comparison with the goodness of God. There is a degree of goodness in saints, though it is mixed with great imperfection. But in God there is all that goodness, which can make the infinite Jehovah absolutely perfect. No creature can wish him to possess more goodness than he does possess. Any kind or degree of alteration in his nature, would render him imperfect, and make him less good. If then goodness be desirable, if it be matter of gratitude and praise, what gratitude! what praise! is due to him who possesses all possible goodness! If the few drops of goodness, which fall on us, should awaken gratitude in our hearts, then what praise is due to Him,

who

who is the boundless ocean of good, from whence these drops flow! This leads me to observe,

2. That the goodness and mercy of God are the fountain and source of all the good and happiness enjoyed in the universe.

From this infinite and inexhaustible fountain flows all the happiness which angels and glorified spirits enjoy in heaven; from hence flows all the happiness that the many millions and millions of mankind, in every part of the world, enjoy; and from hence flows all the natural and animal good, which all the animal creation enjoy. In a word, from this fountain flows all the good, all the happiness, which fills the universe so full, that there can be no more consistently with the most benevolent purpose of the Deity. Surely, then, here is a just foundation for everlasting gratitude and praise. If the streams of divine goodness, which flow to us, ought to excite our gratitude and praise, what gratitude, what praise shall we render to that God who fills the universe with good! God's goodness to other men and to other beings deserves our gratitude and praise, as truly as his goodness to us; and we ought to rejoice as really in the happiness of others as in our own; and if we possess a truly benevolent spirit and temper we shall do it. We find the angels rejoicing in all the good and happiness, which is communicated to mankind. Hence their joy, when God laid the foundations of the world; hence their song of praise, when the Savior

was

SERMON XVII.

was born; and hence their joy at the converſion of ſinners. The goodneſs of God is the proper ground and foundation of gratitude and praiſe; and every inſtance in which God manifeſts his goodneſs, awakens a ſenſe of gratitude afreſh in the minds of holy beings. Indeed, notwithſtanding all the good and happineſs which creatures enjoy, there would be no obligation to gratitude and praiſe, if their good and happineſs did not flow from a benevolent Being. It is not, therefore, the good, the happineſs enjoyed, that is the proper foundation for praiſe; but the benevolent ſource, from which this good and happineſs proceeds. Suppoſe that mankind enjoyed all the outward good and happineſs which they now poſſeſs, yet if this were the effect of chance or accident, there would then be no foundation for gratitude or praiſe. Or ſuppoſe it were all the fruit and effect of their own independent wiſdom, prudence, and induſtry, there would then be no room for gratitude or praiſe. Or if we could ſuppoſe that all our enjoyments proceeded from a Being deſtitute of benevolence and love, who had no friendly and good deſign in giving them, then we ſhould be under no obligation of gratitude for what we enjoy. It is, therefore, the benevolence of the giver that lays us under obligation for the gift; and our obligation to him is great, not always in proportion to the value of the gift, but in proportion to the benevolence of the giver in the beſtowment of it. Hence it appears, that the good-

neſs

ness of God is the foundation of real gratitude and praise. And that this source of gratitude is everlasting further appears, from considering,

3. That the goodness and mercy of God are everlasting and unchangeable—" his mercy endureth forever."

God was the same good and merciful Being before angels, or men, or any creature existed, that he has been since. It was his antecedent goodness and mercy, which led him to create the world and all beings and things. It was this goodness and mercy, which led him to adopt that plan of operation, in which goodness and mercy might be manifested and displayed in the most glorious manner. And the same goodness and mercy which first moved him to create, has governed him, in every part of his conduct, ever since. He is unchangeable in his nature, and therefore his goodness and mercy endure forever. From the beginning of the world to this day, all mankind have experienced the goodness and mercy of God, and from this day forward, as long as the sun and moon endure, they shall continue to experience his goodness and mercy. The goodness and mercy of God do not fluctuate and change, as the benevolence of men often does, but they remain the same, though the dispensations of providence are frequently changing. God is as truly good when he frowns, as when he smiles; when he corrects and chastises his friends for their faults, as when he rewards them

them for their virtues. When we take a view of the moral world, we find that even the church of God in former ages, though the particular object of divine love, was under a dark dispensation, in comparison with the present; but God was no less kind and good in those dark ages, than he is now. And his goodness now, is no less than it will be, when all the saints are made perfectly blessed in heaven. For the Lord is always good, and his mercy endureth forever. Could there be a time when God should cease to be good, we should then be under no obligation of gratitude and praise, even though the effects of his goodness should still remain. But since his goodness and mercy shall endure forever, they must necessarily be an everlasting source of gratitude and praise. I may add,

4. All this goodness and mercy of God is under the direction of perfect, unerring wisdom.

Goodness in God is not the impulse of blind passion, or inclination, as it is in men. It does not consist in the bestowment of a favor, as the humor of the present moment prompts; but it consists in bestowing such a favor, at such a time, and to such an object, as infinite wisdom dictates. For want of this wisdom, men often confer favors on improper objects, and in an unsuitable proportion, and therefore many times find, after they have conferred favors, that they have done wrong in the bestowment of them; that their favors are lost, or worse than lost. But this can never be

the

the case with God; for his wisdom is sufficient, at all times, and under all circumstances, to direct the infinite benevolence of his nature. Hence, he knows perfectly well when to bestow ten talents, when to bestow five, and when but one. In the different distributions of his favors, he is no respecter of persons; he is not partial to one more than to another; but he acts from infinite wisdom in all his dealings towards his creatures. It is not any partiality to *this* man rather than to *that*, which is the cause of his giving to *this* rather than to *that*. Infinite wisdom enables him to see that the greatest good will be promoted by the bestowment of different favors, at different times, upon different persons. Hence it is not only consistent with infinite wisdom, that God should sometimes visit mankind with judgments, but infinite wisdom requires it. And divine judgments make an important part in God's plan of general good. Hence it is, that saints and angels rejoice in God's righteous judgments, as well as in his most beneficent acts of kindness. And those very spirits who at one time sing, "Glory to God in the highest, because on earth there is peace and good will to men," do on another occasion sing, "Alleluia, salvation, and glory, and honor, unto our God; for true and righteous are his judgments." It is, therefore, abundantly evident, that the unchanging goodness and mercy of God are an everlasting source and foundation of gratitude and praise.

IMPROVEMENT.

SERMON XVII.
IMPROVEMENT.

1. If the infinite and immutable goodness and mercy of God be an everlasting source of gratitude and praise; if this be the primary ground of our obligation to praise God, antecedent to the consideration of favors received; and if particular and personal benefits are a secondary ground of gratitude, in proportion to the worth of the gifts and the benevolence of the giver; then how infinitely great are our obligations to give thanks unto the Lord, and to praise the name of the most high God! If we are under obligation to be thankful to God, and to praise him, for the infinite benevolence of his nature, and if this be the primary ground of gratitude, as I think has been abundantly proved, then what an endless and boundless source of gratitude and praise is here opened to our view! Well may we join with the psalmist and say, "Who can utter the mighty acts of the Lord? Who can shew forth all his praise?" It is as much impossible for us to render praise to God equal to his infinite worthiness, as it is to comprehend his infinite majesty. The highest seraph, who stands before the throne, sensible of his utter inability to shew forth all God's praise, bows before the throne, and casts his crown at the foot of the Lamb. Such views of the infinite goodness of God as he has, fills his soul with gratitude, and his mouth with continual songs of praise; and it is the great happiness of all the hosts of heaven to be

continually

continually praising God. And though by reason of our present imperfection, we cannot equal the angels in their songs of praise; yet we can give God some real praise, if our hearts are deeply impressed with a sense of his goodness. And every heart that has once been led to a view of the infinite goodness of God, will feel its obligation forever to praise and adore him. And when the pious person further considers the innumerable expressions of divine goodness to himself, the many, great, and distinguishing favors, which have flowed from this fountain of love, to one so infinitely unworthy, his gratitude rises still higher, and he says, " What shall I render to the Lord, for all his benefits? Bless the Lord, O my soul, and all that is within me bless his holy name. Bless the Lord, O my soul, and forget not all his benefits." Impressed with such a sense of the infinite goodness of God, he will long to have all creatures join with him in praising God. He will not only say, " O! that *men* would praise the Lord for his goodness and for his wonderful works to the children of men;" but will also wish that every thing that hath breath would praise the Lord.

2. The subject leads us further to infer, that every reasonable creature, whatever his circumstances and condition may be, is under obligation to praise God, and will forever remain so.

Wicked men may sometimes feel their obligation to be thankful, when they receive some signal and

and remarkable favor from God; but they cannot feel their obligation to be thankful, when they are in trouble and affliction. They then murmur and complain, instead of giving thanks. They look round on others, who are in outward prosperity, and complain that they are not equally prosperous. They think that those ought to be thankful, but not they themselves. But if the unchanging goodness of God be the highest foundation of gratitude and praise, then certainly they are still under obligation to praise God, notwithstanding all the adversity which they meet with. They ought even now to rejoice, that the goodness and mercy of God endureth forever; and that his wisdom directs him how to exercise his goodness, and how to confer his favors in the best possible manner. They ought to praise him for all marks of divine favor, for all good conferred on all his creatures, and for that good which they themselves enjoy, even in the midst of all their trials, which may also be turned into future and eternal good. They ought to be thankful for those trials, which are designed to ripen and prepare them for endless felicity. It may be, indeed, a hard matter to bring a man, overwhelmed in adversity, to feel his obligation to praise God; but if he be a good man, if his heart be right with God, he will do it. Though he be stripped of all his worldly enjoyments, yet with Job he will say, "The Lord gave, and the Lord hath taken away: Blessed be the name of the Lord."

Thus,

Thus, as the apostle expresses it, he will "in every thing give thanks."

3. If the everlasting and unchanging goodness and mercy of God be a constant and perpetual source of gratitude and praise, and if our obligation to those religious exercises be heightened and increased, by the innumerable benefits conferred on such unworthy and illdeserving creatures as we are; then, how extremely criminal and vile are those, who live continually unthankful, who never praise God for his goodness and mercy, which endureth forever, and which they live upon, and to which they are indebted for all their happiness and hopes!

We all agree to condemn the man, as an unnatural wretch, who is unthankful to an earthly benefactor for his kindness; and more especially if he injure and abuse him, from whom he has received peculiar tokens of favor. But how many thousands of mankind are there, who live continually unthankful to God, and never praise him, either for that goodness and mercy which endureth forever, or for those instances of divine goodness, which they themselves have experienced! If there be any such here present, are they not unspeakably vile and criminal? Do they not deserve to have every favor taken from them? Do they not deserve the wrath and displeasure, instead of the kindness and favor of God? And now let me ask, Is not this the character of some of you? Did you
ever

ever feel real gratitude to God, and truly praise him for his goodness? The unrenewed heart is ever an ungrateful heart. Gratitude and praise are the exercises of a gracious heart; and therefore a great part of mankind are strangers to these exercises. And O! how criminal are such!

The great business of today is, in a public manner, as well as private, to express our gratitude and praise to God, for his goodness and mercy, as the source from whence every favor flows to all his creatures; to praise him for his renewed goodness to us, to the people of this land in particular, in the course of the present year. But how can those express gratitude and praise, whose hearts never felt any gratitude? How can those offer praise to God, who are destitute of a thankful heart? You, therefore, who have a sense of divine goodness, must perform the delightful duty of this day. Bless the Lord, O house of Israel. Bless the Lord, O house of Aaron: Praise ye the Lord. ————AMEN. ALLELUIA.

SERMON XVIII.

The Gospel Method of instituting and ordering Churches.

TITUS, i. 5.

For this cause left I thee in Crete, that thou shouldest set in order the things that are wanting, and ordain elders in every city, as I had appointed thee.

AT the first establishment of christianity in the world, and the institution of christian churches, much was necessary to be done by the apostles, which was peculiar to that particular period. The christian church was established upon a plan, in many respects, different from that of the Jewish church. And when christian churches were set up, where paganism had prevailed, there was much to be done to set every thing in proper order. This made it necessary for the apostles, who had been particularly instructed by Christ in the things pertaining to his kingdom, and who were also under the special influence and direction of the Holy Spirit, not only to give particular directions to

those

those ministers of the churches, who had not been personally acquainted with Christ, nor divinely inspired; but also to write those epistles to them, and to the churches, with which we are favored in these latter days. Besides, this new state of the churches made it necessary for these great apostles to revisit the churches which they had planted, to know their state, and to set in order the things that might still be wanting to render them completely beautiful and regular. Hence St. Paul, after having given many directions, says, " The rest will I set in order when I come." He was now about to depart from Crete, a large island, where he had established a number of christian churches; and accordingly determined to leave Titus, whom he had not only been the instrument of converting, but whom he had consecrated to the work of the ministry, to pay further attention to the state and circumstances of those new formed societies. This he tells him and us in the words of my text : " For this cause left I thee in Crete, that thou shouldest set in order the things that are wanting, and ordain elders in every city, as I had appointed thee." The last clause, " as I had appointed thee," makes it evident, that Paul had, previously to his leaving him at Crete, given him many particular directions and instructions as to his work. But of so much consequence and importance was his work, that he thought it advisable, at least, to give him those further or repeated

repeated instructions, which are contained in this epistle.

Our attention is called up to the work which was assigned to Titus, and the inquiry is, What had he to do? What was the business which Paul left him to perform? The answer is contained in the text, and is divided into two general branches.

I. To set in order the things that were wanting: And,

II. To ordain elders in every city.

I. The first general branch of duty, which Paul mentions as incumbent on Titus, and which was one great end of his being left at Crete, was, to set in order the things that were wanting.

It may, perhaps, be as well here as any where, to observe, that Crete was not the name of any particular city or town, but of a large island in the Mediterranean sea, now called Candia, and which, it is said, was once called Hecatompolis, from the one hundred cities that were in it. (See Henry.) It is beyond a doubt, therefore, that when Paul says, " and ordain elders in every city," he means every city on this island; at least, in so many of them as had received the gospel, and in which particular churches had been established. Hence it appears probable, if not certain, that there were many churches under the inspection of Titus, because destitute of particular elders or ministers to take the oversight of them. This being supposed, and it being well known, that these churches

es were but newly established, and that Christianity itself, especially as to its external order and institutions, was a new thing in the world, it cannot be doubted, but that there were many things wanting, which needed to be set in order. Though there might be real religion, where many things were wanting; and though there might be true christian churches, where some things were out of order, in this their infant state; yet it was not only desirable that what was wanting should be supplied, and that what was out of order should be put in order; I say it was not only desirable, but the will of God, that these things should be done: For God is not the author of confusion, but of peace, as in all the churches of the saints; and therefore requires that all things be done decently and in order. Order and regularity are discoverable in all the works of God. The christian church, which is spoken of as Christ's body, is a beautiful, regular, harmonious body; and particular care has been taken, by the Head of this body, that there should be no schism, no disorder in any of the members. Hence every institution and appointment, relative to the church at large, and to every particular branch of it, is wisely adapted to promote the order, harmony, and regularity of the whole. The church of Christ, in the collective sense, is one body; yet as there are different branches of it, consisting of saints in different places, united together for the mutual edification

cation of each other, thefe are fpoken of as fo many feparate and diftinct churches. Hence the expreffion juft now mentioned, " God is not the author of confufion, but of peace, as in all the churches of the faints:" Hence all thefe feparate churches of the faints, are diftinctly organized, by the great head of the church, with an head or ruler under Chrift, and have their laws and rules prefcribed by Chrift; their modes of adminiftration of the word, the ordinances, and the gofpel difcipline or government within themfelves, as fully and entirely, as though they comprehended the whole church of God. Thefe things being carefully obferved, may help us to underftand what Titus had to do, to fet in order the things that were wanting in every city. He was to fee that all the diftinct churches were duly organized; that they underftood their duty as churches of Chrift; that they conducted all their ecclefiaftical affairs, in a decent regular manner, as became chriftian brethren, whom God had joined together for their mutual edification and comfort, and for the greater advancement of the Redeemer's kingdom. We may now attend to the fecond branch of duty, which Titus was to perform, and that was,

II. To ordain elders in every city; or in other words, to fee that each church in each city was provided for and fupplied with a faithful paftor, teacher, ruler and guide; for all thefe epithets belong to fuch perfons as the apoftle calls elders, and

whom

whom Titus was to ordain in every city. It is quite foreign from my prefent defign to enter into a critical diftinction between bifhops, elders, paftors, teachers, &c. and, to fhow what was the difference, if there were any, in the dignity, power, or duty annexed to each. It is fufficient to obferve, that the apoftle, in his writings, ufes thefe appellations promifcuoufly, to denote perfons of the fame office. One important branch of duty, which Titus had to perform, was, to ordain minifters in all the cities, or to fee that each church was furnifhed with a faithful paftor; for a " church, without a fixed ftanding miniftry in it, is imperfect, is wanting." A church, without a fixed miniftry, is not properly and completely organized. And it is abundantly evident from the facred fcriptures, that it is the will of God, that every chriftian church and fociety fhould be furnifhed with a ftated minifter. This fuppofes and neceffarily implies, that it is the duty of chriftians to form themfelves into focieties; to unite together to obferve divine inftitutions; to maintain the worfhip and ordinances of God; to watch over one another in love; to counfel, warn, reprove, encourage, and affift each other in duty. In this way is the vifible church fupported in the world: Or this is one fpecial and important mean, in the hand of God, of keeping alive the real and true church, and of maintaining true religion. It is evident, that this was the way, in which the apoftles practifed; and furely no

chriftian

christian will object against their practice. When they went and preached the gospel in any city or town, and found a number ready to embrace the gospel and profess religion, they there instituted a church. And those christians entered into covenant with God and one another, to walk together in the faith and order of the gospel. Such churches being instituted, as soon as there could be found able and faithful men, who possessed such a character as Christ required his ministers to possess, they were set over them in the Lord. And this was one important duty, which Titus had to perform at Crete—to ordain elders in every city—to see that each church was furnished with a faithful minister. This certainly is implied in his ordaining elders in every city, that is, that every city might be supplied with a stated pastor.

Now, that it is the will of Christ, that all his churches should be furnished with a fixed and stated ministry, appears from the practice of the apostles in ordaining ministers in all the churches. That this was their practice is evident, not only from the text, but from Acts xiv. 23. "And when they had ordained them elders in every church," *i. e.* in every church in Lystra, in Iconium, and in Antioch, "and had prayed with fasting, they commended them to the Lord, on whom they had believed." And then they, *i. e.* Paul and Barnabas, departed. They had then set in order the things that were before wanting in those churches, and accordingly

SERMON XVIII.

accordingly went on to Pifidia, and Pamphylia, and Perga, and Attalia, to fet in order the things that were there wanting. It was the grand bufinefs of the apoftles to plant the chriftian religion—to eftablifh churches—to ordain elders in every church. And when they had done this, and completely organized the churches, and fet every thing in order, they commended them to the grace of God, and left them. Thus it appears, that every chriftian fociety, every gofpel church, had its particular minifter, whofe office it was, to prefide in the church, to pray with the church, to preach to the church, to adminifter the ordinances to the church, to rule and govern the church, according to the laws which Chrift had enacted in his fpiritual kingdom. Permit me further to obferve, (becaufe I think the fubject of fome importance in the prefent fituation of things, and that it is part of my duty to make the obfervation, in order to give a portion in due feafon) permit me, I fay, further to obferve; that it is the will of Chrift, that his churches fhould be furnifhed, each and every one of them, with a fixed and ftated miniftry, appears from the names given to minifters, or the titles by which they are diftinguifhed.

They are not only called teachers, becaufe it is one part of their duty to preach the word, but they are called paftors or fhepherds, becaufe it is their duty to take care of fome particular part of the flock, or of fome particular flock. And certainly

tainly the shepherd cannot take care of the flock, unless he be with them and among them. They are also called overseers and watchmen, because it is their duty to take particular notice of their christian brethren, and see that they are faithful to their great **Master**. He who watches over others must be with them, that he may observe their conduct. They are, moreover, called rulers, because, under Christ, they are to govern the church, or to lead in the discipline of it. And to do this, they must necessarily be with the church. Christ is, indeed, the only King, Lawgiver and Ruler **in his church.** He is fully able to rule and govern all his church, how widely soever it is extended, and notwithstanding it is divided into many distinct societies. He can be spiritually present with them in all places. But because he cannot be personally present; when he left the world, and ascended up to heaven, he gave gifts unto men; and among all his gifts this was one of the most essential—Ministers to rule and govern, as well as to teach and instruct, in all his churches. The ministers of Christ act under him in those particular churches, over which the Holy Ghost hath made them overseers. This suggests to us a further evidence, that it is the will of Christ, that there should be stated and fixed ministers in each and all the churches, viz.

The duties, which he has expressly enjoined upon ministers to perform, clearly suppose and imply that they are fixed and established in some particular

ular place, and have the immediate watch and care of some distinct society, or body of christians.

They are thus directed: "Feed the flock of God which is *among you*, taking the *overfight* thereof, not by constraint, but willingly, not for filthy lucre sake, but of a ready mind, neither as being lords over God's heritage, but being ensamples to the flock." Every expression here made use of supposes, that those elders or ministers were fixed and established among a society of professed christians. This is implied in their feeding the flock of God among them. This is implied in taking the oversight of the flock. They could not take the oversight of those who were afar off. So when they are directed, not to be the lords over God's heritage, it supposes they have a power in and over the church, which they must exercise, not in a sovereign and arbitrary manner, but with meekness, and according to the spirit of Christ. So again, when they are directed to be ensamples to the flock, it supposes that they dwell among the flock, and that their good example may have a good influence upon them. These, and other duties, which are enjoined upon the ministers of Christ, can never be performed, unless they are fixed and dwell statedly among their flock. They can neither know the state of their flock, nor give to every one a portion in due season, unless they are stated pastors.

The duties, which are enjoined upon people with respect to the ministers of Christ, also clearly prove, that

that minifters are confidered as dwelling among them. "Know them that labor among you and are over you in the Lord, and admonifh you; and efteem them highly in love for their work fake. Obey them which have the rule over you, and fubmit yourfelves, for they watch for your fouls as they that muft give account. Is any fick, let him call for the elders, and let them pray over him." All the duties here enjoined upon the people, plainly fuppofe, that there was in the days of the apoftles, and ought to be now, a fixed minifter in every particular church.

Now, it is abundantly evident, that our Lord Jefus Chrift has made ample provifion for the edification, comfort, eftablifhment, peace, order, and government of all his churches, by a flated, fixed, and fettled miniftry in them. And every church of Chrift, that obferves his directions, fhall be fupplied. It is a peculiar favor to be thus fupplied; and it is a fore judgment of heaven upon any people to be left long deftitute of the fettled miniftry. This is confirmed by melancholy experience. For it is commonly the cafe of a deftitute people, that they are broken in pieces, and fcattered as fheep having no fhepherd. Diforder and confufion naturally take place, and religion commonly decays among them.

And now, my brethren, let me afk you, whether thefe things be not true, and agreeable to the law

and

SERMON XVIII.

and the testimony? But if these things be true, then the following inferences must also be true.

1. That it is clearly unscriptural and disorderly to form a particular church or christian society, of persons or members, who live scattered in divers towns and places, which are remote from each other.

It is abundantly evident, that the apostles practised differently. They went into cities, towns, and villages, and preached the gospel; and when a number in one place embraced the christian religion, and professed their faith in Christ, they formed them into a church state; and so they did in every place, where they found believers enough for a particular church. And when they had formed particular churches, they supplied them as soon as possible with stated ministers, and put every thing in order according to the rules of Christ's family. Hence we read of the church at Jerusalem—the church at Corinth—the church at Ephesus, &c. These churches, composed of members, who could meet together in one place, walking in the faith and order of the gospel, had peace, and were edified. There was no such thing, in the days of the apostles, as a person's living among christian brethren at Corinth, and yet joining himself with the church at Jerusalem, or at any other place. This would have been disorderly, because it would have counteracted the end and design of the institution of christian churches in different places. It is evident, that when christians, residing in different

towns

towns and remote places, form themselves into one church, it is impossible for them regularly to support and attend upon the public worship and ordinances of the gospel, or to meet together, as they ought frequently to do, to encourage, comfort, strengthen, and animate each other. And it is extremely difficult, if not impossible, for christians, in such a situation, to watch over each other, and maintain that discipline in the church, which is of great importance, and expresly enjoined. It appears to be kindly and wisely ordered by Christ, that churches should be composed of christians near together, who have frequent opportunities to see and converse with each other; and especially to unite together every Lord's day, in the public and social duties of the sanctuary. From this it appears, that it is unscriptural and disorderly, to form a church of christians residing in different places, and remote from each other; unless it be where the smallness of the number of professing christians will not otherwise admit of their enjoying gospel ordinances.

Should it be here objected, that there are christians of different denominations, who vary so much in their articles of faith and practice, that some cannot conscientiously join with the church where they live, and therefore they may go and join themselves with some church not far distant, with whom they can agree and hold fellowship and communion, without walking disorderly. To this I reply, no
such

such thing was known in the apostles' days. Christians were not then so divided in sentiment, but that they could hold communion together, nor ought they to be now. No doubt but christians differed, then, in some articles of faith and practice; but they did not differ so much but that they could unite, as brethren, in the worship and ordinances of the gospel. Nor ought any thing to disunite christians, in the present day, so far as to prevent christian communion together, unless it be such fundamental errors, as leave no ground to hope that those who profess them are real saints, or a true church of Christ. Why *may* not christians, why *ought* they not, to unite with christians among whom they live, in the worship and ordinances of the gospel, though they may differ in some less important things?

2. From the view we have taken of the practice of the apostles, in regularly and orderly forming christian churches, and ordaining stated ministers to carry on the work of the ministry, in their own particular charges, we learn, that it is unscriptural and disorderly, for christian churches willingly to remain destitute of a settled ministry, and to depend upon *itenerant* preachers. And it is equally unscriptural and disorderly, for christian ministers to travel about from place to place, under pretence of building up other churches, where christian churches are already established. Certainly, if it be evident and beyond all dispute, that it is the will of Christ,

Christ, that christian churches should be furnished with fixed and stated ministers; if the apostles took special care that every particular church might be furnished with a settled minister, and considered things as wanting in any church where this was not done; and if there be such obvious good reasons for doing this, and such manifest disadvantages in neglecting it; then the consequence is as clear as the sun in the firmament, that it is the duty of every christian church, to take all care and pains to furnish themselves with a settled minister, and steadily and faithfully to adhere to him, agreeably to the divine direction: " Know them that labor among you, and are over you in the Lord, and admonish you; and esteem them highly in love for their work sake." And it is unscriptural and disorderly, for a church willingly to remain destitute of a settled ministry, and to depend upon they know not whom and what; to depend upon travelling preachers, whom they are unacquainted with, and whose character and conduct they are strangers to; for be they ever so good men, ever so good preachers, ever so exemplary in their conduct, it is impossible for the churches to receive that benefit from them that they might, if they were fixed and settled among them.

Furthermore, from the care which the apostles took to have ministers settled in every church, and from the consideration, that almost all, if not every direction given to ministers, as to their duty, seem

evidently

SERMON XVII.

evidently to refpect them as being fixed, fettled, and having the particular care of fome particular church, and from all that has been faid above, it appears plainly unfcriptural and diforderly, for minifters to travel about from place to place, and efpecially to go into places where there is a chriftian church eftablifhed, with a view to draw off a party and fet up a new church, or to induce fome to join a diftant church. This certainly is not to fet in order the things that are wanting, as is the duty of a gofpel minifter; but it is to put things out of order, and introduce confufion in the church of Chrift.

But it may be objected here—

It is evident that the apoftles travelled about from place to place, preaching the gofpel, and why may not gofpel minifters do fo now? The anfwer is plain. Chriftianity was then new. The apoftles travelled to fpread the knowledge of Chrift, where he was not known, and where no chriftian churches were eftablifhed, nor chriftian minifters ordained. And in this way minifters may now travel and preach the gofpel from place to place, agreeably to the example of the apoftles. They may now go into our new fettlements, or among Jews, Mahometans, and Pagans, and there preach the gofpel, and erect churches, without breaking the order which Chrift has eftablifhed in his fpiritual kingdom.

But it may ftill be faid, That Paul and other apoftles did revifit the chriftian churches, which they

they had established. True, they did, and in many instances, no doubt, where ministers were settled. But they went to perfect what was wanting, to confirm and establish the saints in their christian faith, order, and obedience to those who were set over them in the Lord; and not to make converts to a party. Paul did not go where Peter had been, and had established a church, and ordained a minister, and endeavor secretly to draw away some from his ministry. The conduct of the apostles was far different from the modern itenerant preachers, who come in privily to interrupt the order which Christ has established in the churches. It is, therefore, clearly evident, that it is unscriptural and disorderly, contrary to scripture example and precept, for professed ministers to go about into places, where christian churches are established, and regular ministers of Christ ordained; and especially to do this in opposition to, and with a design to draw away people from, those ministers, who have been placed in the churches, by and according to the rules of Christ's kingdom. And it must be, for the same reason, improper and disorderly, for professing christians to countenance and encourage such ministers.

But it may be further objected against what has been said,

That it is evident, that God has, in many instances, manifested his approbation of such ministers and their conduct, by blessing their labors, for the
conviction

conviction and conversion of sinners, and the building up of the church of Christ; and can it be wrong for them to do what God owns and approves? To this I reply, Granting the premises to be true, the conclusion does not certainly follow. God may, and often does, bring good out of evil; but this does not destroy the evil, or alter the nature of men's actions; God may, and sometimes does, accomplish his benevolent and gracious designs, by wicked men and wicked means; but still they are wicked men and wicked means, notwithstanding the good effected by them. We may not do evil that good may come. If it be unscriptural and disorderly, for such men to go about in such a way as has been mentioned, we may not justify it, because some good has been done by them.

But, perhaps, all that good may not be done, which we imagine. Some, possibly many, of those whom we imagine to be converted by their means, may be deceived, may be built upon a sandy foundation; may be but stony ground hearers, who will endure but for a while, and then fall away. No good effects can justify unchristian and disorderly conduct; and it is clearly evident, that such conduct is unchristian and disorderly. We are expressly told, that in the latter days perilous times shall come—that there will be peculiar trials—such trials as would, if it were possible, deceive the very elect. These are the latter days; and the enemy of Christ and the souls of men is peculiarly busy.

Every artifice is tried. Satan can transform himself into an angel of light. Let no man deceive you. Search the Scriptures. Prove all things, and hold fast that which is good. Be watchful, and strengthen the things which remain, and are ready to die. Remember, therefore, how thou hast received and heard, and hold fast and repent. Behold, says Christ; I come quickly; hold that fast which thou hast; let no man take thy crown.

SERMON XIX.

Times of Refreshment.

ACTS iii. 19.

Repent ye, therefore, and be converted, that your sins may be blotted out, when the times of refreshing shall come, from the presence of the Lord.

THE preceding chapter gives us an account, of the extraordinary effusion of the Holy Spirit on the apostles, and disciples of Christ, by which they were, in a very extraordinary and miraculous manner, furnished to the arduous and important work, of building up the kingdom of the divine Redeemer. It also opens to view the glorious success, which they had, in consequence of this power, which they received from on high. The first discourse, which Peter delivered to the people, who were present at the time, and who saw the effects of this gift of the Holy Spirit, this first sermon, had such an effect upon his hearers, that the same day there were added unto the Church, about three thousand souls. This chapter opens another

pleasing

pleasing scene, which probably took place, towards the evening of the same day, when Peter and John went up to the temple to attend evening prayer. There they found, and there they wrought a surprising cure upon, a man lame from his mother's womb. This miracle arrested the attention, and excited the admiration of the multitude, who were there convened; and afforded Peter another excellent opportunity, of preaching Jesus, and the resurrection from the dead, which he gladly improves. He began his discourse, by disclaiming the credit of the miracle, wrought on the lame man; assuring them, that it was not by their power, or holiness, that the cure was wrought; but that God was, in this way, glorifying his Son Jesus, in whose name the miracle was performed, whom they had wickedly put to death. He then calls upon them, in the words of my text, "Repent ye, therefore, and be converted, that your sins may be blotted out, when the times of refreshing shall come, from the presence of the Lord." And he follows this exhortation with all the motives and encouragements, which the gospel exhibits. How surprising, that the first offers of pardon and eternal life, through the merits of Christ's blood, should be made to those wicked men, who were peculiarly instrumental in shedding it! and that these, or at least some of them, should be among the first, who experienced the saving benefit and efficacy of it! Surely, God's ways are not as our ways, nor

his

his thoughts as our thoughts. But herein God has acted perfectly like himself; has shewn what mercy and forgiveness there are with him. And this example may afford encouragement, to the greatest of sinners, to hope in the mercy of God; and in that blood, which thus cleanses from all sin, even from the heinous sin and guilt of shedding it. But to attend more directly to the words of the text, let us

I. Inquire, what is intended by times of refreshing from the presence of the Lord.

II. I shall endeavor to shew, that such times of refreshing shall come. And,

III. What is personally necessary, in order to our participation of the refreshing, which they will furnish.

I. What is intended by times of refreshing from the presence of the Lord? Expositors, I believe, generally suppose, that St. Peter has particular respect to the judgment of the great day, or Christ's second personal appearance. This will undoubtedly be a time of refreshing from the presence of the Lord. His presence will be the refreshment of all the saints. It will complete their redemption. It is what all the saints are looking and waiting for, as the blessed hope before them. This will be the day of the restitution of all things. But I am unwilling to suppose, that the words are to be confined to this time of refreshing only. For the apostle speaks not barely of a *time* of refreshing, but of the *times* of refreshing. And it is certain, that the church has experienced many times of refreshing from the presence of the Lord; times of great joy and comfort; times of great prosperity, increase, and revival. These have been times of refreshing to the church; and the word of God gives us reason to expect, that the church will yet see a time of far greater refreshing from the presence of the Lord, than it has ever yet experienced, previous to the final appearance of Christ to judge the world.

There is, in many respects, a beautiful similarity, between the natural, and the moral world; between material and spiritual things. In the natural, or material world, all things have their periods of labor, toil, and fatigue; of depression and exhaustedness; and they have, also, their times of ease, rest, and refreshment. The natural body has its labors and toils, its pains, burdens, and sorrows; its times of weariness, hunger, and thirst. It has also its intervals of rest, ease, joy, and comfort. It has its times of refreshment, from food and drink. The same is the case with the spiritual body, or the church. This has its times of persecution and suffering; of weakness, weariness, and decay. It has, also, its times of rest, revival, and refreshment. Every one, acquainted with the sacred scriptures, is sensible, that spiritual things are there frequently compared to natural; that the gift of divine grace, and the bestowment of divine influences, are often represented by feeding the hungry, and giving drink to the thirsty. And the saints, in this life, are

are spoken of as hungering and thirsting; and as being fed with the bread of life, and drinking of the water of life. It is peculiar to the heavenly state, to hunger no more, and thirst no more; to eat continually of the tree of life, and to drink continually of the river of the water of life. Hence, spiritual blessings are spoken of as the refreshment of christians. For they give joy and comfort, new life and vigor, to the soul; as rest, meat, and drink, do to the weary, hungry, and thirsty body. But reference is, perhaps, more commonly had to the material world, or the earth, which bringeth forth fruits, when a comparison is made between earthly and spiritual things. This earth, we know, is often impoverished and exhausted. It needs, and it enjoys, its intervals of rest and refreshment. The God of nature has as wisely ordered the revolutions of times and seasons, of days and nights, for the benefit and refreshment of the earth, as for the bodies of men. While the human body, wearied with the toils of the day, enjoys rest and refreshment, the earth, heated by the scorching summer sun, and its moisture in a measure is dried up, is refreshed by the cooling shade and gentle dews of the evening. Under these metaphors, God represents his cheering, refreshing, influences on his church and people. The Lord God is a sun to his people, not only to enlighten them in their way, but to warm their hearts with divine love and grace. His divine influence, on their hearts, is often com-

pared

pared to fire and heat; but his refreshing influences are more frequently compared to the dews and rain. God says, in the beautiful language of the prophet Hosea; "I will be as the dew unto Israel. He shall grow as the lily, and cast forth his roots as Lebanon. His branches shall spread, and his beauty shall be as the olive tree, and his smell as Lebanon." Though they were as withered dying grass, or as the drooping lily, scorched by the heat of the sun, yet his divine influences upon them should revive and refresh them, as copious dews do the withered grass, or dying flower. So the prophet Isaiah, speaking of spiritual and divine influences on the people of God, says, " Thy dew is as the dew of herbs," or refreshing as the dew is to the herbs. So heavenly doctrine, or the word of God, is compared to dew, on account of its spiritual influence. " My doctrine shall drop as the rain, my speech shall distil as the dew, as the small rain upon the tender herb, and as the showers upon the grass." But the influences of the Divine Spirit on the hearts of men, are more frequently compared to rain, than to dew; especially the plenteous effusions of the Divine Spirit, to effect great revivals, and general reformations. These are compared to large and copious showers, or even floods of waters. The prophet Isaiah, to represent the abundant influences of the Divine Spirit, in the gospel day, says, " In the wilderness shall waters break out, and streams in the desert; and the

SERMON XIX.

the parched ground shall become a pool, and the thirsty ground springs of water." So, again, " I will pour water upon him that is thirsty, and floods upon the dry ground. I will pour my spirit upon thy seed, and my blessing upon thine offspring. And they shall spring up as among the grass, as willows by the water courses." Hence Christ, " on the last day, that great day of the feast, stood, and cried, saying, If any man thirst, let him come unto me and drink." And this is the language of gospel grace, " The Spirit and the bride, say, Come ; and let him that heareth, say, Come ; and let him that is athirst come ; and whosoever will, let him come, and take the water of life freely." Thus it is clearly evident, that the influences of the Divine Spirit on the hearts of men, are compared to dews, showers, rivers, wells, fountains, and springs of water ; to denote their reviving, refreshing, and fruitful nature. And particularly times of the gift of the Holy Spirit, and uncommon divine influences on the hearts of men, are, with beautiful propriety, called times of refreshing.

The influences of the Divine Spirit, whenever imparted to any soul, are far more refreshing to that soul, than rest to the weary, or food to the hungry, or drink to the thirsty body. Hence the psalmist, with reference to these divine influences, says, " There be many who say, Who will shew us any good ? Lord, lift thou up the light of thy countenance upon us. Thou hast put gladness in

my

my heart, more than in the time, that their corn, and their wine increased." The influences of the Divine Spirit are far more refreshing to the soul, than rest to the weary, as they afford, not only joy and comfort, far beyond what any of the enjoyments of this life can give, but as they add new life and vigor to the soul; they give the soul fresh beauty, as the cooling and refreshing dews do to the flowers of the field. And they give the soul new and additional strength, so that it can mount with the wings of faith and love, as eagles, towards heaven; and can run, and not be weary, and can walk, and not faint, in the way of duty. When God sheds his divine influences on the soul, in rich abundance, the soul is feasted, as with marrow and fatness. Its joys, its comforts, its refreshments are such, as the world can neither give, nor take away. O how sweetly refreshing, beyond all expression, are these divine influences! The renewed soul does not always feel these sweetly refreshing influences. If it did, it would anticipate the joys of heaven, and almost fly away from dull mortality. But it has some times of refreshing, in which it can, with real feeling joy, say, "O taste, and see, that the Lord is good." And it is truly a time of refreshing to every particular soul, when that soul experiences the influences of the Divine Spirit, in blotting out its sins, renewing and sanctifying it, or increasing and enlarging and exciting the graces of renewed nature.

But

SERMON XIX.

But those, especially, are times of refreshing, when God is pleased to pour out of his Spirit, from on high, on those who were before dead in trespasses and in sins: When many, in any particular town, or society, are effectually awakened, convinced, converted, and brought home to God: When true religion revives, and flourishes; when many are added to the church, of such as shall be saved. Still more are those times of refreshing, when this is the case in many places; when God causes it to rain this heavenly influence, not on one city only, but on every city. This has been, in a great measure, the case in this our happy land, as some of you, I trust, can well remember: When God poured out his Spirit on most of our towns, and churches; and converts were multiplied, as the drops of the morning dew. That was a sweetly refreshing time to the church. She put on her beautiful garments, and in some degree "looked forth as the morning, as a morning without clouds, as the clear shining of the sun after rain." But how much more emphatically will that time be a time of refreshing, when "the Spirit shall be poured out upon *all flesh*; when all flesh shall see the salvation of God; and the whole earth shall be filled with the knowledge of the Lord, even as the waters fill the seas." Then "shall the tabernacle of the Lord be with men, and God will dwell with them, and they shall be his people, and God himself shall be with them, and be their God."

Times of reformation, of revival of religion, of the out pouring of the Spirit on any people, are times of refreshing to such a people, not only as those are refreshed thereby, who are the happy subjects of these divine influences, in being brought out of darkness into light, and turned from the power of Satan unto God; but as they are reviving, refreshing, comforting, to all the saints. To those who have themselves before experienced the same heavenly influence, it gives new and additional joy. For their highest joy, their greatest comfort, their sweetest delight, is to see the prosperity of Zion, the flourishing of the Redeemer's kingdom. This also inspires them with fresh courage and zeal, and with additional fervor, in the service of God: This affords them renewed experience of the power and grace of God, and is a new proof of the faithfulness of the divine promises. It is a refreshment, not only to those saints, who live where such reformation takes place, and who are eye witnesses of it; but it is, also, a refreshment to all the saints in every part of the world, who hear of, and are made acquainted with it. For all the saints are members of the same body; and if one member rejoice, all the members rejoice with it. Yea, it may be said to afford refreshment to the saints and angels in heaven. For if there be joy over one sinner that repenteth, much more, will there be joy there, when many sinners repent, when converts are multiplied, and multitudes are joined unto the Lord.

Lord. We find, in the Revelation of St. John, that when a signal favor is granted to the church on earth, when it is enlarged and increased, when its enemies are destroyed, and it is in a peculiarly flourishing and prosperous condition, the angels have a new song of praise to sing on the occasion. With the utmost propriety, then, may such times be called times of refreshing.

It only remains here that we inquire, Why these times of refreshing are said to come from the presence of the Lord? The propriety of this expression will appear at once, when we consider, that the revival of religion, the increase of the church, the out pouring of the Holy Spirit, is ever the work of God. And it is his most glorious work. "When the Lord shall build up Zion," says the psalmist, "he shall appear in his glory." This is the most glorious manifestation, which God can make of himself, previous to his appearance at the judgment of the great day. When a soul is converted from the error of his ways, God appears in his glory to such a soul. God manifests himself, as the most glorious of all beings. There is nothing that so clearly manifests the glory and perfection of the Deity, as this. The Holy Spirit, the immediate author of this divine refreshment, comes, with all his heavenly influence, from the presence of God. And, indeed, when and where this heavenly influence is felt, there God is, there he comes, and dwells. There he takes up his abode. So says

the

the blessed Savior : " If a man love me, he will keep my words, and my Father will love him, and we will come unto him, and make our abode with him." So the forecited passage from the Revelation : " Behold the tabernacle of God is with men, and he will dwell with them, and they shall be his people, and God himself will be with them, and will be their God."

Here we may, with propriety, make a pause in the discourse, and indulge a profitable reflection. If the revival of religion, the out pouring of the Spirit of God, occasions so much joy, comfort, and refreshment, not only to those souls, who are renewed thereby ; but also to all saints, to the church of Christ in heaven, and on earth, then, how earnestly should we desire, how fervently should we pray, that not only we in this place, but that people in every place, may enjoy such a time of refreshing from the presence of the Lord. It is usually in answer to the fervent prayers of the saints, that God pours out his Holy Spirit on mankind ; or, in other words, previous to such a time of refreshing, he commonly excites in his people an earnest desire, and united fervent prayer, for such a blessing. And we are informed, that the effectual fervent prayer of a righteous man, even of one righteous man, availeth much. How much more the effectual fervent prayers, of many righteous men ! " Shall not God avenge his own elect, who cry to him continually ? Yea he will avenge them,

and

and that speedily." "O pray for the peace of Jerusalem. They shall prosper that love thee." We pray for worldly prosperity; we seek for the outward honors, and enjoyments of the world. Shall we not much more seek the honor of God, the glory of his name, the revival of his work, and the refreshment of his saints? Nothing can so effectually promote the refreshment of the world as this. Let us unite our most fervent prayers for this greatest of all blessings.

SERMON XX.

Times of Refreshment.

ACTS iii. 19.

Repent ye, therefore, and be converted, that your sins may be blotted out, when the times of refreshing shall come, from the presence of the Lord.

WE have already considered, what is intended, by times of refreshing; and have found, that times of reformation, of revival of religion, of the out pouring of the Spirit, of divine influences on the hearts of men, are, with propriety, called, times of refreshing. For they are reviving, comforting, and cheering to the soul, as any, and more than any outward refreshment, can be to the body. They are refreshing, and reviving, to the moral world, as the gentle dews, or copious showers of rain, to which they are compared, are to the natural world, or to the drooping, languishing fruits and flowers of this earth, when parched, with the heat of a summer's sun. And these refreshments are, with propriety, represented as coming from the

presence

presence of the Lord, as they are the fruit and effect of his influences; they are his gift and his work; and they prove that God is especially present with such a people, and that he dwells among them. We now proceed, agreeably to the method proposed, to shew,

II. That such times of refreshing shall come.

This is evidently supposed in the manner of expression in the text. " Repent ye, therefore, and be converted, that your sins may be blotted out, when the times of refreshing *shall come* from the presence of the Lord." If there were no times of refreshing to come, the strength of the argument or motive would be lost. Indeed that is a time of refreshing to every particular soul, when it does truly repent, is converted, and its sins are blotted out. But something more than this seems evidently intended, and it is, as has been before observed, generally supposed, that St. Peter has particular reference to the judgment of the great day; when the sins of all penitent believers will be finally blotted out from the book of God, and they refreshed, with a complete and everlasting fulness of all divine influences. But, previous to this, it is evident, that there shall be many times of sweetly refreshing influences, from the presence of the Lord. That was a time of refreshing, from the presence of the Lord, when the apostle delivered this discourse. Then, as he observed in the preceding chapter, God was fulfilling the promises made to the prophet Joel, as well

well as other prophets, of the plentiful and refreshing influences of the Divine Spirit. And he believed, yea the Spirit of Divine Infpiration affured him, that there fhould yet come times of refreshing from the prefence of the Lord, even times of greater refreshment than that was. Then, notwithstanding the plentiful effufions of the Holy Spirit, with which the church was favored, yet, it was fcorched with the heat of perfecution. And fince that time, the church has often experienced times of great and fore trial and affliction. It has been often weakened, reduced extremely low. It has many times appeared to be languifhing, drooping, dying. It has then again felt the fweetly refreshing influences of the Divine Spirit, reviving, reftoring, ftrengthening, and increafing its beauty, and vigor. Such periods have often fucceeded each other, fince the day of St. Peter's delivering this difcourfe. And it may well be queftioned, whether there has ever been any lengthy period, in which the church has not experienced more or lefs of thefe divine refreshments. Indeed if there were not frequent refreshments, the church would, long fince, have wholly died. And fo long as the church remains on earth, there muft be fome meafures and degrees of this refreshing influence. But there have been fome times of very great refreshment, fome feafons of the plenteous influences of the Divine Spirit. This happy land, as well as moft, if not all chriftian countries, has experienced times

of

SERMON XX.

of peculiar refreshment, times of great revival of religion. And we have reason to hope, nay, we may with confidence expect, that there will, at least, be *a time*, when all the earth shall feel this refreshing. Low as the present state of the church appears to be, and languishing and drooping as she seems, almost ready to faint and die; yet, there are some happy places, which enjoy a time of great refreshment. Divine influences are felt. Religion revives. The church raises its drooping head towards the heavens, from whence these influences come, and waits for more, and longs for a rich and full supply. Nor will God forsake her, nor forget her mourning state.

> "Zion still lives within the heart
> "Of everlasting love."

Hear the language of his heart to her. "For a small moment have I forsaken thee, but with great mercies will I gather thee. In a little wrath I hid my face from thee, for a moment; but with everlasting kindness will I have mercy on thee, saith the Lord, thy Redeemer. For this is as the waters of Noah unto me; for as I have sworn, that the waters of Noah should no more go over the earth; so have I sworn, that I would no more be wroth with thee, nor rebuke thee. For the mountains shall depart, and the hills shall be removed; but my kindness shall not depart from thee, neither shall the covenant of my peace be removed, saith the Lord, that hath mercy on thee." So again,

"Can a woman forget her sucking child, that she should not have compassion on the son of her womb? Yea, they may forget, yet will I not forget thee. Behold, I have graven thee upon the palms of my hands; thy walls are continually before me." There are a number of great and precious promises in the word of God, to his church, which are yet to be fulfilled. There must, and will be yet a time of greater, and more general and universal refreshment, than the church has ever experienced; a time, when "the gospel shall be preached to every creature; when every knee shall bow, and every tongue confess that Jesus is Christ, to the glory of God the Father;" when the Jews shall again be brought in, with the fulness of the Gentiles; and the coming in of the former, shall be as life from the dead to the latter. These are promises, which God has made, which have not yet been fulfilled. And "God is not a man that he should lie, nor the son of man that he should repent. Hath he said, and shall he not do it? Hath he spoken, and shall he not make it good?" The church, in almost every age, have believed these promises, and have been waiting for their accomplishment. They have been looking for this blessed hope, this glorious appearing of the great God, and our Savior Jesus Christ. The time is indeed prefixed for the commencement of this happy refreshment, and it is pointed out particularly by the spirit of prophecy. And was it not for the darkness and obscurity of the language

of

of prophecy, the church might certainly know when the time would be. But, notwithstanding this darkness of prophetic language, it is clearly evident, that the time is drawing nigh. O that all the church of God might be prepared to welcome the glorious and happy day! This would naturally lead to the third inquiry, viz. What is personally necessary, in order to our participating in the refreshment, which will be furnished. But it reoccurs to the mind, that most expositors consider the time of refreshing, as referring to the judgment of the great day. This will be a time of refreshing, a time of joy and gladness to all the saints. This glorious day will complete their redemption. It will not only redeem the body from the grave, and refresh it with unfading beauty, and immortal vigor, with eternal health, ease, and comfort; but it will refresh their souls with the tree of life, which is in the midst of the paradise of God; and with that water of life, which flows, in a never ceasing river, from the throne of God. Then there shall be no more curse. The inhabitants shall no more say, "*I am sick.*" For the people shall be forgiven their iniquity. Their sins shall be blotted out. All sorrow and sighing shall flee away. All tears shall be wiped from the eye; and divine influences shall be given, not as they are in this world, in an imperfect measure, and at some particular seasons; but they shall be filled, with the fulness of that God, who filleth all in all. They shall forever enjoy God, and to the utmost that their capacities will admit. They shall serve him day and night, rejoice in his presence, and reign with him forever and ever. But even in this time of refreshing, all shall not be refreshed. Some shall awake to everlasting life, and some to shame and everlasting contempt. Our next inquiry, therefore, appears greatly important, which is,

III. What is personally necessary, in order to our participating in these times of refreshing, from the presence of the Lord? In answer to which, we may say, that the same is necessary to fit us for the joy and comfort of those times of refreshing, which the people of God enjoy on earth, which is necessary to fit us for the sweeter, fuller, and more lasting refreshments of the heavenly world, viz. That we belong to the number of God's true people, or that we repent, and be converted. Without true repentance, and conversion unto God, our sins can never be blotted out, but they will stand charged to our account, and we must be cast into the prison of divine justice, where we must remain until the utmost farthing be paid, which can be done only by our everlastingly suffering the penalty due for our crimes. There, in that gloomy prison of hell, no refreshments ever come, not so much as a drop of water to cool the tongue, tormented with unquenchable fire. No beam of hope, no ray of joy, illuminates that doleful prison. There none of the vain and empty enjoyments of this life, none of its

delusive

delusive pleasures, can find admittance; but the smoke of their torment ascendeth up forever and ever; and they have no rest day nor night. This is the miserable doom of all the wicked. For unless ye repent, says the Savior, ye shall all likewise perish. The design of all those divine refreshing influences, which God imparts to his people on earth, is to fit and prepare them for those greater, richer, and sweeter influences, which flow in, from his presence, in the heavenly world. They are designed to make them meet for the inheritance of the saints in light. Now he that hath wrought them for the selfsame thing is God, who hath also given them his Spirit, with all its refreshing influences. The church in this world must be purified and cleansed, that it may finally be presented a glorious church, without spot or wrinkle, or any such thing. For this end, all that are brought into the true church of God are made truly humble, and penitent; they are converted, or turned from the love and practice of sin, to the love and service of God. They are brought to prefer God to every thing, and to rejoice in him as their chief good, and thus they are prepared to rejoice forever, in his presence, and in the enjoyment of him.

The same humble, penitent heart and temper, is necessary, to fit the soul to participate, joyfully, in divine influences, or those spiritual refreshments, which flow from the presence of God, in this world. "For unto this man will I look," says God, "even to him that is poor, and of a contrite spirit, and trembleth at my word." Again, it is said, "God resisteth the proud, but giveth grace to the humble." The impenitent, unrenewed heart, cannot receive the refreshing influences of the Holy Spirit. It has no taste nor relish for those divine joys and consolations, which flow from the presence of God. It says unto God, "Depart from me, for I desire not the knowledge of thy ways." But, when the soul is humbled, when it is brought to see the evil of sin, and to hate it; when it mourns its past offences, and turns from them unto God; when it gives up itself entirely to God, and longs for none but him; then the heart is open to divine refreshments, nor will God fail to afford them. Private christians are, in this way, prepared for the reception of these divine influences, from God, who is present with them, though the world may see and know little of it.

The same spirit and temper of mind is necessary, to prepare us for the gloriously refreshing time, when the whole earth shall be filled with the knowledge of the glory of God, and all shall feel this divine refreshment. Indeed, the design of this great and glorious effusion of the Spirit, is to refresh the world; to refresh all nations; to cause all to rejoice in God. But the first step towards this object, will be, to humble the pride of sinners; to lead them to true repentance and conversion unto God. Before any are made to partake of divine joys and consolations,

consolations, they must be brought to mourn and lament their sins. They must feel bitterness of heart. They must be humbled, before they can be exalted. The impenitent and unrenewed are wholly unprepared for the joy and comfort, the sweetly refreshing influences of that happy day. The impenitent and unconverted, are not prepared to rejoice in the glorious coming and reign of the Prince of Peace. But the saints, all the true church and people of God, all penitent and converted souls, are in some measure prepared, for such a glorious event; as their hearts are formed by divine grace to relish these influences. And O how sweet will these refreshments be, to the church and people of God! With heartfelt joy will they be ready to adopt the language of the holy prophet, and say, " Sing, O ye heavens, for the Lord hath done it. Shout, ye lower parts of the earth; break forth into singing, ye mountains, O forest, and every tree therein; for the Lord hath redeemed Jacob, and glorified himself in Israel." And again, " Break forth into joy, sing together, ye waste places of Jerusalem; for the Lord hath comforted his people, he hath redeemed Jerusalem. The Lord hath made bare his holy arm, in the eyes of all the nations; and all the ends of the earth shall see the salvation of our God." How happy those who are prepared to welcome this glorious day! How happy those, who are prepared to enjoy the comfort and refreshment of it! Happy those, who shall live

when

when God doth this. But still more happy are those, who are prepared for, and received to partake of, the more divine refreshments of the world above.

IMPROVEMENT.

1. If there be yet times of refreshing to come from the presence of the Lord; and these refreshments afford so much joy and comfort, then let the believing prospect of this afford us some consolation, in the present gloomy state of the church on earth. When we seriously contemplate the present state of the church, in general, and the particular state of this church, it appears covered with a melancholy cloud. It seems as though God had forgotten us, and our God had forsaken us. But God has not cast off his church, he has not forsaken his inheritance. "In a little wrath I have hid my face from thee for a moment, but with everlasting kindness will I have mercy on thee, saith the Lord, thy Redeemer." It is true, particular churches may be lost, or the church may be lost in particular places; but it shall not be lost from the world. And we would hope and trust, that it will not finally be lost, even here. A glorious and happy day of the church's prosperity shall come; and he that shall come, will come, and though he tarry, yet let us be found waiting for him. It is usually the case that darkness precedes the light; that sorrow precedes joy. Religion is indeed in a very low and languishing

languishing state. And while false prophets and teachers arise, and dangerous and destructive errors are taught, and many depart from the faith once delivered to the saints, and the way of truth is evil spoken of; while vital piety and godliness are renounced, from a belief, that all, of every character, however infamous, will finally be saved; while these things appear, what serious, what benevolent heart, can avoid being pained and distressed? But yet, in the midst of all our grief, a firm belief, and a lively prospect, of a time of refreshing, from the presence of the Lord, as certainly approaching, may, and will afford some comfort to every christian. This may afford a pleasing consolation to the faithful minister, who is laboring and striving to effect a reformation among a people, even though he sees, for the present, no good effect of his labors; for they shall all, in some way or another, contribute to, and prepare for, a time of refreshment yet to come. The seed may be long buried in the dust; but it shall not be lost. Nor shall one prayer of the saint be lost, who fervently prays for a time of refreshing from the presence of the Lord. Though he may possibly be gathered to his fathers, and laid in the dust, before his prayers are answered; yet every such prayer shall come up as a memorial before God, and shall there be remembered by a prayer hearing, and answering God, and the praying saint shall, in a state of glory, be a witness to God's answering of it.

2. If

2. If repentance, and conversion to God, be so necessary to prepare us for pardon, and to partake of the joy and comfort of times of refreshment, in this world, as well as in the world to come, then, with what propriety may I address you, my friends, in the language of my text: " Repent ye, therefore, and be converted, that your sins may be blotted out, when the times of refreshing shall come from the presence of the Lord." You have heard what is meant by times of refreshing from the presence of the Lord, in every sense; you have heard what joyous, happy, reviving times these are, to every renewed soul in particular; as well as to the church in general; you have heard that such times of refreshment, not only have been, but are yet to come; and that, unless you repent, and are converted, or turned unto God, you cannot be prepared for, nor partakers of these divine refreshments. What is sin, that you should be so fond of it? Is it not opposition to the blessed God, the fountain of all good? What are the momentary pleasures of sin, that you should prefer them to the soul reviving, and refreshing influences of the Divine Spirit? With what stings and lashes of a guilty conscience are the pleasures of sin followed, while the love and service of God is attended with the noblest joy and comfort? What evils and miseries has sin already brought upon our guilty world? And how many millions, of the human race, has it already sunk down into endless misery? On the other

other hand, repentance and conversion have saved thousands from these torments, have procured the sweetest divine influence, joy, and comfort, in this world, and endless refreshment, from those rivers of pleasure, which flow at God's right hand, in heaven above. Would you avoid the endless pain and misery of the wicked, would you enjoy those divine, and soul reviving, and happifying refreshments, which flow from the presence of God, then repent, and be converted, that your sins may be blotted out. " Repent, for the kingdom of heaven is at hand."

SERMON XXI.

Fidelity in Preaching Desirable.

WHEN I rise in this sacred Desk, you naturally expect that I call your attention to some particular passage of sacred scripture; and that I address you on some religious subject. This you consider as the proper duty of my office, as if it were my trade, my employment: But should I do this, as most men go about their worldly business, merely to get a living, I should certainly be highly and peculiarly criminal. No man may, at any time, lawfully act from this motive in any thing. We are commanded to aim at the glory of God, in every thing we do. Were we made only for this world, we might then live and act for this world only; but it is certain we are not. There is, my friends, a vast, a boundless, an all important eternity before us; and every thing we do, every thing we say, and every thing we think, will have influence into that future and everlasting state, and increase our happiness or misery there forever. How important then is life! how important every day,

day, hour and moment of life! How important is it that I preach, and that you hear, as those who must give account to God the judge of all! In this view of things, what portion of scripture can be more proper for our present contemplation, than those words of old Eli to young Samuel, recorded in the first book of Samuel, iiid chapter, and 17th verse?

What is the thing that the Lord hath said unto thee? I pray thee, hide it not from me; God do so to thee, and more also, if thou hide any thing from me, of all the things that he said unto thee.

THE occasion of these words you will easily recollect. Eli had, but a little before, been informed, by a man of God, of judgments soon to come upon his family, for the great wickedness and impiety of his children. This prediction was confirmed to Samuel, in a manner described in the preceding part of this chapter. On a certain night, when Eli and Samuel were both lain down to rest, each one in his separate apartment, the Lord called and said, Samuel; and Samuel answered, Here am I; and he ran to Eli and said, Here am I, for thou calledst me. Eli said, I called not; lie down again. No sooner had Samuel lain down, but the voice called again, Samuel! He went to Eli as before, and was informed as before. The same was done three times. Eli was then convinced, that it was God who spake to Samuel; and he told him, that if he
should

should hear the voice calling him again, to reply, "Speak, Lord, for thy servant heareth." He departed and lay down, and the Lord called the fourth time, Samuel! Samuel! Then Samuel answered, "Speak, Lord, for thy servant heareth." God now informs Samuel of his determination to fulfil all that he had before denounced against the house of Eli. Samuel after this lay until the morning, and when he arose he was afraid to inform Eli what he had heard. Eli having just before received a disagreeable message from the man of God, was apprehensive that the vision of Samuel foreboded evil to himself; and therefore he calls for Samuel, and addresses him in the language of our text. "What is the thing that the Lord hath said unto thee? I pray thee hide it not from me; God do so to thee, and more also, if thou hide any thing from me, of all the things that he said unto thee." Eli was truly desirous of knowing the worst of his case, and not only requested Samuel to deal plainly and faithfully with him—" I pray thee hide it not from me"—but he most solemnly adjures him to do it, under the awful penalty of feeling the curse himself, if he concealed the truth—" God do so to thee, and more also, if thou hide any thing from me, of all the things that he said unto thee." Whereupon Samuel told him every whit. Like a faithful watchman, he did not shun to declare unto him all the counsel of God. In treating on this solemn passage, I shall pursue the following method.

I. Show

I. Show that it is of the greatest importance to a people in general, and to every particular person, that ministers be plain and faithful in delivering the truth to them.

II. That such as are truly wise will wish and desire this of their ministers—" I pray thee hide it not from me."

III. That an awful curse awaits those ministers, who are unfaithful in declaring the counsel of God, or who keep back the truth—" God do so to thee, and more also, if thou hide any thing from me, of all the things that he said unto thee."

I. That it is of the greatest importance to a people in general, as well as to every particular person, that ministers be plain and faithful in delivering the truth to them; that they do not conceal the worst of their case from them.

The truth of this proposition must appear evident to every one, who duly considers it. God, in infinite wisdom and goodness, has seen fit to reveal to mankind many things, which greatly concern their present and future happiness, and which it would have been impossible for them to have known, had he not revealed them. Or if any truths of divine revelation could have been known without a revelation; yet they could not certainly have been so clearly and distinctly known, as they may be now. Every thing, that God has revealed in his word, concerns us, and concerns us in our eternal interest. " Secret things belong unto the

Lord our God, but those things which are revealed belong unto us, and to our children." Whatever God has seen fit to reveal must certainly be worthy of our notice; if it had been of no importance to us to know it, surely God would not have revealed it; for he does nothing in vain. Can any one suppose, that God should speak any thing that is not worthy of the attention of his creatures? Shall he call and say, " If any man have ears to hear, let him hear?" and can we suppose it is of no consequence whether we hear or not? A divinely inspired apostle has assured us, that " all scripture is given by inspiration of God, and is profitable for doctrine, for reproof, for correction, for instruction in righteousness: That the man of God may be perfect, throughly furnished unto all good works." If so, then, it is important for us to know the scripture, to be well acquainted with the whole will of God. Besides, there is such a beauty, such a harmony and connection in the whole revealed will of God, that no one can know any thing as he ought to know, who does not know the whole. The proper knowledge of any one truth of divine revelation involves in it the knowledge of the whole. How can any one understand the gospel method of salvation, by the free grace of God through a Redeemer, unless he knows the wretched and deplorable condition into which man is fallen? And this implies the knowledge of the amazing depravity of the human heart, man's utter

aversion

aversion from God, his helpless state in himself, his need of the power and grace of God in regeneration, and the free, rich and sovereign grace of God in the sanctification and complete salvation of saints in heaven. There is, therefore, such a connection of one truth with another, that the whole gospel plan or scheme must be unfolded in order to our properly understanding any part of it. And it has pleased God to appoint an order of men, whose particular work and office it should be, to study the sacred scriptures, to search out the mind and will of God, as it is revealed in his holy word, and to unfold the mysteries of godliness to mankind. Nothing, therefore, is more evident, than that plainness and fidelity in ministers is of great importance—that they do not handle the word of God deceitfully,—that they do not corrupt the word of God; but as in sincerity, but as of God, in the sight of God, they speak the truth in Christ; and by manifestation of the truth, commend themselves to every man's conscience in the sight of God. The design of the gospel ministry is not answered, if the preacher be not plain and faithful in his preaching: On the contrary, the souls of men are injured, the gospel ministry is perverted, and the cause of Satan promoted, by the unfaithful preacher. Truth is the great support of Christ's kingdom. Truth affects the hearts of men. It is the truth that humbles the sinner's heart, strips him of all his excuses, lays him at the

foot

foot of a sovereign God, and makes him free from the law of sin and death. How important is it, then, that the truth be clearly, plainly, and faithfully preached ? So far as the truth is kept out of fight, so far Satan's kingdom and cause are supported. His kingdom is a kingdom of falsehood ; he keeps sinners quiet and secure, by blinding their minds, and shutting the light of divine truth from their understanding. Hence sinners are ever represented as having their understandings darkened, their eyes closed and shut—as ignorant, blind, and walking in darkness. The design of the gospel ministry is to open blind eyes, to give light to them who are in darkness, and to bring men to the knowledge of the truth. This can be done only by preaching the truth clearly and plainly. Nothing, then, can be more desirable than to have the truth taught in the most plain and faithful manner. He, who disguises the truth, and keeps back any part of the whole counsel of God, does the greatest injury to the souls of men. Truth will come to light, it will one day appear, and sinners will be made to see and feel it. If we conceal it from you now, for fear of offending or displeasing you, it will all appear, if not before, yet at the judgment of the great day. And the manifestation of the truth *then*, will overwhelm the guilty soul with unutterable anguish. It will carry such conviction to the conscience, as forever to silence all his excuses and all his complaints. If we conceal from you, or endeavor

deavor to extenuate the wretchedness of your condition; if we pretend that you are not so very bad, not so entirely corrupt and depraved, not such enemies to God as some assert; yet the truth of your character, and the dreadfulness of your condition, will hereafter appear in a more awful light than they can now be represented. It is, therefore, a matter of the utmost importance and consequence to you, that we do not, in any measure, conceal your character from you, that we do not represent your condition any better than it is; but that we plainly and faithfully tell you what you are, and what you have to expect. In this way, we may become the happy instruments of awakening, convincing, and converting you; of turning you from the error of your ways, to the wisdom of the just. I proceed,

II. To show that such as are truly wise will wish and desire ministers to preach plainly and faithfully. They will adopt the language of Eli to Samuel in the text. " What is the thing that the Lord hath said unto thee ? I pray thee hide it not from me."

It is possible that every one may think that he desires this; but it is not possible that it should be true, that every one does desire it. There is something in the truth too painful to the wicked hearts of men to make them love it. The light of divine truth, when let into the heart of the sinner, discovers such a dreadful sight, opens to his view

such

such an awful scene, that he cannot bear to behold it. He shuts his eyes against it, he turns away from it, and endeavors to persuade himself, that it is all delusion, that it is only the imagination of a disordered mind. That this is the truth, I appeal to Christ, the faithful and true witness. He says, "This is the condemnation, that light is come into the world, and men loved darkness rather than light, because their deeds were evil. For every one that doeth evil hateth the light, neither cometh to the light, lest his deeds should be reproved." And Christ had abundant reason to bear such a testimony, not only because he knew the hearts of men, but because he saw them act out this character in their conduct towards him. He came a light into the world; he taught the truth in the clearest and plainest manner; he set before sinners their true character; therefore they hated him, and told him that he reproached them—they were offended at him, and sought to kill him. And it has ever been found to be the case, in every age of the world, that plain and faithful preaching will give offence to many. But this does by no means prove, that such preaching is not desirable, and that those who are truly wise will not desire it. It is desirable, and those who are truly wise will desire it, as much as Eli desired Samuel to be plain and faithful with him, in telling him every thing that God had said concerning him.

This they will desire,

1. Because

1. Because they know that every thing which God has said is true, that it is worthy of their notice, and that it is important to them to attend to.

There is nothing, which God has revealed in his word, but what is true. All his declarations are true—all his promises are true—and all his threatenings are true. It is impossible for God to lie, or to deceive. He does not need falsehood or deceit to carry on his cause and support his kingdom. He does not need to terrify or frighten men with dreadful descriptions and representations of what shall never come to pass; but when he tells us what sinful creatures we are, how odious sin is in his sight, what it deserves, and what the sinner shall actually meet with if he continues in it, he does this that we may not be ignorant of ourselves; that we may not go blindfold to destruction; that we may not say that he did not give us warning of our danger. And such as are truly wise are sensible of this; they know that it is important that they become acquainted with their true character, and that they know the whole truth that respects them. They are sensible that the truths of God's word are realities, and that they are infinitely worthy of their notice. They will, therefore, desire to hear and know the mind and will of God; they will prize his word above gold; yea, above much fine gold. They will be ready to say, "Speak, Lord, for thy servant heareth;" they will watch the priest's lips, and seek the law at his mouth; they will sit as at the feet of Christ to hear him. They find that truth is sweet, and in itself desirable; and the soul is fed and nourished by it. "As new born babes they desire the sincere milk of the word, that they may grow thereby." They, therefore, seek for knowledge as for silver, and search for it, as for hid treasures; they delight in the word of God, and meditate in it day and night. This leads me to add,

2. Such as are wise will desire ministers to be faithful, because of the benefit and advantage which they find from plain and faithful preaching.

It is certain that the great design of the institution of the gospel ministry is to promote the good and benefit of mankind, and the edification of the Church, which is the body of Christ. And the more plain and faithful ministers are, the more good they will do. There is a much greater probability, that sinners will be awakened, convinced and converted, under plain and faithful preaching, than under that which is more loose, declamatory, and indefinite. It is true, it is not in the power of the most plain and faithful preacher to speak to the hearts of men. Paul may plant, and Apollos water, but it is God who must give the increase. The excellency of the power is not of man but of God. Yet, as God ordinarily makes use of second causes to effect his purposes; so there is a much greater probability that faithful and plain preachers will be successful, than those who daub with untempered mortar.

mortar. Hence the apostle Paul exhorts Timothy to be faithful from this consideration. "Take heed unto thyself, and unto the doctrine; continue in them: For in doing this thou shalt both save thyself and them that hear thee." Every one, therefore, that truly desires an interest in the benefits and blessings of the gospel, and that salvation which it contains and reveals, will sincerely desire, that ministers should preach plainly and faithfully. Though such plain and faithful preaching may give pain, though it may awaken conscience to condemn them; yet they know that this is necessary in order to their spiritual healing. The sick man knows that it is necessary for him to take disagreeable medicines, in order to his recovery; and if he is wise he will wish the physician, not to consult his present appetite, not to consider what will be most agreeable, but what will be the most beneficial. So the wounded man will desire the surgeon to search his wound thoroughly, and to make proper applications, with respect to his complaints. And so will the truly wise do, with respect to their spiritual physician. They will wish the minister to deal plainly and faithfully with them; not to flatter them with hopes of peace and safety in a Christless state; not to smooth over things, and leave them to perish in their sins; but to make them see the worst of their case, and tell them the whole counsel of God—" I pray thee hide it not from me." But the real christian, in particular,

whose

whose heart has felt the transforming power and influence of divine light and truth, will especially desire the most plain and faithful preaching of the word. He finds, by his own happy experience, that such preaching makes him wiser and better; he grows up under it in knowledge and grace. He learns more of God, sees more of the glory of the divine nature and character, and God appears more glorious, amiable, and excellent. He sees more of the perfection of the ways and works of God, the beauty, harmony, and consistency of his great plan, as it is revealed in his word. And even the awful displays of God's vindictive justice tend to fill his mind with the greater awe and reverence of the divine character. In a word, he finds that the plain and faithful dispensation of the word of God, serves to awaken him to a holy fear, lest he should finally come short of eternal life; that it animates him to diligence and fidelity in his christian course; that it inspires him with ardent desires of growth in grace; that it increases his joy and comfort, and affords him daily delight in the house of his pilgrimage. The more clearly, plainly, and faithfully, the whole counsel of God is exhibited to view, and the more the truths of his word are opened and explained, the more proficiency he makes in the divine life, and finds and feels that he is ripening and preparing for that happy state, where he shall see, not through a glass darkly, but face to face; where he shall see as he

is

is seen, and know, even as also he is known; where all the mists of ignorance and error, which now darken the counsel of God, and make mysteries in his word, shall be dispelled, and unclouded light beam fully and clearly upon his ravished soul. This will constitute one important part of the happiness of heaven; and for this reason, the more a christian desires to be prepared for the state of the blessed, the more he will desire that ministers should unfold the great truths of the gospel, and preach in the most plain, faithful, and edifying manner.

SERMON XXII.

Fidelity in Preaching Desirable.

1 SAMUEL, iii. 17.

What is the thing that the Lord hath said unto thee? I pray thee hide it not from me: God do so to thee, and more also, if thou hide any thing from me, of all the things that he said unto thee.

THERE can scarcely be a greater blessing to any people, than a wise, prudent, and faithful minister; one who is truly acquainted with the word of God; who knows how to open and explain the sacred Scriptures, to represent divine truth in the clearest and plainest light; and who is not afraid or ashamed to do this. On the other hand, there can scarcely be a greater curse to a people, than a teacher or instructor in religion, who is ignorant, unskilful, and unfaithful. He, who is ignorant of divine truth himself, can never give light and knowledge to others. He may amuse and he may please, but he cannot profit; he will lead his hearers in the dark, and there is

the

the utmost danger left blackness and darkness, forever, be the portion of both minister and people. Ministers are set up to shine as lights in the world; they are called the light of the world; if, therefore, the light that is in them be darkness, how great is that darkness! But we are not without temptations to be unfaithful; yea, the temptations are many and great. It is by no means defirable to be the bearer of evil tidings; it is not pleafing to deliver things that will give offence to any; it would be more agreeable to prophefy fmooth things, and to fpeak peace and fafety, as the falfe prophets did, and like them to gain the good will of the people. And the temptation is the greater, when this is the moft common and fafhionable way. How great was the temptation to Micaiah, to join with the multitude of falfe prophets, in encouraging Ahab to go up to battle againft Ramoth Gilead? They all with one voice bid him go and profper. He afks Micaiah. Micaiah knew that the king hated him, and would not be likely to pay any regard to what he faid, if he did not agree with the reft. He, therefore, at firft, bids him go and profper. It is probable, however, that by the manner of his fpeaking, Ahab queftioned whether he was in earneft, and therefore faid, "How many times fhall I adjure thee, that thou tell me nothing but that which is true, in the name of the Lord?" Micaiah now feels the importance of plainly and faithfully delivering the word of God; and he does it, though he incurs the

wrath

wrath and displeasure of the king. The prophet Jeremiah was in a similar situation, and conducted in a similar manner. Ministers, like other persons, are not fond of speaking things that will give pain and offence; they do not love to provoke the wrath and resentment of men. Samuel was afraid, as we are informed, to shew Eli the vision which he had seen, or to declare what God had told him concerning him. Not, probably, afraid that Eli would be angry with him, for this was inconsistent with Eli's character as a good man; but he was afraid to grieve and trouble the good old man. He knew that Eli had before been informed of judgments to come upon his house, and if he were now forward to be the bearer of these evil tidings, it might look as though he hoped to build his own family on the ruins of Eli's. But Eli was desirous of knowing the worst of his case, as we before observed, and, therefore, he not only earnestly entreats him not to hide it from him; but also solemnly adjures him, in God's name, and on penalty of the divine displeasure, to be plain and faithful in delivering the messages of heaven. "God do so to thee, and more also, if thou hide any thing from me, of all the things that he said unto thee."

You, doubtless, remember the method proposed; agreeably to which we have shown, that it is of the greatest importance to a people in general, and to every particular person, that ministers be

plain

plain and faithful in delivering the truth to them; and that such as are truly wife will wish and defire this of their ministers. I now proceed to show,

III. That an awful curse awaits those ministers, who are unfaithful in delivering the counsel of God, or who keep back or conceal the truth from their hearers—" God do so to thee, and more also, if thou hide any thing from me, of all the things that he said unto thee." As if he had said, " I doubt not but God has told thee of awful judgments, which he is about to bring upon my wicked family, but I wish to know them; and may all the judgments, great and dreadful as they may be, fall and light upon your head, if you conceal them from me." Such shall the doom be of every one, who is unfaithful in delivering the messages of God. If ministers do not warn sinners of the wrath of God, which is coming upon them, they bring upon themselves that wrath and curse, which they should have denounced in God's name, against those who go on still in their trespasses. This is agreeable to the declaration of God to the prophet Ezekiel. " Son of man, I have made thee a watchman unto the house of Israel; therefore hear the word at my mouth, and give them warning from me. When I say unto the wicked, thou shalt surely die; and thou givest him not warning, nor speakest to warn the wicked from his wicked way to save his life; the same wicked man
shall

shall die in his iniquity ; but his blood will I require at thine hand. Yet if thou warn the wicked, and he turn not from his wickedness, nor from his wicked way, he shall die in his iniquity ; but thou hast delivered thy soul." It appears, then, that an awful and aggravated curse awaits those, who are unfaithful in delivering the messages of God to the people, to whom they are called to minister. But in order to set this truth in the clearest point of light, you will suffer me to observe,

That the work of the ministry respects the greatest of all public concerns, or it respects the highest possible interests of mankind, as well as the honor and glory of God—that love to men, as well as a regard to the glory of God, requires ministers to be faithful in it—that God has expressly enjoined fidelity upon them—and that he has denounced the most awful threatenings against those who are unfaithful.

Fidelity in every kind of business and employment is required of every man, by the laws of nature, of nations, and of God. And he who is unfaithful in any kind of business entrusted to him, is an odious character ; he deserves to be despised by every good being in the universe. But the sin of unfaithfulness increases, in proportion to the importance of the trust committed to our charge. He who is unfaithful in improving the goods or worldly estate of another, which is committed to his trust, is just-

ly

ly odious in all civilized society. He, who is unfaithful in preserving the life and health of another, which is committed to his trust, is still more criminal than the former. But he, who is unfaithful to the souls of men, is of all others the most criminal, because these are infinitely more important than every thing else. For one soul is of more value than all the wealth of the world. The gospel ministry is certainly designed to promote the salvation of souls, and primarily and immediately respects the great things of our everlasting peace. He, therefore, who is unfaithful in the ministry, is unfaithful to the souls of men. He does, as it were, defraud men, not of their daily bread, but of the bread of life. He keeps from them that provision, which God has made, and which, as a faithful steward, he ought to give them to live upon forever. He starves and famishes their souls. And God is hereby robbed of that honor and glory, which is due to him; not only from the unfaithful minister, but from his people, whom he ought to have endeavored to lead, by his preaching, to glorify God, both with their bodies and spirits, which are his. A regard to the honor and glory of God, therefore, as well as love to mankind, strongly urges fidelity upon the preacher. Can it be supposed, that any man truly loves his neighbor, who is not concerned for his happiness, and who will not do any thing in his power to promote it? Most certainly, that man gives a poor proof of the kindness and goodness of his heart, who can see his neighbor in the utmost danger, and yet take no care nor pains to save him from ruin. Love to the souls of men will lead every faithful minister to do every thing in his power, to save them from eternal death. He will not shun to declare unto them all the counsel of God, nor cease to warn them night and day; nor can he be faithful to God, nor to the souls of men, nor even to his own soul, if he neglects to do this. For, God has expresly enjoined fidelity upon him. The directions to fidelity to men of every class and character are many, but to ministers they are still more numerous and pointed. It may suffice, however, to mention a few. " Take heed, therefore, unto yourselves, and to all the flock of God, over which the Holy Ghost hath made you overseers, to feed the church of God. Take heed to thyself and to thy doctrine. Labor in word and doctrine. Study to shew thyself approved unto God, a workman that needeth not to be ashamed, rightly dividing the word of truth. Preach the word; be instant in season and out of season, reprove, rebuke, exhort with all long suffering and doctrine." They are directed " to cry aloud, and spare not, to lift up their voices like a trumpet, to shew God's people their transgressions, and the house of Israel their sins; to cause them to know their abominations; to speak God's word faithfully." And the forecited passage from Ezekiel is, if possible, more exprefs and full than any which have just been mentioned.

mentioned. "Son of man, I have made thee a watchman," &c.

Here we see that the injunctions to fidelity in ministers are enforced by the most awful sanctions. The blood of those who perish, through their unfaithfulness, will be required at their hands. And if no one can bear the wrath of God due to him, how can ministers bear the accumulated weight of the sins of others? If God denounces judgments against others, and they refuse to declare them, God will do so to them and more also; greater and more awful curses shall light upon them. St. Paul, in God's name, curses those who preach another gospel. And St. John says, in the conclusion of the cannon of Scripture, "If any man shall add unto these things, God shall add unto him the plagues that are written in this book: And if any man shall take away from the words of the book of this prophecy; God shall take away his part out of the book of life, and out of the holy city, and from the things which are written in this book." Who can tell how many curses the unfaithful minister shall have in a world of misery, from those who perish through his unfaithfulness! How will such curse him for concealing from them the truth of their character and situation; and how tormenting must it be to hear them say, If you had done your duty, and dealt plainly and faithfully with us, we might have escaped this everlasting torment! How dreadful then will be the condition of the unfaithful minister, who keeps back the truth from his hearers! And how important is it, both to ministers and people, that ministers be plain and faithful in their preaching! O, that we might all feel the importance of this subject!

IMPROVEMENT.

1. Preaching is a solemn business, it is truly an important work!

I doubt not but you are ready to think, that it is really solemn and important to the preacher. But let me tell you, that it is more than probable that you do not always view it in this light, that you do not always feel sensible of it. Preaching is not designed for an amusement; it is not designed merely to pass away the Sabbath, which hangs heavily upon those, who have not this to while away the time. But it is a divine appointment, and designed for the spiritual good and benefit of mankind. It is one part of that plan, which infinite wisdom has devised for the recovery of a lost and ruined world; and the ordinary method, in and by which sinners are converted to God, and prepared for heaven. It is, therefore, too solemn a business to be trifled with. It ought not to be performed by such as take no care and pains to prepare for it, and who say any thing and every thing, as it comes to mind in the moment of speaking; and whose sermons, or rather whose talking (for it is not fit to be called a sermon) is like the original chaos, without form and void, and darkness

ness is upon the face of it. Such discourses cannot give light or instruction.

Preaching is also too solemn a business, to be performed only to give lessons of heathen morality. The gospel preacher must collect his sermons from the sacred scriptures, and not from the writings of Seneca, Plato, Confucius, or any other human compositions. He must unfold the great mysteries of godliness, and preach the truth as it is in Jesus. You must expect to hear truths that are not pleasing to the carnal heart. You must expect that the faithful preacher will come home to your consciences; that he will shew you your sins; that he will endeavor to make you feel them, and convince you of your guilt and danger. The minister, who never takes pains to convince sinners of their guilty and miserable condition, can never be a faithful and profitable preacher. He will never lead sinners to Christ; for the whole need not a physician, but they that are sick; and they must be sensible that they are sick, before they will apply to a physician. If you are sensible that preaching is indeed such a solemn and important work, you will wish your preacher to feel it, and to be plain and faithful in his preaching. You will wish him to keep back nothing that is profitable for you. You will wish him not to confer with flesh and blood, but to consult the word of God, and to declare his messages plainly and faithfully. Hence we are led to reflect,

2. That

2. That it is a solemn thing to hear preaching, or it is a matter of great importance how we hear. If it were not a matter of importance how we hear; if it were not a solemn thing to sit under the plain and faithful preaching of the word, it would not be such a solemn and important thing to preach. Much of the solemnity and importance of preaching arises from the effect which it has upon the hearers. Therefore, it is a solemn thing to hear preaching, and especially to hear plain and faithful preaching. It would not be a solemn and important thing, to preach to the walls, or to preach to beasts; but it is to preach to men; because it will have some great effect, either good or bad. Hence it appears to be important to hear. It is a solemn consideration, that every sermon you hear will have some effect upon you. You cannot hear a plain and faithful sermon, without being made better or worse by it. If you are not benefited by it, you will be the worse, you will be more criminal, you will be more hardened in sin.

And you are also to remember, that you must give an account to God, for the improvement of every advantage you enjoy. If you abuse the means of grace which you enjoy, if you refuse the calls and invitations of the gospel, if you slight and despise the warnings and admonitions, which God sends you; you will find, that you have a dreadful account to give at a future day. Only allow that preaching is a divine appointment, that it is an in-

stituted

stituted mean of grace, and designed for the good of mankind; and you must at once be convinced, that it is a matter of importance that you attend upon preaching; that you do not needlessly absent yourselves from it; that you come with a teachable temper and disposition; that you be willing to hear and know all the Lord hath said; that you do not quarrel and contend with the truth; that you do not shut your eyes against it—but that you receive it with faith and love, lay it up in your hearts, and practise it in your lives. If you can now sit and hear the most plain and faithful preaching, and remain unmoved and unaffected by it; if you can now hear the most solemn and important truths delivered, and yet not feel the weight and power of them; yet, the time will come, when you must feel the power of truth. Truth will appear at the judgment of the great day, if it does not before, and it will make men feel then, if it does not now. If it be of any importance, that ministers be faithful to the souls of men in their preaching, (as I doubt not but you think it is) then it must be of importance to their hearers, that they be faithful to their own souls in hearing. You must let the word of God sink down into your ears and into your hearts, and consider yourselves as deeply interested in it. You need to be extremely careful not to determine, that any thing is not true, because you are unwilling that it should be true, because you do not love it, because it is

against

against you. It is not uncommon for men to find fault with the truth, to complain of preaching, because it does not suit their corrupt hearts. But if you would act a wise and faithful part to yourselves, you must be willing to come to the light, and let the light of divine truth come home to your hearts. You must not act like children, who cannot bear to have their wounds dressed, because it hurts them and makes them smart; but you must be willing to suffer pain now, rather than bear it to all eternity.

And now let me put the question to each one in this assembly, Can you really and heartily adopt the language of the text, and say, " What is the thing that the Lord hath said unto thee ? I pray thee hide it not from me !" Or, in other words, Do you wish me to be a plain and faithful preacher ? Do you wish me to deliver the whole counsel of God, to keep back nothing of all that God has said ? Do you wish to be dealt plainly with, and to have your true character set before you, and your dreadful condition described ? Will you not quarrel with me if I do this ? Or if you do not quarrel and contend with me, yet will you not secretly and in heart find fault with the truth ? You cannot but own, that it is desirable to have the truth preached ; to have it preached plainly and faithfully too. You cannot but own, that it is a solemn thing to do this, both to me and to you. Will you then suffer me to deal thus plainly and
faithfully

faithfully with you? I will not say, that I have been the faithful Minister, that I have in any respect done my duty as I ought—I know that in many things I offend, and in all things come short—But I think I can say, that I have not knowingly concealed the truth, and kept it back from you. I have meant to be plain and faithful in my preaching; and in doing this no doubt I have displeased some. But shall I, for fear of this, neglect my duty? Shall I be less plain and faithful, for fear of giving you uneasiness? This would be unkind to you, offensive to God, and injurious to my own soul, as well as yours. Rather let me be, if possible, more plain, more clear and full in representing the misery and danger of a natural state and condition. And let me entreat those of you, who are sensible of this deplorable situation of sinners, that you would beg of God to make me more faithful in preaching his word, and delivering his messages to the people. Suffer me further to ask you, Whether you have been faithful in hearing the word of God? Have you attended to the preaching of it, as you ought to do? Have you applied divine truths to your hearts? Have you carefully sought for instruction? Have you given truth a friendly reception, and fed upon it for your spiritual nourishment? Certainly this has not been the case with all of you. If it had been, there would have been more real religion, more true, vital piety than is found among us. Where is the appearance of your profiting by my ministry? Is the fault in me alone? Is it not in any part in you? Let us each one ask his own heart, Is not the fault in me? It will not be long, that I shall have an opportunity to preach, or you to hear. It will not be long, before we must all appear before our Judge, to give an account how we have preached and heard. It will, my hearers, be a solemn day, when we shall meet before the bar of God—when this day, which we now enjoy, and this hour in the house of God, will come into view—when this sermon will come to light, and it will be certainly known, whether I have been plain and faithful in preaching it, and whether you have been faithful in hearing it. For all these things God will bring us into judgment. In the view of this awful day, and of this solemn account, let me call upon you today to hear the voice of God, and not harden your hearts against his calls. Let me call upon you now to repent, and believe in the Lord Jesus Christ with all your hearts. Let me tell you, that now is the accepted time, and now is the day of salvation; that if you will not accept of his offered grace today, you may justly be denied any lot or portion in it tomorrow. For he that being often reproved, hardeneth his neck, shall suddenly be destroyed, and that without remedy.

SERMON XXIII.

Truth Painful to a Wicked Heart.

ACTS, ii. 37.

Now when they heard this, they were pricked in their heart, and said unto Peter, and to the rest of the apostles, Men and brethren, what shall we do?

THE event here referred to is this. The disciples of Christ, agreeable to the direction of their Divine Master, given when he was taken up from them, were waiting at Jerusalem for the descent of the Holy Ghost, which was, in a singular and miraculous manner, shed down, to furnish them for the work, which Christ had assigned them. On the day of Pentecost, a feast day, when there was a large and unusual collection of people, from all parts of the country, and also a great number of proselytes from many other nations, and when all these, with the disciples, were collected in one place, the promised communication was granted, in the appearance of cloven tongues as of fire, which sat upon each of them, and they were filled

with

with the Holy Ghoſt; and began to ſpeak with other tongues, as the Spirit gave them utterance. So that thoſe, of every nation, who were preſent, heard them, each one in his tongue or language. This diverſity of languages, ſpoken by them, appeared to ſome to be only a confuſion of noiſe, and they imputed it to the diſciples being drunken. Upon this impious ſuggeſtion, Peter aroſe, and the other diſciples ariſing to ſupport him, he addreſſed the multitude, in a moſt ſerious, ſolemn, and affecting manner; aſſuring them that the aſtoniſhing ſcene, to which they were witneſſes, was not the effect of intemperance, but the fulfilment of an ancient prophecy of Joel, which was to be accompliſhed in the latter days. He then proceeds to preach Jeſus, and his reſurrection from the dead; and to aſſure them, that what they now ſaw and heard was indeed the work of Chriſt, the gift of that Holy Spirit, which Chriſt had received from God, and which, in this truly miraculous manner, he had ſhed upon them. And that this was a full and convincing demonſtration, that God had made that ſame Jeſus, whom they had crucified, both Lord and Chriſt. The effect of this diſcourſe of Peter, in addition to what they had before ſeen and heard, is mentioned in the text, and in the following verſes. "Now when they heard this, they were pricked in their heart, and ſaid unto Peter, and to the reſt of the apoſtles, Men and brethren, what ſhall we do? Then Peter ſaid unto them,

SERMON XXIII.

them, Repent, and be baptized, every one of you, for the remiſſion of ſins, and ye ſhall receive the gift of the Holy Ghoſt. For the promiſe is unto you, and to your children, and to all that are afar off, even as many as the Lord our God ſhall call. And with many other words did he teſtify, and exhort, ſaying, Save yourſelves from this untoward generation. Then they that gladly received his word, were baptized; and, the ſame day, there were added unto them about three thouſand ſouls." In theſe verſes we have the happy effect of the outpouring of the Divine Spirit upon the hearers, as before we had upon the preachers of the goſpel. "We have here, as one obſerves, the firſt fruits of that large harveſt of ſouls, which, by the goſpel, were gathered in to Jeſus Chriſt. Come and ſee, in theſe verſes, the exalted Redeemer, riding forth in theſe chariots of ſalvation, conquering and to conquer." But what we propoſe more particularly to attend to, in this diſcourſe, is this ſentence, "They were pricked in their heart." That is, their conſciences were awakened to a ſenſe of their ſin and guilt. They ſaw themſelves condemned, and in danger of everlaſting miſery. They felt an inward pain and diſtreſs, as poignant as if a ſword had pierced them to the heart. When divine truth comes home to the conſcience, and men are made to feel the power and efficacy of it, they muſt be pricked and pained in the heart, unleſs, at the ſame time, the heart is reconciled to the

truth,

truth, and bowed in humble submission to it. Hence the words will naturally suggest to us this important and affecting observation:

That divine truth is painful to a corrupt and wicked heart; and the more the truth is realized by such a heart, the more uneasy will it be.

I shall now endeavor,

I. To illustrate and confirm the truth of this observation, or shew, that divine truth is painful to a corrupt and wicked heart.

II. Endeavor to shew why it is so.

I. I shall attempt to establish the truth of the observation, and shew that divine truth is painful to a corrupt and wicked heart; and that the more the truth is realized by such a heart, the more uneasy it will be.

Here it will be necessary, first of all, to remark, that when we say, that divine truth is painful to a wicked heart, we do not mean that every wicked heart is always pained at reading, or hearing, or meditating on divine truth: We do not mean, that divine truth can never be represented, without giving pain and uneasiness to the corrupt and wicked heart. For experience proves the contrary. Probably, the experience of every one present has proved the contrary. Nor is it meant, that no one truth can be delivered, without giving pain to the wicked heart. Experience proves, that wicked men, in general, are not pained with divine truth. They can, for the most part, read

and

and hear the moſt plain, important, and fundamental truths of the Bible, without feeling any great uneaſineſs, any conſiderable pain, anxiety, or diſtreſs. The reaſon of this is, The truth is not ſeen, realized, or felt, by ſuch perſons. It is not apprehended in its reality and importance. By far the greater part of wicked men are in a kind of ſtupid and unfeeling ſtate, with reſpect to divine and eternal truth. They have eyes, but they ſee not the light of truth, which ſhines around them. They have ears, but they hear not the voice of God, ſpeaking to them in his word. Hearts have they, but they underſtand not divine things. In them is fulfilled the ſaying of St. John: " The light ſhineth in darkneſs, and the darkneſs comprehendeth it not." This is the reaſon of the quietude and ſecurity of a wicked world. This is the reaſon why wicked men cry, Peace, peace, to themſelves, while God ſaith, " There is no peace to the wicked." But notwithſtanding this, it may be true, that divine truth is painful to a corrupt and wicked heart. When the truth is apprehended, realized, and felt, by the corrupt and wicked heart, it undoubtedly is ſo. And the more the truth is realized and felt by the wicked heart, the greater will its pain and uneaſineſs be. When the great and important truths of God's word come home to the conſciences of wicked men, and they ſee them in their reality and importance, when they feel the weight of truth, it is a burthen too heavy for them to bear. They are

then

then pained and pricked in the heart; and, with those in our text, cry out, What shall we do? It is the truth of God's word, applied to the heart, that awakens and alarms the guilty sinner; that fills him with the most painful apprehensions, and gives him no true peace or rest, until he can either shut out the light of truth from his heart, and return to his former ignorance and blindness, or his heart be renewed and changed, and he become cordially reconciled to the truth, and receive it in the love of it. That divine truth is painful to a corrupt heart, and that the more such a heart realizes and feels it, the greater its pain and uneasiness will be, is clearly evident, from scripture declaration, and from history. Christ says, "Every one that doth evil hateth the light," *i. e.* the light of divine truth, "neither cometh to the light, lest his deeds should be reproved." What light is to the natural world, or to the bodily eye, that truth is to the moral world, or to the eye of the understanding. Truth discovers things to the understanding, as they really are, and opens to the view of the sinner such a scene as gives him pain and uneasiness. His deeds are reproved. He is convinced of sin. He is condemned by his own conscience, and he finds that he is condemned by that God, who is greater than his heart, and knoweth all things. Hence, he is opposed to the light of truth, and endeavors to keep it out of sight. That this is indeed the case, is confirmed by the whole tenor of

scripture

scripture history. Any one, who reads the Bible with attention, will find, that a wicked world has ever been opposed to divine truth, and in proportion as wicked men have seen, realized, and felt the truth, have they been pained and disgusted by it. Many have at least affected to treat the great and important truths of God's word with scorn and contempt. They have made a jest of sacred things. But there is at least reason to believe, that the great cause of this is, finding and feeling that the great truths of God's word, if they be indeed truths, are too painful for them to bear. Hence they wish to make themselves believe that they are not truths. It is certain, from their own declaration, that some of the greatest infidels were, antecedent to their infidelity, in some sense believers in divine Revelation, and had been awakened, alarmed, and pained with the great truths of revealed religion. And is it not probable, that they flew to infidelity, in order to avoid the pain, which they felt from the truth, and which they knew not how to bear? But however this may be, it is clearly evident, that truth has been painful to many a wicked heart. If we look into the word of God, we shall find this to be the case, in many particular instances. In a variety of cases, wicked men have discovered their pain and uneasiness with divine truth, by their passionate, angry and malicious conduct, towards those who set divine truth before them. Ahab hated Elijah, because he was faith-

X ful

ful in setting divine truth before him. He called him his enemy, and treated him as his enemy. He sought to put him to death. And the only reason was, he could not bear the truth, which Elijah delivered to him. It pained and disgusted his wicked heart. Elijah condemned his wicked conduct. So the same Ahab said of Micaiah, a faithful prophet, "I hate him, for he doth not prophecy good concerning me, but evil." It is said of the Jews, as a people, in the days of the prophets or seers, that " they said unto the seers, See not, and to the prophets, Prophesy not; prophesy not unto us right things, prophesy unto us smooth things, prophesy deceits." They could not bear right things, that is, the truth. They wanted smooth things; things which would give no pain or uneasiness to their wicked heart; which would not disturb them in their sinful slumbers. And the prophets, in general, complied with their wishes. And God says, that they prophesied lies in his name. If we look to the New Testament, the truth of our observation, that divine truth is painful to the corrupt heart, and that the more clearly it is seen, the more offensive it is, will appear with additional evidence. When John the Baptist preached the truth before Herod, it exasperated and provoked him so much, that he took him, and shut him up in prison, and finally put him to death. But nothing ever gave so much pain and uneasiness to the wicked heart, as the plain and faithful preaching of
Christ.

Christ. No man ever taught the way of life so clearly as he did. Never man spake the truth like this man. He spake as one who had authority. His words took hold of the heart and consciences of wicked men, and they so far saw and felt the truth, as to find that it evidently condemned them. They considered themselves as reproached by him. Hence they were exceedingly enraged and provoked. They said all manner of evil concerning him. They treated him with every kind of indignity, insult, and abuse, and at last put him to the most ignominious and painful death. And all this they did, because he told them the truth, because he was plain and faithful in setting the truth before them. And the same was the cause of the persecutions and sufferings of the apostles. It was their plainness and fidelity, in preaching the truth, which pained the hearts, and provoked the resentments, of wicked men. A most affecting instance of this kind we have recorded in the viith chapter of the Acts, where we find Stephen preaching a most solemn and affecting sermon, delivering the most solemn and weighty truths, in the most engaging manner. We are told the effect it had. "When they heard these things, they were cut to the heart, and gnashed on him with their teeth. They cried out with a loud voice, and stopped their ears, and ran upon him with one accord, and cast him out of the city, and stoned him to death." But divine truth does not always have this effect upon the hearts of wicked men, who are pained by it. It does not always exasperate and provoke so highly. It does not always awaken the wrath and indignation of those, who feel the power of it. It sometimes carries such conviction to the conscience, as that sinners cannot but know and feel that it is indeed the truth; and then, instead of being so highly exasperated, they are greatly distressed and concerned, and, like those in the text, they cry out, What shall we do? In this way, God is pleased, not only to discover what is truth, with respect to himself, and what is the truth with respect to them, but, many times, he is pleased to overcome the opposition of their heart, by renewing and changing it, and bringing them to receive and embrace the truth in the love of it. We proceed,

II. To shew why it is that divine truth is painful to a corrupt and wicked heart, and why the more clearly the truth is seen and felt, by such a heart, the more uneasy it is. We have endeavored to make it evident, that this is the case; and that it is indeed so will farther appear from considering the reason of it. Here, then, we say,

1. Divine truth is directly opposed to all sin. Hence it must give pain and uneasiness to a corrupt and wicked heart. It is absolutely impossible, that a heart, under the power and dominion of sin, and in love with it, as every corrupt and wicked heart is, should ever love and approve di-

vine

vine truth. On the contrary, the heart that loves sin must be opposed to the truth. For the truth condemns sin. Hence, Christ says, "Every one that doth evil hateth the light, neither cometh to the light, lest his deeds should be reproved." And hence, also, he said, "And this is the condemnation, that light is come into the world, but men have loved darkness, rather than light ; because their deeds are evil." Men do not always feel the opposition of their heart to the light of truth, because they do not always see the light of truth. The light shineth in darkness, and the darkness comprehendeth it not. When the truth is really apprehended, seen, and felt, it will then be seen that it is opposed to all sin, and so opposed to the feelings of a corrupt heart.

2. Divine truth is painful to a corrupt and wicked heart, because, as it condemns such a heart, it shews the sinner, that he is exposed to the wrath and curse of God. Truth, when it is seen, realized, and felt to be truth, by a corrupt and wicked heart, shews the sinner what a being God is ; how much he is opposed to all sin ; how plainly and awfully he condemns him. Truth, at the same time, shews him, that he is a sinner. It shews him the plague of his own heart. It discovers to him, not only that he is a sinner, but that he is wholly under the power and dominion of sin. Truth teaches him, that he has a carnal heart, enmity against God, not subject to his law, neither indeed can be,

while

while it remains carnal. Divine truth discovers to him, the nature, extent, and spirituality, of the law of God; that it reaches the heart, and all the secret and hidden springs and inclinations of it. Truth, at the same time, arraigns the sinner, before the bar of conscience, a tribunal erected by the Deity in every human breast, and there accuses him of ten thousand crimes; proves him to be verily and greatly guilty; and, at the same time, strips him of all his excuses, leaves him self condemned, and shews him that the wrath of an angry and omnipotent God abideth on him, while he continues in an impenitent and unrenewed state. In proportion as divine truth is realized and felt by the sinner, these things are felt to be true, and these truths must be painful to the heart. It is impossible that the heart should see and realize its own character, and know itself to be in a state of condemnation, under the wrath and curse of God, and yet not be pained and uneasy. When the truth comes home to the conscience, and the sinner feels it, he must and will be pricked, and pained in the heart; he must be in great distress. No sinner can be quiet and easy, while he feels himself condemned, while he sees and knows, that he is under the curse of a broken law, and that he is liable every moment to drop into endless misery. And divine truth, realized and felt by the sinner, will convince him, that this is his situation, and this will be painful to him. These truths are all opposed to the feelings of a

wicked

wicked heart. The unrenewed heart, in view of these truths, is disposed to quarrel and contend with God, and to say, that the way of the Lord is not equal. The sinner quarrels and contends with the law and government of God, and finds no peace. I add,

3. Divine truth is painful to a corrupt and wicked heart, because it tends to exalt and magnify God, and to humble and abase the sinner very deeply. Truth evinces and illustrates the moral rectitude and unlimited glory of God, the rectitude of his government and law, the grandeur of his works, the supremacy and absolute sovereignty in which he moves at the head of the whole moral system, the irresistibleness of his power, and the infinite obligations all creatures are under to obey and honor him, with all the heart. It, therefore, exhibits him, to all creatures, and even to the conscience of the sinner, as an infinitely glorious being. Truth, with equal force of demonstration, shews the sinner how hateful, vile, and guilty he is before God, shows him his dependence, his accountableness, and his incapability of escaping out of the hands of the holy God, who is a sovereign God, who has a right to do as he will with his own, and who will save or destroy just as he pleases. Truth, therefore, infinitely honors the Being, whom the sinner opposes most; and sinks low, even into the depths of dependence, loathsomeness and danger,

the being whom he loves moſt, himſelf. This is perfectly galling to his pride, and painful to his heart. O how painful! It is too painful to be borne.

I obſerve, once more,

4. Divine truth is painful to a corrupt and wicked heart, becauſe it cuts off all ground of hope, on the ground on which the ſinner at preſent ſtands. Though it is a great and important truth, a faithful ſaying, and worthy of all acceptation, that Jeſus Chriſt came into the world to ſave ſinners; yet, this gives no juſt ground of hope to the ſinner, whoſe heart is under the power and dominion of ſin, unrenewed and unſanctified. He is ſtill in the gall of bitterneſs and bond of iniquity. He is not in a better ſtate, becauſe a Savior is provided, ſo long as he continues to deſpiſe the Savior, and reject his offered grace. He is, indeed, the more aggravatedly guilty; his condemnation the more juſt; and his miſery will be the more intolerable, if he continue in his preſent ſtate. Truth, therefore, gives the impenitent ſinner no kind of encouragement to hope, that he ſhall eſcape the wrath and curſe of God, while he continues in his preſent ſtate. On the contrary, it cuts off all hope of ſafety, and leaves him wholly in the hand of a ſovereign God, who can do with him as he pleaſes, and who has mercy, on whom he will have mercy, and whom he will he hardeneth. Divine truth, therefore, muſt be painful to the

wicked

wicked heart; and the only reason why all wicked men are not pained in the heart with the truth, must be, either because they do not believe the truth, or because they do not see and feel it.

Truth Painful to a Wicked Heart.

ACTS, ii. 37.

Now when they heard this, they were pricked in their heart, and said unto Peter, and to the rest of the apostles, Men and brethren, what shall we do?

SOLOMON says, "The spirit of a man will sustain his infirmity; but a wounded spirit, who can bear?" By which he undoubtedly intends, that man can, by the strength of merely animal spirits, fortitude, and resolution, bear the infirmities or burdens of this life; but when the heart is wounded, when the soul is pierced with the arrows of deep conviction, and divine truth comes home to the heart, this would be intolerable, was there no relief to be had. There is nothing wounds and pains the heart, like divine truth. Nothing gives so much uneasiness and distress to a heart unreconciled to God, as plain, important truth, seen, realized, and felt, by the wicked heart. The power of truth is great, and it will finally prevail,

vail, to the joy and comfort of all the friends of God, and to the confusion and misery of all his enemies. Truth is the great weapon, which God makes use of, in the hand of the Holy Spirit, to support and establish his throne and government, and to confound, disappoint, and subdue his enemies. His cause is the cause of truth and righteousness. And he makes use of nothing but truth to support it. Truth is mighty, through God, to the pulling down of the strong holds of sin and Satan, casting down imaginations, and every high thing, which exalteth itself against the knowledge of God, and bringing into captivity every thought to the obedience of Christ. Sinners make lies their refuge, and hide themselves under falsehood. Truth sweeps away the refuge of lies, and destroys the falsehood under which they attempt to hide. But, in doing this, it gives great pain to those, who have been resting in falsehood, and seeking ease under a covert of lies. Truth, when it comes home to the heart, and is realized and felt by the sinner, pierces him through with sorrow, and makes him cry out, in anguish and distress, " What shall I do?"

Divine truth is painful to a corrupt and wicked heart; and the more truth is realized and felt by such a heart, the more uneasy it will be. This was the doctrinal observation drawn from the text, and discussed in the preceding discourse. It was endeavored to be illustrated, and confirmed, and some reasons were given why it is so. What remains

mains is by way of improvement, in some inferences and reflections, arising from the subject.

I. If divine truth be painful to a corrupt and wicked heart, then it is no evidence that a doctrine is not true, that wicked men find fault, quarrel, and contend with it. It is clearly evident, that wicked men often have, and do, quarrel, and contend with the truth, and with those who set the truth plainly before them. We have found, that this has been the case in every age. It was so in the days of the Old Testament prophets; and it was so in the days of Christ. No one, who believes the divine authority of the scriptures, and who acknowledges that Christ was a teacher, sent from God, can question, whether Christ preached and taught the truth, nor whether he preached it in the most plain and intelligible manner. It is evident, that he did; and, that his hearers often saw and felt the power of it. It was this that offended and enraged them to such a degree, that they put him to the most painful and ignominious death. And in every age since, there have been many who have hated, quarrelled, and found fault with the plain and faithful preachers of the truth. So that it cannot possibly be any evidence, that any doctrines are not true, that many men find fault, quarrel, and contend with such doctrines, and with those who deliver them. Nor is it a certain evidence, that they are not true, that they do not contend with them. For many do

not

not always see and feel the power of truth. There are many men, who quarrel and contend with the truth, who yet do not do it openly. Many contend with the truth, who yet dare not complain and contend with the preachers of it. They are, in heart, greatly uneasy, but yet dare not openly complain. Indeed, if divine truth be painful to a corrupt and wicked heart, then a corrupt and wicked heart will always be uneasy with divine truth, when it really and truly sees and feels it. The corrupt heart cannot relish, or love, but must be opposed to divine truth. Hence, wicked men often find fault and contend with the truth. They cannot bear to think that the plain declarations of scripture are true. They wish and endeavor to find some way to evade the truth, either to disbelieve it, or think it not applicable to themselves. How many are there, who hate to hear those doctrines, which show the total depravity and wickedness of the human heart; which represent the sinner as dead in trespasses and sins, and an enemy to the real character of God! How many, who cannot bear to hear of the sovereignty of God, and of his doing all things after the counsel of his own will! Such doctrines disturb the peace and quietude of sinners, and their hearts will rise up against them, if they have any sense of the truth of them. Hence it is no evidence whatever, against the truth of any doctrine, that many men cannot bear to hear it, but do really quarrel and contend with it.

2. If

2. If divine truth be painful to a corrupt and wicked heart, then we learn, that wicked men are peculiarly expofed to embrace error; and why it is that there are fo many errors among mankind. That the hearts of all men are naturally corrupt and finful, is a truth too evident to need any labored proof; and that truth is painful to fuch a heart, is, we think, alfo evident. Hence it is, that mankind are peculiarly expofed to reject the truth, and embrace error. Men naturally wifh to avoid, or get rid of that, which gives them pain. This is equally true of mental, as of bodily pain. Yea, as mental pain is often much greater, and more intolerable, than bodily, we are more defirous of getting rid of it, than of that, which pertains to the body. Hence it is, that the world of mankind in general are defirous of remaining in a ftate of finful quietude and fecurity. They do not love to be difturbed in their finful flumbers. They choofe to keep off convictions of their loft, undone, and perifhing condition. They refufe to come to the light, left their deeds fhould be reproved, and they find themfelves condemned. For this reafon, when divine truth begins to come home to the confcience, and finners begin to be alarmed, and, like Felix of old, to tremble under the awful apprehenfions of a judgment to come; like him, they fay to their fears and convictions, "Go thy way for this time." They endeavor to perfuade themfelves, that there is time enough yet; that there is no need

of

SERMON XXIV.

of being in any hurry. And if this plea does not quiet their fears, and stifle their convictions, they have recourse to some other method. And the most common of all methods is, to hide the truth from the view of the mind, to persuade themselves, that their character is not so bad, and that their danger is not so great, as has been represented; that God is not so strict and severe as they have been ready to imagine; that he is more pitiful and compassionate, more kind and benevolent, than to punish them forever for their sins. Any thing that will give them a hope of peace and safety, is very readily embraced and believed; and the enemy of souls always stands ready to say to them, "Thou shalt not surely die." When the mind is in this situation, the heart opposed to the real truth of God's word, and yet seeking for something to quiet and calm its fears, how much exposed is it to embrace any error, which speaks peace unto it! Truth will not afford peace, while the heart is unrenewed. It was truth which wrought conviction. It was truth, which occasioned the pain and distress. And truth will continue and increase the conviction, and pain, until the heart be overcome, and be brought to receive the truth in the love of it. Hence it is, that God says, that "there is no peace to the wicked;" that "the wicked are like the troubled sea, which cannot rest, whose waters cast up mire and dirt." In this situation, either the heart must bow to the truth, and give up its

controversy,

controversy, by an unfeigned and unconditional surrendery to God, or it must make lies its refuge, and hide itself under falsehood, in order to avoid its distress. Hence, men, under strong convictions of conscience, are exceedingly prone to lay hold on that, which will promise them safety, though they are unreconciled to God. Error is the only thing, which has a flattering appearance. It will, therefore, be welcome. Hence it is, that there are so many errors among mankind; and that so many of mankind are led to embrace them. Truth gives pain to a corrupt and wicked heart, because it is opposed to the feelings and happiness of such a heart. But error affords present relief. It seems to promise peace and safety to the sinner. In this view, it appears not at all strange, that there are so many, and such various errors, even in a christian land; and that men are ready to lay hold on any thing, rather than the plain and fundamental truths of the Bible. When a sinner has been under great awakenings, and strong convictions of conscience, of his sins, and danger, if he be not truly converted from sin to God, he usually falls into some gross error. And many, because they can get relief in no other way, have recourse to infidelity, or, as is frequent in the present day, to Universalism. And some, who, for a long time, have entertained a hope of their good estate, afterwards finding reason to question their safety on this ground, fly to the modern sentiment of no punishment after this life.

And

And it becomes, afterward, truly painful to them to hear of the future and everlasting punishment, of the impenitent and ungodly.

3. If truth be painful to a corrupt and wicked heart, then we learn, that the heart must be renewed, and changed, before it can truly love and relish divine truth. To receive the truth in the love of it, is made a part of the christian character. The good man not only assents to the great and important truths of God's word, as being true, but he is said, in the word of God, to *receive the truth;* which expresses a cordial approbation of it. So he is said to love the truth, and to walk in the truth, and to rejoice in it. The good man has an high esteem of the truth. He values it above gold; yea, above much fine gold. It is sweeter than honey to his taste. He has taken it as his heritage forever. It is the rejoicing of his heart. But wicked men hate the truth, and will not come to it. They reject the counsel of God. They resist the light of truth, and shut their eyes against it. Hence, it is necessary, that the heart be renewed and changed, before it can ever receive the truth, in a spiritual and saving manner. Many wicked men, however, can very well bear to hear truth delivered, because they do not understand it, or do not see and feel the nature and effects of it; or because they think that it does not apply to them. But the heart cannot love and rel-

ish the truth, until it be renewed by the power and grace of God. Hence,

4. We learn, that the power and grace of God must be employed to change the heart. Means are, of themselves, ineffectual. Means are, indeed, used; and the great mean made use of is the word of God, the word of truth. This is the rod of God's strength, or his strong rod, with which he subdues the heart of the sinner, slays the enmity of his heart, and brings him to receive the truth in the love of it. But what can the word of truth do towards changing the heart, which is opposed to the truth? The more clearly the truth is set before the sinner, and the more the wicked heart feels and realizes it, the more it opposes it. Hence, nothing short of a divine power can change the heart, and cause it to receive the truth in the love of it. As divine truth is opposed to the feelings of a corrupt heart, it is absolutely necessary, that the heart be subdued; that the sinner be brought to give up all controversy with God; that he may no longer dispute and contend with him; that he may no longer complain, that the way of the Lord is not equal; but that he cheerfully own the justice and righteousness of God, and his entire dependence on the free and sovereign grace of God.

5. If divine truth be painful to a corrupt and wicked heart, and if the more such a heart sees and feels the truth, the more uneasy it is, and the more it opposes it; then we learn the exceeding sinfulness,

sinfulness, and aggravated criminality, of such a heart. Certainly, it must be extremely criminal for a guilty sinner to oppose, resist, and contend with eternal truth and rectitude. To do this, is to contend with God, and to impeach his character and conduct. Truth is the essential basis of God's throne, and the first principle of his government. It is the rule, by which he always acts. To contend with truth is, therefore, to contend with God. To hate the truth, is to hate God. To oppose the truth, is to oppose God. Truth is unchangeable in its nature, as God is: It is, therefore, amiable and excellent, as God is. How exceedingly vile and criminal it is, then, to resist and oppose the truth! And how aggravatedly guilty are those, who oppose and resist the truth, in proportion as they see and feel, the reality and importance of it. This was what made the Jews, in Christ's day, so exceedingly guilty and criminal. Christ says, "If I had not come and spoken unto them, they had not had sin; but now they have no cloke for their sin:" *i. e.* If Christ had not come and spoken the truth to them, in the clearest and plainest manner possible, they would have been innocent, in comparison with what they now were. Their sin would have been comparatively small. But now, when they had been taught the truth, when they had both seen and heard it, they had no kind of excuse; they were aggravatedly guilty. And this is the condemnation of every impenitent sinner.

Hence, Chrift fays, "This is the condemnation, that light is come into the world, and men love darknefs rather than light, becaufe their deeds are evil." And this fhews the propriety and juftnefs of Chrift's pronouncing fuch great and aggravated woes, upon thofe places, in which moft of his mighty works were done. They finned againft greater light, againft ftronger convictions, againft more plain and obvious truth. And this fhows why finners, under the gofpel, fhould meet with more aggravated condemnation, than thofe, who live in heathen lands.

6. If divine truth be painful to a corrupt and wicked heart, then it muft be a hard and felf denying duty to a minifter, to preach thofe truths, which will give pain and offence to many of his hearers.

Plain and faithful preaching often gives offence, and expofes the preacher, to reproach, to contempt, and, fometimes, to violent perfecution and death: As was the cafe with Chrift, and his followers, and many of the prophets before them, and many of his faithful minifters fince. And this affords a ftrong temptation to minifters, to preach fmooth, foft and eafy things, which will not give offence. This may account for the exiftence of fo much preaching, of that kind, at the prefent day. The temptation is ftrong to preach the truth, if indeed it be preached, in fuch a manner as not to wound or hurt the feelings of the hearers. It muft require a good degree of self denial to deliver, plainly, the truth, when there is reason to believe that it will give offence. But this the faithful minister will do. This Christ did. And this his followers did, not counting their lives dear to them, in such a cause as they were engaged in. But though there be no great cause to fear giving general offence, by plain and faithful preaching, yet every minister must know, that the truth will give uneasiness to many of his hearers, if they realize and feel it. And this he must desire, i. e. that they may feel the truth; that it may come home to the hearts of his hearers, and disturb their sinful quietude. In itself confidered, it is not defirable to give pain to any heart. But as it is necessary to the attainment of true peace, it is pleasing to a benevolent mind, to see men pricked in the heart, and crying out, in anguish, " What shall we do?" Every wise and good minister wishes to preach, not barely to the ears, but to the heart, and to the consciences, of his hearers. He wishes to make them see and feel the truth, however painful it may be to them. He knows, that unless what he delivers reaches the hearts of his hearers, it will do them no good. It will be only as water spilt upon the ground, that cannot be gathered up. Good men are not profited by the word preached, unless it reach their heart. Then it will comfort, quicken, and animate them. Wicked men are not profited, unless they see and feel the truth, and are pained by it. The faithful and good minister, therefore, will wish to reach the hearts of his hearers, however displeased or offended they may be with him for it. This was what made Christ such an excellent preacher. It was, that all his discourses were calculated to reach the heart. " Christ never drew a bow at a venture, but always directed the arrows of truth at the hearts of his hearers. He described the character of the saint, and the character of the sinner, with so much truth and propriety, that every person might easily distinguish the one from the other, and know which belonged to himself. Nay, he did more than this. For he directed every man's eyes inward, and obliged him, by the light of truth, to see and feel his own character. This is that peculiar excellency in preaching, for which the finest encomium, perhaps, ever bestowed on a preacher, was given by Lewis XIV, to the eloquent Bishop of Clermont, Father Massillon. After hearing him preach at Versailles, he said to him, " Father, I have heard many great orators in this chapel. I have been highly pleased with them. But for you, whenever I hear you, I go away displeased with myself; for I see more of my own character."* Would such a preacher, my hearers, be pleasing to you ? Would to God I could deserve such a character, however painful it might be to you.

7. If divine truth be painful to a corrupt and wicked heart, and if the more the truth be realized

and

---

* See Emmons's Sermon, on " Christ the Standard of Preaching."

and felt, the more uneasy and distressed such a heart will be, then how dreadful and intolerable will hell be to the wicked! In that world of misery, truth will not only be known, but it will be seen, and understood, and felt, to the utter confusion and torment of the wicked. In the present state, wicked men are greatly ignorant of divine truth. The God of this world hath blinded their eyes, so that they cannot see the light of truth. But, in the state of final punishment, sinners will be fully and perfectly acquainted with all truth. They will then know what a being God is. They will then know, that he is a sovereign God, who hath, from eternity, concerted his plan, and in every age of time, performed every thing according to the counsel of his own will. In the world to come, truth will be stripped of all disguise. It will appear to be what it is. There will then be no more uncertainty what truth is. There will be no more difference in sentiment and opinion, as to what is truth. But all will see the truth clearly, understand it perfectly, and feel it most sensibly. The friends of God, whose hearts are reconciled to him, and who have received the truth in the love of it, will forever rejoice in the truth, and walk in the light of it; and the more they see and know of it, the greater their joy will be. But the enemies of God, whose hearts are opposed to the truth, will feel their pain and torment increased, by the clear discovery of it. They will not then be able to get

rid

rid of truth. All their refuges of lies will then be deſtroyed. There will be no hiding place, no way for the wicked to deceive themſelves. Nothing will remain to divert the mind from attending to the truth. But every thing will ſerve to preſent the truth in the cleareſt poſſible manner. In this world, the wicked have many ways to ſhut out the light, and prevent the truth from taking hold of their conſciences. But there they muſt ſee, and hear, and know, and feel the truth. There they cannot run away from the truth. They cannot there avoid knowing it, as here they can. Though they will then hate the truth, far more than now they can do, yet they will not be able to avoid it. What an inconceivable ſource of pain and miſery will it be, to find and feel the truth to be, what they hate, and to know that they always oppoſed and reſiſted it. Now ſinners hate to hear ſome of the moſt plain and important truths, becauſe ſuch truths diſcover to them their own wickedneſs, which they are unwilling to ſee. But then, God will make them to hear, and ſee, and feel, the truth. Truth will then appear clear and bright as the ſunbeams; and like the heat of the ſun will then burn and conſume the wicked, and they ſhall be forever pained with it.

8. If divine truth be thus painful to a corrupt and wicked heart, then, of how great importance it is, that we all become friendly to the truth, willing to know the truth, and that we receive it in the

love

SERMON XXIV.

love of it. It is certainly the height of madness and folly, for any one to be unwilling to know and believe the truth; especially as it relates to God, and the things of eternity. For the knowledge of the truth is of infinite importance. Men must and will, sooner or later, know it. God is determined to make his truth known. He has taken many ways, and made use of various means, to exhibit divine truth. He has revealed it in his word, and men might and would see and know it, if they were willing to come to the light. And all God's works of nature, providence, and grace, are calculated to make God known, and to manifest the truth. And he will not finally fail of accomplishing his end. It is certainly a very desirable thing to know the truth, if it may be. And men do desire, in every instance, to know what is true, except in the infinitely important things of religion. Here they are unwilling to come to the light, and know the truth, because it gives them pain. But if it does, is it not better to endure pain in this life, than forever to feel it in the life to come? Is it not better to know and embrace the truth now, than to know and hate it forever in a world of misery. Whatever the truth may be, the heart must love it, and embrace it, or it cannot be happy. God has established his throne in truth and righteousness, and it shall stand forever; and none, but the friends of truth, are, or can be, the friends of God. It is, therefore, of infinite importance, that we become

cordially

cordially reconciled to the truth, and that we receive it in the love of it. It is of as much importance, as it is that we be saved. For we cannot be saved, without the knowledge and love of the truth. For, says Christ, "This is life eternal, that they might know thee, the only true God, and Jesus Christ, whom thou has sent." To know them, is to know them practically. This knowledge involves, not only the assent of the understanding, but the consent of the heart. To love the truth, and be willing to receive and embrace it, is the exercise of a renewed heart. This is what Christ calls coming to the light. And men's hating the light is expressive of the opposition of their heart to the truth. But this opposition of heart to the truth must be removed. Then the soul will love the word of God, will delight in it, as true, and love it, because it is precious and important truth. And then the heart will not only be reconciled to some truths, but to all truth. It will then rejoice in the universal dominion and government of God. It will then be entirely swallowed up in the divine will. There are many things, taught in the word of God, which many men do not believe, such as the doctrine of the divine decrees, the absolute and universal sovereignty of God, that he doeth all things after the counsel of his own will. But it would be well for such as disbelieve these doctrines, to ask their own hearts, whether the only reason why they do not believe them, is not, because

they

they are unwilling they fhould be true; that they are unwilling that God fhould be a fovereign, doing juft as he pleafes; and whether, in this, they are not in heart oppofed to God, and unwilling that he fhould be God, and have the throne to himfelf. If fo, does not this manifeft a heart unreconciled to God?

O my hearers, the day, the awful day, is juft at hand, when we fhall all know what is truth; and if our hearts are reconciled to the truth, we fhall be forever happy. But if, in heart, we are oppofed to the truth, we muft be unfpeakably miferable. For the truth is great, and it will prevail.

www.ingramcontent.com/pod-product-compliance
Lightning Source LLC
Chambersburg PA
CBHW030007240426
43672CB00007B/864